The Clinical Neuropsychologist, 24: 373–390, 2010
http://www.psypress.com/tcn
ISSN: 1385-4046 print/1744-4144 online
DOI: 10.1080/13854040903264154

Psychology Press
Taylor & Francis Group

ADVOCACY 101: A STEP BEYOND COMPLAINING. HOW THE INDIVIDUAL PRACTITIONER CAN BECOME INVOLVED AND MAKE A DIFFERENCE

Laura L. S. Howe[1], Jerry J. Sweet[2], and Russell M. Bauer[3]
[1]*VA Palo Alto Health Care System, Palo Alto, CA,* [2]*NorthShore University HealthSystem, Evanston, IL, and University of Chicago, Pritzker School of Medicine, Chicago, IL, and* [3]*Clinical and Health Psychology, University of Florida, Gainesville, FL, USA*

There are critical issues facing the neuropsychological community, such as inadequate reimbursement for services, a lack of familiarity among public policy makers regarding the science and practice of neuropsychology, and a lack of public policy awareness among professional neuropsychologists. Advocacy for the field is the most effective way to undertake positive change. Currently, a minority of psychological professionals actively engages in an advocacy process, while the majority is not involved, or is involved periodically or passively. With weak advocacy our field risks slower development in key areas, and without strong and constant advocacy we risk losing ground previously gained. The purpose of this article, and those that follow in this special issue of The Clinical Neuropsychologist, is to: (1) convey the importance of advocacy, (2) address and dispel unfounded mental obstacles that inhibit involvement in advocating for the specialty, and (3) aid neuropsychologists in preparing to join the advocacy process. To accomplish this, we acquaint readers with the advocacy process, delineate to practitioners how they can become involved, and encourage participation in advocacy.

Keywords: Neuropsychology; Advocacy.

INTRODUCTION

Advocacy is "the act of pleading for or actively supporting a cause or proposal" (*Black's Law Dictionary*; Black et al., 1999). In everyday life there are many examples of individuals advocating for particular ideas, activities, and philanthropic causes. For example, when attending a movie or going to dinner with a friend one may advocate for a personal favorite. At one time or another we all engage in persuasive actions as we attempt to have our needs met and our opinions heard. Most psychologists, however, do not extend this advocacy behavior into their professional lives. Professional psychologists often appear to display an "advocoagnosia," feel powerless to effect change, seem to feel uncomfortable

Address correspondence to: Laura L. S. Howe, VA Palo Alto Health Care System, Psychology Service (116B), 3801 Miranda Avenue, Palo Alto, CA 94304, USA. E-mail: lauralshowe@yahoo.com
Accepted for publication: August 17, 2009. First published online: October 20, 2009.

with the process, and do not know how to become involved (Bauer, 2006). Because of this, a *minority* of psychological professionals actively engages in an advocacy process, while the majority is not involved, or is involved periodically or passively. With weak advocacy, our field risks slower development in key areas in which we are subject to external statutory or economic forces that determine or at least affect the quality of our professional lives. Of equal importance, without strong and constant advocacy we risk losing ground previously gained. For example, although Medicare reimbursement rates have been increased and work effort has finally been recognized for neuropsychological assessment services, Medicare reimbursement reductions are constantly threatened in today's economic climate. Constant vigilance is required in order to maintain the status quo, and active participation is required to continue to gain ground in the economic and political arenas. When only a few psychologists engage in advocacy activities, a relatively small percentage of individuals are encumbered with the work that really requires more effort shared more equitably among a larger group. Like moving large rocks, the tasks before us require large amounts of energy and substantial momentum, and are better accomplished by large crowds than by small dedicated groups.

At the broadest level the American Psychological Association (APA) has been, and continues to be, a prominent and shaping force advocating for psychology, including the specialty of clinical neuropsychology. Gerald Goldstein's paper "Advocacy for Neuropsychology in the Public Sector" in this special issue illustrates some of the means by which APA has positively impacted psychology and neuropsychology in the public sector. A wide range of opportunities exist for individuals to become involved in advocacy efforts, ranging from involvement with larger organizations, such as APA, to smaller more specialty-focused professional organizations, such as the American Academy of Clinical Neuropsychology (AACN), to much more local efforts that can be made within an individual's office, such as placing brochures explaining the purpose and benefits of neuropsychology in the waiting room or office lobby.

The purpose of this article, and those that follow in this special issue of *The Clinical Neuropsychologist*, is to: (1) convey the importance of advocacy, (2) address and dispel unfounded mental obstacles that inhibit involvement in advocating for the specialty, and (3) aid neuropsychologists in preparing to join the advocacy process. After first discussing the main features of the advocacy process, we offer alternative routes to practitioners regarding how they can become advocates, and, finally, we encourage involvement. The individual articles that follow in this special issue discuss some of the specific areas that are currently relevant and would benefit from advocacy efforts. These articles will also inform individuals how to immediately become involved in those areas.

WHY SHOULD THE INDIVIDUAL PRACTITIONER ADVOCATE?

Advocacy can be conceptualized as directing one's emotional and intellectual efforts toward a cause. Advocacy can take many different forms. Some forms of advocacy attempt to effect change in policies or laws. Other forms of advocacy seek to alter the practices of people or organizations. Advocacy can be private (e.g., educating a patient or family member on what constitutes quality in service delivery) or public (e.g., testifying before Congress), and can be local or global. Most forms of advocacy seek to provide education about a particular issue or problem. At its core, advocacy involves increasing awareness of particular issues and educating a target audience about those issues, with the goal of bringing about a particular result.

It is important for all professionals to educate policy makers, among others, as much as possible regarding the science and practice of neuropsychology. In this regard it is important to remember that we are the current stewards of our profession, and it is our responsibility to protect and enhance the profession so that its benefit to individual patients and to society can continue to be realized and expanded. A primary motivation to engage in advocacy should be found in the stark realization that *most critical decisions that affect neuropsychological practice are made by non-neuropsychologists*. These decisions may have profound effects, negative and positive. It is our responsibility as neuropsychologists to educate policy makers so that decisions are made with a full understanding of relevant issues and potential consequences. For example, suppose a state legislature is considering repealing a mandatory motorcycle helmet law. Such a decision will likely have consequences in which neuropsychologists have expertise, including potential increases in disabling injuries, attendant medical and rehabilitative costs, and reduced quality of life. Without strong advocacy and educational efforts, neuropsychologists cannot reasonably expect policy makers to fully understand such consequences. When proposed actions have the potential to benefit or harm the profession or the patients we serve, we need to argue for or against, as appropriate, such courses of action.

It is often apparent that policy makers, the general public, other disciplines we work with, and sometimes our own patients know very little about neuropsychology. Advocacy includes informing others of the nature and benefits of our services in a language they can understand. What matters to patients may not matter to politicians, and what matters to politicians may not matter to insurance executives. Many professionals are not familiar with clinical neuropsychology as a practice specialty, except perhaps in those allied disciplines (neurology, neurosurgery, psychiatry) whose members populate the same interdisciplinary health care teams as we do. However, many of these professionals have inaccurate or incomplete knowledge of the benefits of neuropsychological services. This can lead to inappropriate referrals or referral questions, a lack of referrals, resistance to the participation of neuropsychologists in cases, inappropriate expectations when neuropsychologists are involved in cases, or other negative consequences. Such consequences illustrate why we need to educate the general public, other disciplines, and policy makers about our specialty. Moreover advances, such as increased integration of neuropsychological services within hospitals, proper reimbursement for work product, and increased awareness and utilization of neuropsychological services by the general public, will not occur unless we educate people about what neuropsychology has to offer and why particular changes should occur. This advocacy activity must begin at the local level, where the individual neuropsychologist seeks to convince health care colleagues that neuropsychological assessment and rehabilitative services can help them treat and understand their patients better and can thus lead to improvements in care.

Currently, there are many critical issues facing the neuropsychological community. For instance, inadequate reimbursement for services and marginalization of some neuropsychology departments in medical centers are two examples of issues practitioners sometimes complain about. Marginalization of neuropsychology refers to when practitioners feel as though their services are underutilized in medical centers and that they are not treated with the respect that should be given to a colleague. Advocacy regarding our training background and our skill set is an important part of the process of change that can eventually lead to advancement. Complaining without taking action, however, will not lead to change. We all need to step up, step in, educate, and advocate for our field.

WHAT HAPPENS WHEN PEOPLE DO NOT ADVOCATE?

As many as 10,000 bills may be introduced in the US Congress each year and approximately 6% become laws that govern various aspects of our lives. Extensive advocacy and lobbying efforts occur as bills are introduced and considered (and are important factors in their success or failure), and so it is important to recognize that advocacy plays a key role in all stages of legislative debate, not just the 6% of bills that are enacted as laws. In addition to bills introduced at the federal level, state and local policies are continually being made and changed. When professionals are not vigilant regarding what bills and policies are being introduced at all levels, and do not act when needed, detrimental effects may occur. For example, California Senate Bill 229, which extended the psychology licensing board, was up for renewal in 2005. At the time, there was a fear that Governor Schwarzenegger would veto the bill once it was passed and then create a new "Mental Health Board." This new board potentially could have included multiple mental health disciplines, such that psychology would no longer have a discipline-specific board governing psychological practice. If the "Mental Health Board" concept had been adopted, the composition of the Board would have included only one doctoral-level psychologist, thus significantly eroding the voice that professional psychologists would have in practice governance. Due to the efforts of a significant grassroots coalition of psychologists both in and out of the State of California, Governor Schwarzenegger heard psychology's message and did not veto the bill. If psychologists had not been vigilant, and if they had not acted to show their opposition to the proposed action, the bill may have been vetoed and then other disciplines and members of the public would have become the main decision makers in the regulation of psychological practice in California. One way elected officials determine what bills to support and what stances to take on proposed bills is to determine what their constituents favor. The only means available for policy makers to determine where neuropsychologists stand on an issue is for individuals within our specialty to speak up and make themselves heard. Luckily, in this instance, many psychologists stood together and spoke with one voice and the proposed development of the Mental Health Board did not come to pass.

The California Licensing Board issue is only one of numerous examples. Similar issues occur on a regular basis across the country, most of which affect regional or local affairs but have potentially broader implications. These issues are not "announced with trumpets" and may escape notice, unless psychologists get involved in the advocacy process. Individual practitioners are more likely to hear about policies or regulations that directly impact practice for better or worse. Changes in billing codes and reimbursements are key examples. Practitioners are less likely to hear about victories that maintain the status quo.

Neuropsychologists need to be sufficiently familiar with existing rules and laws to be alert to adverse legislative interpretations that significantly affect practice. For example, in 2003 New York State passed a scope of practice law for psychologists. The New York State Department of Education interpreted a section of this law as excluding the use of technicians by psychologists, stating that technicians would be engaged in the independent practice of psychology. As might be predicted, this inaccurate interpretation of actual practice in neuropsychologists' offices could have a widespread negative effect on the practice of neuropsychology in New York State.

The interpretation barring the use of testing technicians is at variance with the established standard of practice in the field of clinical neuropsychology. The use of technicians is not only standard practice, it is the modal arrangement currently adopted by practicing neuropsychologists. More than half of the neuropsychologists who responded to the NAN/Division 40 Practice survey (Sweet, Peck, Abramowitz, & Etzweiler, 2002) and to the AACN/TCN "Salary Survey" (Sweet, Nelson, & Moberg, 2006) reported using testing assistants in their practices. Several major psychological organizations have published Position Statements supporting the use of testing technicians—American Psychological Association (Report of the Division 40 Task Force on Education Accreditation, and Credentialing, 1989); American Academy of Clinical Neuropsychology (AACN, 1999); National Academy of Neuropsychology (NAN, 2006)—and there are published guidelines regarding psychologists' use of nondoctoral-level testing assistants (APA, 1987, 2002; Report of the Division 40, 1989, 1991). These documents, as well as professional practice surveys dating back to the 1980s, are evidence of the standard use and acceptance of testing technicians in clinical neuropsychology. Of critical importance is that restricting the use of neuropsychological testing assistants decreases the number of patients a neuropsychologist can evaluate, thereby reducing access to care for some patient populations. A potential consequence of reducing access to care could be that patients in the lower socioeconomic status range, who have poor insurance coverage or who cannot otherwise pay for services, are left without services. It seems possible that disadvantaged members of minority groups (e.g., African-Americans, Hispanics, etc.) might be disproportionately affected. Additionally, the negative effects of this interpretation are not isolated to New York State. The interpretation could ultimately set a precedent for restricting the use of testing assistants in other states. This topic is discussed in greater depth by Festa, Barr, and Pliskin in "The Politics of Technicians" within this special issue.

These examples illustrate the importance of advocacy for our field. In the California situation psychologists organized an in-state effort, as well as an out-of-state effort, to create a grassroots initiative. Many psychologists within and outside of California responded by sending letters, emails, and faxes and made phone calls to the Governor that demonstrated the field's stance on the topic. The same has been true with the ongoing New York scenario.

COMMON RATIONALIZATIONS THAT DISCOURAGE INVOLVEMENT IN THE ADVOCACY PROCESS

There are many reasons given by psychologists when explaining why they are NOT actively involved in advocacy. In this section we describe some of the more common reasons, which we characterize more specifically as rationalizations (aka excuses) that inhibit individual practitioners from becoming involved in the advocacy process.

It's not in my backyard

Sometimes individuals do not take action and advocate regarding a particular issue because they think an event or policy will not directly affect them and therefore it is of little or no concern. Events are, in fact, often more interconnected than they may first seem. Any practicing neuropsychologist outside New York who thinks that the scope of practice interpretation in that large and influential state has no relevance to their practice does not comprehend the full implications of that single state's crisis for practice nationwide. Just as the judicial system and courts look to decisions from other jurisdictions for guidance, local and state policy makers look to other jurisdictions for guidance as well. Rules, laws, policies, and procedures enacted and followed in one jurisdiction can and may impact how neuropsychology and psychology is practiced in other jurisdictions. This is one means by which events isolated in one geographic area may actually affect practice in other areas.

A variant of the "backyard" rationalization occurs when practitioners ignore science advocacy issues, and those engaged primarily in research ignore practice advocacy issues. The fact that the scientist-practitioner model is the dominant paradigm in our field means that any advocacy need that falls anywhere along the *science–practice* continuum is in our backyard and impacts all of us, regardless of whether we identify more with being researchers or practitioners. In order for our field to accomplish larger goals, neuropsychology needs to act in a more concerted and cohesive fashion. Researchers and clinicians can accomplish much more if they work together.

Nothing is wrong, so we do not need to act

This rationalization is also known as the "head in the sand" or "ostrich" rationalization. Prevailing evidence from the decision-making literature in cognitive psychology suggests that most people prefer to maintain the status quo, even if the status quo is not optimal or does not allow them to reach their goals (Kahnemann, Knetsch, & Thaler, 1991). Although we have seen some recent improvements in principles of reimbursement for psychological services (with the recognition in 2006 of a "physician work component" associated with neuropsychological service delivery), we are still threatened by looming cuts in reimbursement by federal programs, which are byproducts of the current economic environment. The "status quo" will, without advocacy, result in declining reimbursement in the coming years because of reductions in overall appropriations for health care, and because we will be competing with more highly mobilized and vocal entities supported by our colleagues in other health care disciplines. This is a continual and often cyclical struggle, with good times followed by bad times, and so on. Nothing is ever solved forever. Neuropsychology needs to have a constant presence and individuals committed to working towards maintaining and increasing funding for the science and practice of neuropsychology.

Others are taking care of it. There's no need for me to get involved

This frame of mind leads to a phenomenon known as the "bystander effect" in social psychology, wherein diffusion of responsibility leads to a lack of assistance or intervention by bystander witnesses to a crime or accident. Although others are advocating on behalf of the profession, there is a proportionally large group of "bystanders" who are not involved. Interestingly, research indicates that as the number of bystanders increases, the likelihood that someone will intervene decreases (Latané & Darley, 1970). There exist areas in which advocacy efforts are needed: however, the person power to meet those needs does not currently exist. Reinforcements are also needed in areas in which advocacy efforts are already underway. Neuropsychology needs its own version of a "troop surge." One key example is advocacy for education and training funds. Until the Graduate Psychology Education Program (GPEP) was approved in 2002, there were NO federal monetary appropriations whatsoever for organized training of psychologists at the graduate or internship level. Through excellent and dogged advocacy led by APA's Education Directorate, a modest appropriation was approved and 25 programs successfully competed for training funds. Compared to federal appropriations for Graduate Medical Education in Medicine, however, the initial $2M appropriation for GPEP was miniscule in comparison to the billions available for Graduate Medical Education, and in the current economic climate the appropriation for GPEP has been threatened with reduction or elimination nearly every year since. Every neuropsychologist who is involved in the education and training of tomorrow's cadre of neuropsychologists should be involved in advocating for the enhancement of GPEP or other programs designed to achieve a fairer, more level playing field with our colleagues in other health care disciplines. In this example others are minding the store, but they are grossly understaffed and would significantly benefit from additional reinforcements.

I can't make a difference, so why bother?

Individuals can make a difference, and providing clear examples of how this can occur is one goal of this special issue of *The Clinical Neuropsychologist*. Every good idea or potential solution begins in the mind of an individual. Each individual practitioner and the effort they exert for the field makes a real and tangible difference. "Constituents are the most important influence on a

Member's voting decision" (APA, 2009, *A Psychologist's Guide to Federal Advocacy*, p. 13). Grassroots advocacy and letter writing have been shown to be very effective in influencing political decision making. One reason why grassroots efforts work so well is that elected officials are concerned with and responsive to issues that affect the voting population. Letters to elected officials seek to inform and persuade them on issues. Even if officials do not read every single letter, their staff prepares tallies and reports concerning letters received for and against a particular position. When only a few letters are received regarding an issue, the content of that letter becomes proportionally more important and may have a real impact in guiding the policy maker's decisions. If politicians hear from enough individuals, the weight of the mail may counteract lobbying efforts in opposition to a position. This is what occurred in the 2005 California Licensing Board issue described above. Individual practitioners can make a tangible difference by responding immediately when there is a call to action from one of the neuropsychological organizations.

I don't have time

Many neuropsychologists do not get involved in advocacy because of busy patient schedules, reports that are due tomorrow, supervision and other meeting demands, or the paper that needs to be finished. While these are all legitimate excuses, advocacy doesn't always take extended time and can be woven into the everyday activities of most neuropsychologists. For example, increasing the general public's and other professions' awareness of neuropsychology is a form of advocacy. Having neuropsychology brochures available in the waiting room or for distribution to other healthcare professionals (excellent brochures can be downloaded free of charge from the Division 40 website[1]) can increase the public's awareness of neuropsychology and may reach patients, families, or professionals who are not actively seeking neuropsychological services at that time. Additionally, when co-workers and friends ask what neuropsychology entails, being prepared with a succinct and understandable answer that conveys some of the benefits and usefulness of neuropsychology is another form of advocacy for the field. Answering requests from news organizations to provide an opinion about a relevant issue can greatly increase public awareness of the field (particularly if the opinion is reasonable and evidence-based). Furthermore, when our larger organizations, such as APA's Practice Organization, request a call to action (a so-called "action alert"), the emails soliciting help often contain sample letters and where to send the letter, email, or fax. When balancing the time required to slightly alter the form sent in the email and direct it to the appropriate target versus the impact of non-action by practitioners, it should be clear that each practitioner has and should take the minimal amount of time required to respond to action alerts. Advocacy can occur at multiple levels and does not always require inordinate or burdensome time commitments.

[1]http://www.div40.org/Resources_Pages/neuropsychology_brochures.htm

I don't know how to get involved, even if I wanted to

This is a stumbling block with which many practitioners may resonate. A first reaction to identifying a problem, even if there is a desire to become involved and advocate for the field, may be "But I don't know how." In reality this is sometimes a rationalization for anyone who has even a small awareness of the specialty-focused organizations related to clinical neuropsychology or to APA. In a sense, this response conjures up the old psychodynamic concepts of denial and repression, which in this instance would serve to block the person from the anxiety or anticipated stress of recognizing resources that are already well known, and then becoming involved. One of the concrete goals of this article and special issue of *TCN* is to show practitioners how they can immediately become involved on several different levels, from learning about key issues and becoming a part of an advocacy network, to contacting organizational chairs and offering to help with particular causes.

Advocacy is uncomfortable because it is emotional, not scientific

While our education and training prepares us for practice and research, it does not commonly prepare us for advocacy. We are taught to think as scientist-practitioners, using an evidence-based approach to patient care, and keeping clinical relevance in mind when conducting scientific research. We are taught to be objective in our interpretations and in our methods. Advocacy is sometimes perceived as violating our adherence to objectivity because it can be viewed as "emotionally championing a cause." In our view, while advocacy does entail an emotional commitment, it best proceeds if one's argument is rooted in scientific data and outcomes. In arguing for the importance of neuropsychological services we must be prepared to cite evidence of utility, of cost-effectiveness or cost-offset, or of positive outcomes in support of our position. We must be able to show, in behavioral and economic terms, that our positions are based on credible data. These are the products of clinical research studies, and many more data on cost-effectiveness of neuropsychological procedures are needed. This illustrates how clinical research findings and advocacy must shake hands firmly if we are to make progress. Thus it is not the case that advocacy and science are opposed in any meaningful way; in fact, successful advocacy depends on good science, and scientific activity depends on successful advocacy needed to secure funding and training support.

Outcome studies and evidence-based research and clinical practice are discussed in this issue in Chelune's "Evidence-Based Research and Practice in Clinical Neuropsychology" and Prigatano and Morrone-Strupinsky's "Advancing the Profession of Clinical Neuropsychology with Appropriate Outcome Studies and Demonstration of Clinical Skills." It is important to note The American Academy of Clinical Neuropsychology (AACN), via the non-profit AACN Foundation, is focused on funding clinical outcome projects that can demonstrate the cost-effectiveness of our assessment and intervention procedures. The National Academy of Neuropsychology (NAN), via the NAN Foundation, also supports clinical research projects central to our specialty.

HOW TO PREPARE TO ADVOCATE: SOME PRELIMINARY STEPS

Be informed

In order to advocate, the individual practitioner must be informed regarding the issues and concerns confronting the field of neuropsychology. There are many ways to stay informed. One key approach is to obtain formal, regular continuing education on key policy issues and trends in science, practice, and education/training. Most licensed psychologists are required to obtain CE as a condition of maintaining state licensure. Only a minority of states does not have such a requirement, and it seems likely that all states will have this requirement eventually. A good practice is to devote at least some of the required time to advocacy-worthy topics. Several websites that have information pertaining to current issues of concern in psychology and neuropsychology are listed in Appendix A. Listserv membership is a way of immediately hearing about key, time-sensitive calls for action. For instance, the Division 40 listserv sends out practice alerts and calls to action that inform individual practitioners of key issues as they arise. Often, these "alerts" will occur when a bill is being considered, or when a legislative vote is pending, and typically call for immediate action. Additionally, joining listservs (e.g., AACN, NPSYCH) is one way that individual practitioners and scientists can raise issues, propose solutions, and learn about what is currently being done in certain practice areas. Appendix B lists the administrators and how to join a number of the open neuropsychology-oriented listservs. Attending local and national meetings and conferences offers additional routes for practitioners to stay informed.

Assess your strengths and weaknesses

Some people feel that advocacy is not their "cup of tea," and many conjure up images of placard-waving demonstrations or marches on Capitol Hill as their prototypic concept of what it means to fight for a cause. In contrast, advocacy takes many forms and a concerted advocacy effort requires many people with different talents and interests working toward a goal. Figuring out how to "fit in" is the first step. Identifying unique skill sets and matching abilities and resources with potential volunteer efforts is important. For example, individuals who are artists may be able to draw designs for informational brochures. A good speaker may be well suited to volunteer to give a talk at a hospital grand rounds or community center regarding the benefits of neuropsychological services. A good organizer can volunteer to develop a comprehensive distribution list or to organize informational events for the community. For those with less time or who are more comfortable with someone else providing direction, opportunities include volunteering to complete pre-written action alerts, serving on specific committees, and becoming involved in specific ongoing projects. Everyone has something to offer and therefore everyone has a means of advocating for a cause they believe in.

BRIEF OVERVIEW OF FEDERAL ADVOCACY

APA's Public Policy Office has a link to the informational guide *A Psychologist's Guide to Federal Advocacy*, which gives an overview of federal advocacy including a brief and understandable description of the legislative process (http://www.apa.org/ppo/ppan/advocacyguide.html). When engaging in federal advocacy, practitioners need to know who the local members of Congress are and how to contact them. This information for the US House of Representatives is available via the http://www.house.gov/writerep/ website. Senators and their contact information can be found at http://www.senate.gov/general/contact_information/senators_cfm.cfm. Many of the same principles can be applied when advocating on the state and local level. State and local legislator contact information can usually be found easily via the Internet.

GENERAL WAYS INDIVIDUAL PRACTITIONERS CAN BECOME INVOLVED IN ADVOCACY FOR THE FIELD

Individual practitioners can participate at local, state, or national levels. Individuals can participate in issues that affect psychology in general or neuropsychology more specifically. Individuals can concentrate their efforts on one or two particular issues or give general help broadly by responding to action alerts. Several means by which individual practitioner can become involved are discussed below.

Increasing the general public's awareness of neuropsychology

Increasing the public's awareness of neuropsychology is important for our field to grow and flourish. Several benefits could flow directly from increasing the exposure of the general public to the science and practice of neuropsychology. Assuming that scientific advances in preclinical detection of neurobehavioral disorders will continue to advance, and assuming medical advances in treatment of behavioral or cognitive impairment, neuropsychological services could enjoy increasing roles in prevention efforts, much like the roles currently played by mammograms or colonoscopies in preventative health care. If neuropsychology's role in treatment planning is better articulated, individuals may begin to request neuropsychological examinations when they or family members notice changes in cognitive functioning. This would lead to an increase in referrals to practitioners. Aside from financial gains to the individual practitioners, diseases and brain pathology may be identified at earlier stages and treatments could potentially be implemented sooner. With regards to degenerative and progressive diseases, families would have more time to adjust and plan for the future. Each of these effects can potentially improve patient care as well as treatment and patient-centered outcomes.

In addition, if the public was aware of the extensive training and knowledge of brain–behavior relationships required for comprehensive neuropsychological examinations, this knowledge might improve the ability of the public to discern quality of care among professionals who offer neuropsychological services. Increasing such awareness at the professional and legislative levels might lead to more effective definition and quality control of neuropsychological specialty practice. Increasing the general public's awareness of neuropsychology as a science and a practice would also increase awareness of the value of neuropsychology by the public and by other health care professionals. Increasing the general public's awareness of neuropsychology is a goal of several of our major organizations, which is the focus of the article "Increasing Awareness of Clinical Neuropsychology in the General Public" by Attix and Potter in this special issue.

Increasing medical and other healthcare practitioners' knowledge of neuropsychology

Just as it is important to increase the general public's awareness of neuropsychology, it is also important to increase awareness of what neuropsychologists can offer among our interdisciplinary healthcare colleagues. This can potentially increase referrals and allow neuropsychology to achieve a better integration with other services so that neurobehavioral factors are considered in the patient's overall case conceptualization. Individual practitioners can offer to conduct presentations teaching an overview of neuropsychology and highlighting its benefits at local hospitals, nursing homes, other departments, and similar venues. This is direct advocacy for the advancement of our specialty.

Increasing colleagues' awareness of the issues within our specialty

Sharing information with colleagues is crucial. Routes to become acquainted with current topics of concern have already been reviewed. Taking individual awareness a step further, the information should be shared with other colleagues and friends. An organized way to achieve this is to set up a personal email alert list, which can be done easily via an email provider or using a program such as Excel or Outlook. When receiving an action alert from one of the organizations such as Division 40, activating personal alert lists is relatively simple; just forward the email to the designated personal alert list. This results in friends and colleagues who did not receive the alert from the original source now being informed and having the opportunity to act if they wish. Information is empowering because it gives the recipient the choice to act and be heard on an issue.

Increasing knowledge of neuropsychology within the political system

The intersection of psychology and the political system is an important area in which we need to increase the presence and awareness of neuropsychology. This encompasses the intersection of neuropsychology and the law, which includes administrative law hearings and the court system. This also includes the interaction of neuropsychologists and politicians (legislators and other elected officials). There are various ways an individual practitioner can advocate at the intersection of neuropsychology and the political system.

Public hearings. Occasionally there are public hearings on issues that may impact the field of neuropsychology. When these occur, neuropsychologists should attend and voice their concerns. For example, when funding to rehabilitation facilities is being considered for budget cuts, neuropsychologists can accentuate the importance of such services and can explain how losing services will impact the community. When laws potentially affecting public health and safety (e.g., seatbelt restraints/helmet laws, alcohol and drug abuse policies) are considered, neuropsychologists can provide relevant input based on scientific evidence.

Ways to interact with elected officials. There are many routes to interact with elected officials. These typically include letters, emails, phone calls, faxes, and face-to-face meetings. When utilizing any of these routes the individual practitioner should "stick with the facts" even when the issue is one she or he feels very passionate about. Losing one's temper or becoming irrational is a quick way to have targeted recipient disregard the information to be conveyed. Empirical evidence should be used to support positions when possible.

It is important to keep in mind the information overload that often accompanies debate on key legislative initiatives. Elected officials often are very busy and receive hundreds of letters from constituents each day. When writing a letter, email, or fax to an elected official following these simple rules[2] will increase the effectiveness of your efforts. Foremost: be clear, direct, and succinct. If possible, limit the correspondence to one page; each contact should concern only one main issue. Ideally, state the position, support it with facts and information, cite the bill number or legislation concerned, and when possible illustrate long-term negative consequences or how certain populations or areas may be affected. If requesting a response, contact information should be included.

A sample letter utilizing some of these pointers and a guide to making phone calls as a constituent is provided in the APA's *A Psychologist's Guide to Federal Advocacy* which can be found via the APA website at http://www.apa.org/ppo/ppan/advocacyguide.html

Responding to action alerts and grassroots efforts. Grassroots advocacy is action taken by concerned citizens supporting issues of concern to them. Being a part of a grassroots network and responding timely when contacted is an important way for the individual practitioner to be involved in the advocacy process. Every response adds to the cumulative effectiveness of the effort. Our voice is stronger when we stand together, and amounts to only a whisper when we don't.

APA congressional fellowship program. Individual practitioners who want to become intimately involved with policy making can apply for one of the APA Congressional Fellow positions and spend one year working as a special legislative assistant on the staff of a member of congress on a congressional committee http://www.apa.org/ppo/fellows/congressional.html

---

[2]Some of the advice given was taken from the APA's *A Psychologist's Guide to Federal Advocacy*, which extracted the advice from the Congressional Record.

Interactions with our organizations

Support APA. In the past APA has played a central role in major advocacy issues relevant to neuropsychology, including obtaining Graduate Medical Education funding for our educational programs and advocating for better reimbursement for our CPT codes from CMS and AMA/CPT. Undoubtedly, APA's role will continue to be central in the future. Recognition and support of APA is crucial to its ability to provide ongoing support for psychology and neuropsychology. This support can take the form of financial contributions and/or time contributions. Serving on committees within APA that help guide the direction of the organization is an important way to become involved. In addition, the APA has a Practice Directorate and affiliated foundation Association for the Advancement of Psychology (http://aapnet.org/) whose goal is to "make Members of Congress aware of the significant contributions that psychology makes to health, education, human performance and the public welfare" (http://aapnet.org/index.htm accessed March 7, 2009). Supporting these facets of APA, and especially Division 40 (Division of Clinical Neuropsychology), is critically important and considered a primary means of advocating for the field of neuropsychology.

Support the neuropsychology-specific organizations. At a minimum, individual practitioners should join and support the major neuropsychological organizations by paying membership fees and by attending annual meetings. A portion of the fee collected goes towards funding advocacy efforts. Although practitioners may at times disagree with some of the actions of our organizations, overall the organizations have the best interests of the field in mind. It is critical to remember that organizational boards are elected from the membership and that self-nominations are always welcomed. Some perceive the board election process as a club-like atmosphere; the reality is that most neuropsychological organizations actively seek involvement from the membership and benefit when someone self-nominates for an activity or expresses an interest in getting involved. Another way to support our organizations is to encourage colleagues, including students to join the organizations.

One additional way to get involved is to support current efforts to develop studies on neuropsychological outcomes (Outcomes Research Group) sponsored by the American Academy of Clinical Neuropsychology. This initiative is designed to support, through foundation support, studies of the cost-efficacy of neuropsychological services, the effects of neuropsychological services on future health and healthcare consumption, and the incremental value associated with professional neuropsychological consultation in the interdisciplinary health care setting.

Students and practitioners can become involved with our organizations in several ways. AACN, Division 40 within APA, NAN, and INS list board members and committee chairs on their websites. Individuals can directly contact board members and committee chairs to convey that an area is of interest to him or her and offer to help when needed. Additionally, AACN, NAN and Division 40 have extensive committee structures, with many of these committees involved in a range of activities related to advocacy efforts. Calls for volunteers for activities or committee positions are periodically noted in mailings or posted on organizational listervs. Individuals can keep an eye out for theses notices and respond when indicated.

Issue alerts. When an individual practitioner notices a policy, practice, change in law, or occurrence that may affect our field, they can take the initiative and alert one of our organizations (e.g., AACN, Division 40, NAN, APA, state organizations). It is possible the organizations are already aware of the situation, but there may be times (particularly when the issue involves a local or state determination) when they are not yet aware. The sooner our organizations are aware of current issues the better able they are to respond appropriately and effectively.

CONCLUSION

There are many specific topics toward which individuals can direct their advocacy efforts. For example, working toward reasonable reimbursement rates and procedures for neuropsychological services, increasing awareness of neuropsychology in the community, increasing and maintaining funding for neuropsychology training programs, allocation of funding for neuropsychological and neurobehavioral research, and patient services, are topics with which individual practitioners can become involved. Ongoing advocacy efforts are needed related to these and other topics. In coming years, developments in specialty education and training and in the specialty designation of neuropsychologists will raise important issues for how we define ourselves. At the local and state levels the specialty of clinical neuropsychology is uniquely positioned, due to our distinctive knowledge base, to provide important comment on relevant legislation involving public health, safety, or healthcare policies.

We hope and expect that this special issue of *The Clinical Neuropsychologist* will provide a useful review of some advocacy areas in more depth and enable the individual practitioner to become involved in related activities that benefit our field, our colleagues, and the patients we serve. Aside from this introduction and general review of advocacy, there are 12 papers presented within this special issue that cover a diverse range of topics illustrating how individuals can become involved in the advocacy process. The 12 articles address topics such as increasing the public's awareness of neuropsychology, how to advocate for neuropsychology in the government sector, promotion of professional identity and scope of practice, advancement of the science of the field, select issues at the interface of neuropsychology and the law, increasing the diversity of neuropsychological practitioners, and increasing services to underserved populations. One of these contributions also shows how neuropsychologists can become involved and advocate to improve clinical services and quality of life for specific patient populations. It is our hope that this special issue will be a catalyst for positive change within and for the field of neuropsychology, as well as for the society in which we all live and work.

REFERENCES

AACN. (1999). American Academy of Clinical Neuropsychology Policy on the Use of Non-Doctoral-Level Personnel in Conducting Clinical Neuropsychological Evaluations. *The Clinical Neuropsychologist*, *13*(4), 385.

American Psychological Association. (2002). Ethical Principles of Psychologists and Code of Conduct. *American Psychologist*, *57*, 12–28.

American Psychological Association Board of Professional Affairs, Committee on Professional Standards. (1987). General guidelines for providers of psychological services. *American Psychologist*, *42*, 712–723.

American Psychological Association Education Directorate. (2009). *A Psychologist's Guide to Federal Advocacy* (http://www.apa.org/ppo/ppan/advocacyguide.html).

Bauer, R. (2006). President's message. *Newsletter 40*, *24*(1), 26.

Black, H. C., et al. (1999). *Black's law dictionary* (7th ed.). St. Paul, MN: West Publishing.

Kahneman, D., Knetsch, J. L., & Thaler, R. H. (1991). Anomalies: The endowment effect, loss aversion, and status quo bias. *Journal of Economic Perspectives*, *5*(1), 193–206.

Latané, B., & Darley, J. M. (1970). *The unresponsive bystander: Why doesn't he help?*. New York: Appleton-Century-Crofts.

National Academy of Neuropsychology. (2006). The use, education, training, and supervision of neuropsychology test technicians (psychometrists) in clinical practice. *Archives of Clinical Neuropsychology*, *21*, 837–839.

Report of the Division 40 Task Force on Education, Accreditation, and Credentialing. (1989). Guidelines regarding the use of non-doctoral personnel in clinical neuropsychological assessment. *The Clinical Neuropsychologist*, *3*(1), 23–24.

Report of the Division 40 Task Force on Education, Accreditation, & Credentialing. (1991). Recommendations for education and training of non-doctoral personnel in clinical neuropsychology. *The Clinical Neuropsychologist*, *5*(1), 20–23.

Sweet, J., Peck, E., Abramowitz, C., & Etzweiler, S. (2002). The NAN/Division 40 Practice Survey. *The Clinical Neuropsychologist*, *16*, 109–127.

Sweet, J., Nelson, N., & Moberg, P. (2006). The TCN/AACN "Salary Survey": Professional practices, beliefs, and incomes of US neuropsychologists. *The Clinical Neuropsychologist*, *20*, 325–364.

APPENDIX A

Websites that may contain relevant issues and/or advocacy alerts for the field of psychology.

(1) APA's Public Policy Office's website http://www.apa.org/ppo has information on issues of interest and concern to psychology in general at http://www.apa.org/ppo/issues
(2) APA's Public Policy Advocacy Network (PPAN) is located at http://www.apa.org/ppo/forms/joinppan.html
(3) APA's Federal Education Advocacy Coordinators (FEDAC) grassroots network is located at http://www.apa.org/ppo/ppan/fedac.html
(4) Regarding issues of concern specifically related to neuropsychology, practitioners can access the AACN (http://www.theaacn.org/index.php), NAN (http://www.nanonline.org/), or Division 40 (http://www.div40.org/) websites.
(5) The AACN Committees can be found at http://www.theaacn.org/committees.php

(6) The NAN Professional Affairs and Information Committee is located at http://www.nanonline.org/paio/index.shtm
(7) The Division 40 Practitioners Corner is located at http://www.div40.org/Committee_Activities_Pages/Advisory_Committee/prac_corner.htm
(8) Division 40 of the APA has an informational announcement list serve that sends important information to practitioners DIV40ANNOUNCE@LISTS.APA.ORG

APPENDIX B

Neuropsychology-oriented listservs:

(1) The Association of Neuropsychology Students in Training (ANST)

Administrator: John Strang
Participants: Students who are interested in or currently enrolled in graduate, internship, or post doctoral programs focusing on neuropsychology and neuropsychologists.
To join: Send an email to LISTSERV@LISTS.APA.ORG. In the body of the message (not the subject line) type: SUBSCRIBE DIV40ANST.
Listserv address: DIV40ANST@LISTS.APA.ORG

(2) Forensic Neuropsychology (FORENSICNP)

Administrator: Joe Dixon, J.D., Ph.D., HSP-P
Participants: Psychologists and physicians, or psychologists and physicians who are also attorneys.
To join: Send an email to Dr. Dixon at doc.dixon@psychologyandlaw.com with a request to join the forensic neuropsychology listserv. In your email include your professional status (i.e., licensed psychologist, post doctoral fellow, graduate student).
Listserv address: FORENSICNP@BAMA.UA.EDU

(3) Neuropsychology Listserv (NPSYCH)

Administrators: David Loring, Ph.D., ABPP-CN and Laura Howe, J.D., Ph.D.
Participants: Professionals and trainees with an interest in neuropsychology and brain behavior relationships.
To join: Go to http://www.neurolist.com/
Scroll down to the second list that can be joined called NPSYCH. Enter your name, email, and create a password. Within two weeks you will be contacted and directed to indicate your credentials and interest in joining the list serve. Once reviewed, you will be added as a member to the listserv.
Listserv address: npsych@neurolist.com

(4) Pediatric Neuropsychology Listserv (PED-NPSY)

Administrator: Steve Hughes, Ph.D., L.P., ABPdN
Participants: Neuropsychologists and trainees along with professionals from related fields.

To join: Send an email to Dr. Hughes at sjh@umn.edu with the subject line "CREDENTIALS."

In the body of the email include:

(1) Name to add
(2) Email address to add
(3) Highest degree obtained
(4) Licensure status and where issued
(5) Institutional affiliation (e.g., university) or practice group (if applicable).

Listserv address: PED-NPSY@LISTS.UMN.EDU

(5) Women in Neuropsychology (WIN)

Administrator: Chris Morrison, Ph.D., ABPP
Participants: Individuals interested in mentoring and supporting the role of women in neuropsychology.
To join: Send an email indicating interest to Dr. Morrison at chris.morrison@nyumc.org
Listserv address: DIV40WIN@LISTS.APA.ORG

The Clinical Neuropsychologist, 24: 391–400, 2010
http://www.psypress.com/tcn
ISSN: 1385-4046 print/1744-4144 online
DOI: 10.1080/13854040802537668

Psychology Press
Taylor & Francis Group

INCREASING AWARENESS OF CLINICAL NEUROPSYCHOLOGY IN THE GENERAL PUBLIC

Deborah K. Attix[1,2] and Guy G. Potter[2]
[1]Division of Neurology and [2]Division of Medical Psychology, Duke University Medical Center, Durham, NC, USA

We can only benefit from raising public awareness about the unique role of clinical neuropsychology in patient care and clinical research. Public awareness of the distinctive skills of our practitioners and researchers and the utility of our products may well be linked to our viability as a field given the current healthcare and funding climates. This article discusses the goals of public awareness efforts for clinical neuropsychology, and outlines current resources that can be utilized toward this end. We review the process of creating new public awareness resources and discuss ideas for how practitioners can become involved public awareness efforts. We consider some of the many issues driving the need for public awareness activities and resources, highlight the need for practitioners and professional organizations to be self-advocates, and hope to inspire our field to the very feasible process of integrating public awareness efforts into professional practice.

Keywords: Public awareness; Awareness; Communication.

INTRODUCTION

Clinical neuropsychologists are currently in the midst of a changing healthcare climate in which reimbursement for services is increasingly linked to definitions of medical necessity, empirically validated treatment, and cost/benefit outcomes. These definitions require clinical neuropsychologists to clarify to themselves and others what is valuable about their services, and specifically how these services improve patient care and quality of life. Delineation of what differentiates clinical neuropsychology from other fields like occupational therapy, speech pathology, and social work, and how their evaluations differ from school-based evaluations, is also critical. Clarifying the value of neuropsychology within the field can take place though continuing education, activities within professional organizations, and discourse in journals like *The Clinical Neuropsychologist*. Clarifying the value of neuropsychology outside of the field represents a greater challenge because this involves diverse groups ranging from legislators, to insurance companies, to physicians, and of course to patients. The purpose of the current article is to discuss ways in which clinical neuropsychologists can promote public awareness of our field.

Address correspondence to: Deborah K. Attix, Ph.D., ABPP/CN, Box 3333 Duke University Medical Center, Durham, NC 27710, USA. E-mail: koltai@duke.edu
Accepted for publication: October 5, 2008. First published online: March 31, 2009.

What is clinical neuropsychology?

Informing the general public about clinical neuropsychology includes characterizing our science and our practice. When asked, most of us within the field can reliably produce a definition of clinical neuropsychology that is consistent with that provided by the National Academy of Neuropsychology (Barth et al., 2003) or the archival definition of Division 40 of the American Psychological Association (Division 40, 1989). The latter states (p. 22), "A clinical neuropsychologist is a professional psychologist who applies principles of assessment and intervention based upon the scientific study of human behavior as it relates to normal and abnormal functioning of the central nervous system." We have come to understand that this definition may not resonate so clearly with the lay public when we get the response, "So you're a 'clinical nurse-psychologist'?" This definition, however, may also not be clear to our colleagues and referral sources in the fields of psychiatry, neurology, and even those in neuropsychiatry, all of whom devote attention to the interaction of brain and behavior. Although we are a recognized *specialty* with aspirational guidelines for education and training (Hannay, 1998), it is our distinct impression that the depth and breadth of the neuropsychological knowledge base and skill set is not widely known. One of the important characteristics of clinical neuropsychology is that we are trained in the science of cognitive and behavioral assessment as well as intervention; however, when one moves beyond the close circle of those practicing within the profession or those providing direct referrals, there is often misunderstanding, confusion, and gross misinformation about the role and scope clinical neuropsychology. Seemingly prevalent examples within healthcare research settings include the use of neuropsychological instruments in research studies without input from a neuropsychologist, and the perception that any healthcare provider or scientist has the psychometric knowledge necessary to validly administer, score, and interpret neurocognitive measures. Lack of information in healthcare and general public spheres about the science and practice standards of clinical neuropsychology can result in the misuse of neuropsychological measures in a manner that adversely affects both our professional reputation and patient care. Examples of such misinformation are reflected in research reports delineating the structure of human memory based solely on a digit-span test, or the use of cognitive measures to diagnosis "memory" deficits by practitioners without training in brain–behavior relationships, functional neuroanatomy, or neurobehavioral disorders.

It is clear that there is inadequate public information about the role of clinical neuropsychology in patient care and clinical research. Although there may be many things that contribute to inadequate public awareness of neuropsychology, three clear modifiable factors are: (1) our own motivation and sense of responsibility to engage in public awareness education, (2) our knowledge of methods that can be utilized to this end, and (3) our own limited awareness of tools that exist for such awareness efforts. Public awareness education often occurs on the level of practitioner-to-patient and practitioner-to-practitioner interactions. These interactions are likely to be most effective in conjunction with communication tools, such as talks and distribution of printed and web-based materials.

Goals of public awareness

The goals of providing clear information to patients, physicians, and insurers about the expertise and clinical services available from our profession are to (1) increase consumer satisfaction, (2) generate appropriate referrals, (3) promote involvement in multidisciplinary treatment and research teams, and (4) facilitate reimbursement for our assessment and intervention services at a level consistent with our training and expertise. Clarity about the distinctive expertise of clinical neuropsychologists may reduce confusion about our unique contribution to patient care, as well as reduce the use of neuropsychological instruments and provision of neuropsychological services among those who do not have adequate clinical training. Defining the practice standards of clinical neuropsychology to our consumers—patients, parents, caregivers, and referral sources—is particularly important given the lack of enforceable guidelines for the use and dissemination of neuropsychological instruments.

FOCUSED GOALS

The focused goals of this article are to describe how public awareness tools can be created and applied, and to encourage organizational development of these tools to increase public awareness of clinical neuropsychology. Individual practitioners are also encouraged to participate in public awareness efforts. Some tools that may be used toward this end are described as part of this article.

Previous and continuing efforts

We believe it is important to expand the resources that clinicians may draw from to promote public awareness both individually and on behalf of our field. A significant challenge is the lack of a central repository for such work; tools may be available without widespread knowledge of their existence. Tools created by our national organizations can be particularly useful, as they are typically created to be applicable to the broad memberships they serve. The resources available through our professional organizations may allow for the creation of more sophisticated communication tools, and they are often highly visible. Finally, communication tools developed in conjunction with professional organizations typically undergo careful review and sanction, which supports broad utility and minimizes individualistic representations of our profession. At present, Division 40 has two public information brochures that can be located at http://www.div40.org/resources.htm These brochures currently can be downloaded for printing or ordered via direct mailing and are available in English, Spanish, and French. The NAN Professional Affairs and Information Committee (PAIC) has assembled a packet of resources that can be used in educational efforts and to assist in interactions with managed care. This packet presently includes a paper written for legislators, managed care operators, and lay persons (Ball, Stutts, Morgan, Peck & Sari, 2004) and can be accessed via the NAN PAIC or the authors.

Direct outreach to the community is a powerful method of promoting public awareness. An effective method of doing so is to give talks in venues such as hospitals, nursing homes, and schools. Clinical neuropsychologists are well trained to teach the public about a variety of clinical conditions, and patient care organizations associated with these conditions are typically eager for such outreach. Presentations to specific patient interest organizations, such as the Alzheimer's Association, can also be powerful and effective. Some target audiences are listed in Table 1. In our personal experience, outreach to one patient advocacy group often generates requests from other groups, and that content pertaining to the science and practice of clinical neuropsychology is somewhat transferable across groups. Another powerful source of public awareness occurs at the level of individual patients, family members, and physicians. We know that many practitioners have designed information sheets or flyers to raise awareness about their specific services or programs. We also know that clinical neuropsychologists frequently speak in public forums or lecture in teaching settings to professionals who could be important consumers of neuropsychological services (e.g., medical students). These specific and targeted talks, monograms, and other outreach efforts are numerous and impossible to track and acknowledge in a comprehensive manner, but networking within our neuropsychological community can facilitate sharing of experience and resources.

Table 1 Methods of participation

Develop printed information	• Brochures • Flyers • Magazine and newspaper articles
Develop web-based resources	• Information on personal services • Links to neuropsychology sites • Links to associations and organizations
Public speaking	• Schools • Associations and organizations supporting patients and families with central nervous system disorders (e.g., Alzheimer's Association) • Allied health conferences (e.g., neurology) • College, graduate, medical school seminars • Nursing homes • Day care centers (child and adult) • Medical clinics • Community centers
Volunteering	• Division 40 Public Interest Advisory Committee • National Academy of Neuropsychology Professional Affairs and Information Committee • American Academy of Clinical Neuropsychology • American Psychological Association Media Referral Service • State and regional associations and organizations

Another way to promote public awareness of clinical neuropsychology is via targeted forums. Neuropsychologists who are highly visible in the press, who are well published or publicized, or who are known via their institutions, may come across unique opportunities to contribute to public awareness. We encourage individuals to capitalize on these opportunities for public awareness as they arise. These opportunities typically involve low-cost methods of reaching targeted forums to disseminate information and increase public awareness of clinical neuropsychology. While such efforts may be of most benefit to the target audience rather than the practitioner, we encourage participation in such opportunities for the greater good of the field. As an illustration, an article entitled "Depression and Cognitive Impairment in Older Adults" (Potter & Steffens, 2007) appeared in the *Psychiatric Times*. This article was an opportunity to shape the dialogue on an important mental heath condition from a neuropsychologist's perspective, in a forum that reaches a large audience of mental health professionals and the general public. At the time of this writing, it can be accessed at: http://www.psychiatrictimes.com/display/article/10168/54436. Another example (Sullivan, 2007) was published in *The Science Teacher*, entitled "Career of the Month: An Interview with Clinical Neuropsychologist Deborah Attix". At present, this piece can be accessed at http://www.nsta.org/store/product_detail.aspx?id=10.2505/4/tst07_074_01_54. These articles reflect the personal experience of the authors, and numerous examples of the activities or other neuropsychologists also exist. Current events may also provide opportunities for positive public awareness of clinical neuropsychology. The characterization of head trauma as a signature injury associated with the current military activity in Iraq highlights the role of clinical neuropsychologists in the assessment and treatment of brain injuries. This was further highlighted by national interest in the brain injury suffered by journalist Bob Woodruff in Iraq and his subsequent road to recovery. Another example is the work of the actor David Hyde Pierce in promoting awareness of Alzheimer's disease. Neuropsychologists should note the activities of high-profile individuals such as these and make use of the connection perceived by patients and the general public to communicate the role of neuropsychology in the assessment and treatment of neurocognitive disorders. While on occasion this may require the correction of inaccurate portrayals of clinical neuropsychology in the media, on the whole this visibility is highly valuable as it increases our opportunities to raise public awareness and provide quality clinical care to patients with cognitive conditions. The publicity often facilitates communication about the relevant condition, easing the process of bringing attention to and defining them, and making way for clarification of the role and utility of clinical neuropsychology in assessment or treatment.

We encourage efforts among neuropsychological practices and local professional organizations to create communication tools for public awareness and to identify novel ways to disseminate tools to appropriate target audiences. Brochures can be disseminated to patients and families, but can also be networked throughout care settings and forwarded to resources in the community, such as the offices of associations serving those with central nervous system disorders. Most practicing neuropsychologists would have little difficulty identifying and targeting several audiences for public awareness efforts. However, we also raise some cautions when advocating these activities; idiosyncratic definitions of clinical neuropsychology may work against efforts to establish a broad-based, unified characterization and understanding of the field. We encourage consideration of the following steps when developing tools for public awareness of neuropsychology.

FUTURE EFFORTS

The future of public awareness would be markedly enhanced if each clinical neuropsychologist considered and acted on their unique ability to make a contribution. Clinicians in private practice could provide community talks. Clinicians and scientists in medical centers could give grand rounds to reach their colleagues, lectures to reach medical students and other health professionals, and meet with specialty clinics underutilizing neuropsychological assessment or therapy services. Those who are able could network with state licensing boards to provide talks or write public awareness pieces for newsletters. Many state psychology associations are involved in legislation and are thus positioned to influence healthcare policy. Volunteering on committees in the American Academy of Clinical Neuropsychology, Division 40 of the American Psychological Association, and the National Academy of Neuropsychology is another avenue of beneficial service.

Future efforts for increasing the public's awareness of neuropsychology require the creation and dissemination of resources that will support educational and outreach efforts. We will next review the best practices for creating resources, and then give an example of how an existing resource was created.

Creation of resources

Identification of need. It is difficult to communicate effectively about clinical neuropsychology without knowledge of what information is most important to the target audience. When planning a communication tool, it is important to select goals carefully because the effort involved in producing materials to reach the potential targets for public awareness often exceeds the financial and participatory resources. For individual clinicians or practices, it may be useful to consider whether there are specific groups that are under-represented in clinical practice relative to one's expertise. An example of this would be a clinician with expertise in neuropsychological rehabilitation who get few outside referrals for this service due to lack of public awareness. One way to identify needs clearly is to make contact with physicians and community groups that may benefit from neuropsychological services. An informative talk on the neuropsychology of a disorder like traumatic brain injury or childhood learning disorders links back to the approach of public forums and is also a good practice-building exercise; in addition, it also provides a captive "focus group" to learn about areas where public awareness is needed. Mailed questionnaires to potential referral sources may also identify areas where information about the expertise and services of neuropsychologists is needed.

Resource identification and development. Prior to developing a communication tool, it is often useful to canvas existing resources. Good ideas rarely exist in a vacuum, and inspiration can often be drawn from existing neuropsychological materials. Useful information may be found among the communication materials of associations that advocate for specific conditions or diseases, such as the Alzheimer's Association. Reviewing the existing resources of relevant groups may minimize redundant information and direct focus to information specific to neuropsychological services.

Execution. Communication tools can be created by individuals or by committee. The former has the advantage of control and efficiency, whereas the latter has the advantage of differing perspectives. Execution is most efficient when linked to an identified need in accordance with a timeline.

Review. Ideally, communication tools will undergo review and approval before being launched for public consumption. While cumbersome at times, obtaining multiple review perspectives typically yields a more thorough, responsible, and usable product. These perspectives should include colleagues within neuropsychology, other healthcare professionals, and members of the lay public. It is important not to overlook the value of family and friends in reviewing communication tools; in our experience they have not only offered valuable perspectives, but they have also expressed appreciation for learning more about what their friend or family member actually does as a neuropsychologist.

Distribution and evaluation. The dissemination of communication tools is largely guided by the target audience. Options include strategic placement of the product in offices or waiting rooms, mailings, and websites with downloadable pdf files. Once public access is established, the success of the communication tool should be evaluated periodically, with attention to modifying content or distribution to maximize its utility and longevity.

Practical considerations. A few points warrant comment regardless of the specific project planned. The target audience of the communication tool should be carefully considered during the early planning stages of the project. Planning of communication tools should include basic principles for promoting health literacy, which reflects the extent to which individuals can understand basic health information in order to obtain appropriate services and make appropriate health decisions. To the extent that lower health literacy is often related to lower levels of education and acculturation to the majority culture, the failure to incorporate health literacy principles, such as clear organization of key information, plain language at the sixth- to eighth-grade reading level, and acknowledgement of cultural differences, may unwittingly exclude populations that are in greatest need of public awareness outreach. A useful introduction to health literacy communication strategies is the "Quick Guide to Health Literacy" published by the U.S. Department of Health and Human Service's Office of Disease Prevention and Health Promotion. At the time of this writing, the document can be accessed at: http://www.health.gov/communication/literacy/quickguide/.

Whether writing to an audience of laypersons or healthcare professionals, it is important to avoid jargon and terminology that may not be easily recognized outside of our field. The writer is likely to be significantly more invested and interested in the product than his or her audience, and the goal of an effective communication tool is to convert this enthusiasm for our field into audience interest. Simple choices about the media and appearance of the tool can either draw readers toward or away from the content. Readability can be enhanced by using *sans serif* fonts (e.g., Arial or Helvetica) that are at least 12-point size. A 14-point font is preferable if members of the target audience are likely to have visual impairments. Avoid overusing italics, which may decrease readability. Clear symbols, pictures, and diagrams can further enhance the health literacy value of the tool when they are relevant and supplement the text. When within budget, graphic design expertise can facilitate a professional product. Ownership and copyright of materials should be negotiated in advance, and policies for when material should be revised should be set. Distribution and outreach efforts to underserved populations should also be considered, including translation of materials into languages other than English.

Example: Division 40 neuropsychology brochures. Two public awareness brochures were published during one of the author's (DKA) tenure as Chair of the Public Interest Advisory Committee (PIAC) of Division 40 of the American Psychological Association (APA): *Clinical Neuropsychology: A Guide for Patients and Their Families* and *Pediatric Neuropsychology: A Guide for Parents*. The ensuing widespread distribution of the brochure suggested a considerable potential impact on public/consumer understanding of the role of clinical neuropsychology in health care. Here we will discuss how our current recommendations for development and distribution of public communication tools were applied to these projects. Although this was one specific example from a number of public awareness initiatives in our field, we hope that this personal perspective will highlight the time, effort, and cooperation necessary to develop an effective public awareness resource.

The *need* for public awareness tools *was identified* by then president of Division 40, Gordon Chelune, Ph.D. Preliminary efforts at drafting a brochure explaining clinical neuropsychology to the general public had already started. With the composition of the PIAC changing, we launched a renewed public communication effort. *Resource identification and development* began with contacting APA and reviewing the public awareness efforts of our major neuropsychology organizations. At that time, there were no national or organizationally based brochures about clinical neuropsychology. APA forwarded brochures about various psychological conditions, but these differed from what the PIAC was envisioning, which involved a focus on our practice rather than on patient conditions. We did learn through this that APA publications would be competitively priced for the printing and distribution of the brochures. The *execution* of brochure development began in earnest, and we *identified a need* for separate pieces for adult and pediatric populations. The entire committee worked on the first drafts of each, which was challenging in terms of logistics and consensus. As a result, development and review subcommittee teams were formed, each comprised of three members, to first craft and then edit each brochure. These drafts were then presented to the Executive Committee (EC) for input and editing, and then later for *review and approval.*

Based on competitive bids, production of the brochures proceeded through APA. Pricing was set by the EC to cover printing and distribution costs. The membership was notified of the brochures via the Division 40 website (www.div40.org), notices in several bi-annual mailings, mention in the minutes of the EC sessions, and most effectively by mailing a copy of each brochure to Division

40 members. *Distribution* over the first two years was estimated at approximately 140,000 brochures. *Evaluation* of the success of brochures and their likely public awareness impact resulted in the Executive Committee approving distribution of the brochure via downloadable pdf file from the website (http://www.div40.org/resources.htm). In the first year, approximately 2875 downloads of the brochure were logged, and approximately 5467 brochure downloads were logged this past year. To further facilitate public awareness, the brochures have been translated into Spanish and French. In addition to being available via pdf file, the brochures can still be ordered directly at this time. Finally, issues of ownership and copyright were established and policy regarding use and specific alterations of the brochure were set.

HOW TO GET INVOLVED

The need for increased public awareness of clinical neuropsychology is clear, as is the necessity of participation by neuropsychologists in the creation of resources to meet that need. Some ideas for mechanisms of information distribution are listed in Table 1, and include printed material and web-based information. In addition to printed information, community lectures and discussions can be a powerful way of increasing public awareness of clinical neuropsychology. Sample target audiences are listed in Table 1.

Neuropsychologists can also volunteer on committees related to public awareness and education. A current listing of relevant committees and subcommittees can also be found in Table 1; however, the structure and function of these organizational groups evolve over time. Finally, questions we have consistently found to be of the highest relevance in raising public awareness appear in Table 2. Neuropsychologists might consider these key elements when educating patient and referral source consumers via any method. When speaking publicly, neuropsychologists might use these elements to prepare "talking points" most relevant to their target audience. These areas of focus would vary across settings, but such preparation could maximize delivery of information about the function and utility of neuropsychological assessment and intervention in relation to the

Table 2 Public awareness questions and topics

- What does neuropsychological testing involve?
- What is the purpose of testing?
- How are the test results relevant to my life?
- How will the test results improve my care?
- What can neuropsychologists do to help me and my family cope with and compensate for my memory and cognitive problems?
- Is there another way to get the same information?
- What are the limitations or risks of testing?
- How long will the assessment take?
- Are the tests culturally sensitive?
- What will the evaluation cost?
- Does insurance cover this service?

condition of interest. For instance, an important point to make in speaking to dementia caregivers would be to highlight how a timely neuropsychological evaluation might prolong the independence of the patient, inform caregiver and professional support, and assist in care and estate planning. When speaking to parents of school-aged children, an important point to highlight is how a timely neuropsychological evaluation for a child might identify learning strengths that can compensate for learning weaknesses, provide diagnostic information to secure needed services, and provide a mechanism for parents, teachers, and other caregivers to better frame and understand a child's behavior and academic performance. In all public awareness efforts, we encourage inclusion of definitions and illustrations emphasizing both the *role* and *value* of clinical neuropsychology in patient care and research.

REFERENCES

Ball, J. D., Stutts, M. L., Peck, E. A., & Sari, D. (2004). The utility of psychological and neuropsychological assessment in modern health care: A report of the Health Care Benefits Committee of the Virginia Academy of Clinical Psychologists. *Psychogram, 29,* (pp. 4–26). Richmond, VA: Virginia Academy of Clinical Psychologists.

Barth, J. T., Pliskin, N., Axelrod, B., Faust, D., Fisher, J., Harley, J. P., et al. (2003). Introduction to the NAN 2001 definition of a clinical neuropsychologist. NAN policy and Planning Committee. *Archives of Clinical Neuropsychology, 18,* 551–555.

Clinical neuropsychology: A guide for patients and their families. (2002). [Division 40 brochure.] New York: APA Publishing.

Division 40. (1989). Definition of a clinical neuropsychologist. *The Clinical Neuropsychologist, 3,* 22.

Hannay, H. J. (1998). Proceedings of the houston conference on specialty education and training in clinical neuropsychology. *Archives of Clinical Neuropsychology, 13,* 157–249.

Pediatric neuropsychology: A guide for parents (2002). [Division 40 brochure.] New York: APA Publishing.

Potter, G. G., & Steffens, D. C. (2007). Depression and cognitive impairment in older adults. *Psychiatric Times, 24,* 23–30.

Sullivan, M. (2007). Career of the month: An interview with clinical neuropsychologist Deborah Attix. *The Science Teacher, 74,* 54–55.

The Clinical Neuropsychologist, 24: 401–416, 2010
http://www.psypress.com/tcn
ISSN: 1385-4046 print/1744-4144 online
DOI: 10.1080/13854040903313597

Psychology Press
Taylor & Francis Group

ADVOCACY FOR NEUROPSYCHOLOGY IN THE PUBLIC SECTOR: THE VA EXPERIENCE

Gerald Goldstein
Mental Illness Research, Education and Clinical Center (MIRECC), VA Pittsburgh Healthcare System, PA, USA

In this paper important advocacy areas for the VA are described with implications for other psychologists working in institutional settings in the public sector, and some advice is provided concerning how best to advocate in the VA. Distinctions among advocacy issues that are of concern to the general public, those that are of concern to all psychologists involved in healthcare, and those specifically related to clinical neuropsychology are made.

Keywords: Veterans; Advocacy; Neuropsychology; Geropsychology.

INTRODUCTION

Many clinical neuropsychologists work in institutional settings for government. In 1998, government agencies at the federal, state, and local level were estimated to employ 17% of the 166,000 jobs held by psychologists (Website Vet Success, http://www.vetsuccess.gov/resources/occupations/profile?id = 82& PHPSESSID = 082494a0a11410dd41f540f103578440, accessed on May 30, 2009). Therefore almost 30,000 psychologists work for government agencies. The federal government employs a large number of psychologists, mainly in healthcare facilities that it operates. The VA and the Department of Defense (DOD) employ a majority of psychologists working for the federal government. The Department of Veterans Affairs (VA) is the nation's largest single employer of psychologists (Baker & Pickren, 2007). The VA healthcare system itself employs 1200 professional psychologists (Akaka, 2007) plus many trainees, psychology technicians, and program support personnel.

Although there is substantial overlap between advocacy needs and goals within the public sector and private, corporate, or academic settings, in many respects needs and goals within the public sector differ from those of American psychology in private or academic settings. There are also regulatory and business ethics constraints regarding how government employees can advocate for their needs that are not present in other employment settings. This paper describes how this public sector of American psychology has a different pattern of advocacy issues from psychologists working in private or academic settings. It will focus on the VA

Address correspondence to: Gerald Goldstein, VA Pittsburgh Healthcare System (151R), 7180 Highland Drive, Pittsburgh, PA 15206, USA. E-mail: ggold@nb.net
Accepted for publication: September 4, 2009.

because the VA has a long and continuing tradition of employing many clinical neuropsychologists. Indeed, some of the important foundations of clinical neuropsychology in America were developed in VA hospitals and clinics. An understanding of the history of these developments and of the structure of the VA is important for gaining an understanding of advocacy methods and strategies used in support of VA psychologists and their veteran patients. Aside from general clinical psychology positions, the VA typically employs individuals in three areas within clinical psychology including health psychology, neuropsychology, and geropsychology. The requirements for employment as a psychologist are contained on the VA website state "The specialty area of the degree must be consistent with the assignment for which the applicant is to be employed" (USAJOBS: http://jobsearch.usajobs.opm.gov/a9va.asp). Regardless of specialization, all professional psychologists hired by the VA are required to have doctoral degrees (Ph.D. or Psy.D.) from an APA accredited program and an APA accredited internship. No exceptions can be granted. The VA also employs psychology technicians at three levels of complexity (GS-5, GS-7, GS-9) who have Bachelor's degrees with psychology majors or Master's degrees. Many neuropsychological technicians function at the GS-9 level due to the demands of the job description. Most clinical psychologists work in the VA healthcare system, now known as the Veterans Health Administration (VHA), although some work in the Department of Veterans Benefits, mainly in the areas of counseling and rehabilitation. The VHA operates VA hospitals throughout the country, with at least one in every state and in Puerto Rico, Guam, American Samoa, the U.S. Virgin Islands, and Manila. Thus VA psychologists are typically hospital employees and their patients are veterans eligible for treatment and in need of healthcare services. In recent years active military soldiers are also being assessed and treated at some VA facilities under some circumstances. For example, the Polytrauma Inpatient Rehabilitation Centers assess and treat some of the soldiers returning from Operation Iraqi Freedom and Operation Enduring Freedom (VHA Directive 2005–024, January, 2005).

Within the structural and regulatory framework there are numerous restrictions on how psychologists employed by the government can advocate for their needs. Perhaps most significantly, the Hatch Act (5 USC §§ 7321–7326) limits participation in partisan political activities. Federal and certain state and local employees may not be candidates for public office in public elections, use official authority to influence an election, or engage in political activity while on duty. Thus a federal employee cannot support the election of a candidate who is an advocate of a position held by the employee through political activity while on the job, and must abide by rules in this regard. For example, psychologists cannot support the election of a candidate who favors strong mental health legislation by wearing a campaign button while at work, or write an advocacy letter to a Congressman on VA stationery. Employees of the federal government may not contact legislators directly in any official VA capacity while on duty status without specific authorization and direction from the VA. Some political activities may be engaged in off duty hours, but such activities as being an officer of a partisan campaign organization are considered inappropriate, even if that activity is carried out off duty hours. There are channels for advocacy activities, but they are different from what is commonly seen in the private sector. For example, if you are advocating for competitive and fair salaries for psychologists, you cannot strike against the federal government.

The history of advocacy efforts supporting psychology in the VA is quite instructive regarding conduct of such activities in the public sector in general. While perhaps presenting a conclusion before providing the evidence, it may be helpful to indicate in advance that advocacy has been successful in the past for psychology in the VA. This history is recorded in two books (Baker, 2007: Baker & Pickren, 2007) that document the history of VA psychology. One does so anecdotally, and the other historically from World War II to the present. Advocating to lawmakers for the importance of clinical neuropsychology to VA patient care has almost become preaching to the saved, because clinical neuropsychology in recent years has become an established area of specialization in VA psychology, and its importance is widely recognized by the VA and the military. Before that, after many years of struggle and controversy, clinical psychology became recognized as an independent healthcare profession. The advocacy issues that became prominent later became those between clinical neuropsychology that wanted to be recognized as an independent specialty within psychology, and clinical psychology in which there was another widely held view that clinical neuropsychology should be characterized as an area of proficiency within clinical psychology.

FOCUSED GOALS

In this paper important advocacy areas for the VA will be described with implications for other psychologists working in institutional settings in the public sector, and some advice will be provided concerning how best to advocate in the VA. Distinctions between advocacy issues that are of concern to the general public, those that are of concern to all psychologists involved in healthcare, and those specifically related to clinical neuropsychology will be made.

Previous and continuing efforts

Goals shared with the public. VA employees are de facto advocates for veterans. A long-standing goal of the VHA has been to establish and maintain a healthcare system that is equal in quality and outcomes or better than any healthcare system available in the world. VHA has the unique mission of providing state of the art healthcare to veterans who deserve the support of the nation they have served and defended. These goals were first articulated by Abraham Lincoln and now are reflected in the VHA's stated mission and vision (About VHA, http://www1.va.gov/health/ aboutVHA.asp, accessed on May 30, 2009). The public also has a continuing interest in assuring the VHA provides prompt and competent care. This general goal is advocated for and implemented at many levels and monitored by advocacy groups, the press, and the public.

The VA was founded as an administrative coordinating agency in 1930 but is now a Department in the cabinet. Therefore the leader of the VA is now called the Secretary of Veterans Affairs, making the position equivalent to the Secretary of the Treasury or of Commerce. There is a direct line in the chain of command from cabinet secretaries to the President. One of the duties of the Secretary of Veterans Affairs is to support provision of an optimal budget for the VA before Congress. The budget allows for programs and services within the VHA. Additionally, there is typically a strong advocacy effort, also made by veterans' organizations such as the American Legion or Disabled American Veterans through the Secretary of Veterans Affairs, to support favorable legislation for veterans before Congress.

Locally, advocacy for veterans includes grassroots efforts where individuals organize to rectify local VA hospitals' perceived deficiencies or to promote desired improvements in service. For example, difficulty in obtaining specialty appointments or long times spent in hospital and clinic waiting rooms or delays in processing of applications for healthcare services or disability determinations are instances of issues often dealt with locally with VA administrators.

National level efforts of public advocacy typically involve specific matters. For example, there was substantial public support for increased substance abuse and PTSD treatment for veterans returning from the Vietnam war. This effort resulted in the establishment of many new programs at VA hospitals, and opening of Veterans Centers in the community. More recently, in association with the wars in Iraq and Afghanistan, there is substantial advocacy for care of returning veterans, particularly in the areas of PTSD and traumatic brain injury. While one cannot document precisely the impact of these public advocacy efforts, as mentioned above, the VA did establish a number of polytrauma centers for these disorders, with strong involvement of neuropsychology (VHA Directive 2005–024, January, 2005).

The advocacy goals of the general public appear to be reasonably focused. Currently the main public advocacy efforts aimed towards the VA appear to be directed at assuring that veterans returning from Iraq and Afghanistan receive prompt and fully competent treatment for their health problems, and that special efforts be made for treatment of traumatic brain injury and PTSD. The increased instances of suicide among returning veterans has also prompted aggressive outreach and monitoring efforts in the VA. There is also the view that efforts should be made to avoid the unfortunate response to veterans following the Vietnam war involving negative reactions to Vietnam veterans apparently because of objection to the war.

Goals for psychology. Historically, when psychologists were first employed by the federal government they generally conducted civilian or military employment assessments or were involved in vocational rehabilitation (Baker & Pickren, 2007). The VA was established in 1930, in response to rising demands for assistance by veterans of World War I; however, the VA did not employ clinical psychologists in hospital settings to any extent until the end of World War II in 1945. At that time, General Omar Bradley was appointed Administrator of the VA by President Truman, and George H. Kelly, Ph.D. was appointed as the first Consultant for Psychology. Psychologists who worked in VA hospitals typically were placed in a Psychiatry Service and the service chiefs were psychiatrists. Psychology was designated as a "Section" in a larger "Psychiatry Service." An early advocacy goal was establishment of an independent "Psychology Service" directed by a psychologist chief. This goal was accomplished, and larger VA hospitals that treated psychiatric patients formed independent "Psychology Services" beginning in 1957.

While this organizational plan no longer exists in many VA hospitals because of a comprehensive reorganization of clinical services, psychologists still maintain reasonable clinical autonomy in the VA. For example, psychologists may operate within the framework of a mental or behavioral health "product line" in which they may have shared administrative control of mental health services. There are now several mental health product or service lines in VA hospitals. Interestingly a number of VA centers are returning to the articulated and autonomous Psychology Service structure. This change appears to reflect a recognition that psychology's focus on behavioral health outside of core mental health diagnostic entities is an important part of the VA healthcare mission.

Following this establishment of relative independence for the discipline of psychology, a number of other advocacy issues arose. Several of them were associated with perceived inequities among professional groups regarding working conditions, loss of administrative oversight of mental health services previously assured by independent psychology services, and time allocations for various activities such as psychological testing. There were discussions and advocacy efforts regarding the grade levels at which psychologists at different levels of responsibility should be placed. These matters are discussed in detail in Chapter 6 of Baker and Pickren (2007) that provides a history of practice issues for psychologists in the VA.

According to Baker and Pickren (2007) "One of the reasons for VA psychology developing its own advocacy initiatives in the early years was that many practice and employment issues were uniquely defined by practice in a large federal organization" (p.115). This advocacy was conducted on multiple levels ranging from Congress and the administration of the VA itself to a local level with hospital administrators and bureaucrats. Two items significantly aided the advocacy efforts of VA psychologists: The presence of a Chief Psychologist in the VA Central Office in Washington and an active collaboration with the APA. Later, there was the formation of a VA section within the Division of Psychologists in Public Service (18) of the APA and the Association of VA Chief Psychologists. This latter association, now known as the Association of VA Psychologist Leaders (AVAPL), has become the primary independent advocacy organization for VA Psychology; and AVAPL works closely in partnership with Division 18 and APA. The groups organize a joint annual meeting that has a strong emphasis on advocacy and education. This partnership has been of enormous value in establishing and advancing the role of psychology in the VA.

Two not fully resolved advocacy issues are the "ABPP bonus" and "Title 38." With regard to the ABPP bonus, some years ago there was an attempt to provide a financial incentive for VA psychologists to become board certified by the American Board of Professional Psychology (ABPP). Historically, while the VA psychology leadership encouraged psychologists to become Diplomates, no incentive was offered to do so. In contrast, for physicians, board certification had important implications for income and promotion to higher administrative positions. Generally, it is expected that a Service Chief will be board certified in her or his specialty. Numerous legislative attempts were made to provide income supplements to board certified psychologists. Despite strenuous advocacy within the VA and by the APA, the idea was not embraced by VA leadership. The idea was proposed, in part, as a means of increasing recruitment of highly competent psychologists.

The VA leadership responded that their recruiting efforts were already sufficient to fill all vacant jobs with fully competent individuals. Ultimately a bill was passed by Congress, but implementation of the plan calling for a lump sum bonus of $10,000 was never undertaken by the agency and expired. Even so, it would have constituted what may be viewed as a compromise. The original plan to provide all Diplomates a one-time lump sum bonus was never implemented, but in 2006, the VA initiated the policy of having ABPP Diplomates receive a "Special Advancement for Achievement" that increases their grade level (e.g., GS-13) one step. Up to that time steps were increased only on the basis of longevity. It would appear that some degree of success was achieved regarding the ABPP bonus apparently because of strong advocacy efforts by the APA and by the AVAPL. This point should be emphasized because, unlike what might be the case in the private sector, individual VA psychologists writing to their Congressman requesting action on the ABPP bonus probably would have been counterproductive. Additionally, increases in pay cannot typically be given on an individual basis such as they can in the private sector. Salaries in the federal government are controlled by Congress and administered, government-wide, by the Office of Personnel Management (OPM).

Without going into any detail about a highly complex matter, VA psychologists were formerly not employed the same way as physicians. Physicians and a small number of other groups are hired under a special law, called Title 38, while psychologists are hired under Title 5, the law that regulates hiring of all other federal employees. It was generally felt that, on balance, there were significant advantages of Title 38 with regard to the hiring process itself, employee benefits, income possibilities, relating income to merit, and upward mobility. A detailed presentation of the history of VA psychology and Title 38 is presented in Chapter 6 of Baker and Pickren (2007). In 2003 a bill was passed that incorporated components of Title 5 and Title 38 and was therefore called "Hybrid Title 38." Its implementation is just beginning and there have been many "glitches" but it appears that the VA is at the beginning of employing and developing psychologists on the basis of their credentials, merit, and responsibilities rather than the perfunctory administrative standards associated with Title 5. The passage of a "hybrid" law may again have represented a compromise between what was sought and what was achieved, but overall the extensive advocacy efforts made to achieve it appear to have substantially improved the status of psychologists in the VA. ABPP Diplomate Special Advancements for Achievement are now starting to be routinely granted.

A third matter that will only be discussed briefly is prescription privileges for psychologists. VA psychology does not appear to speak with one voice on this matter and the need for advocacy is highly controversial. Some psychologists strongly advocate for prescription privileges, while others are opposed to such efforts, and still others are neutral on the issue. The issue was raised regarding what would happen in the VA hospital (s) in some state if a state law permitting psychologists to prescribe were passed. While there has been no strong, unanimous advocacy regarding this matter among VA psychologists, there is some understanding that the VA will abide by medical practices in the states that hospitals are located, as it does in general. The implication is that VA psychologists may prescribe permitted drugs in states in which it is legal to do so. The writer is not aware of any instance in which a psychologist in the VA is currently prescribing.

When and if the number of states increases in which psychologists can prescribe this matter may become more of an advocacy issue. There are undoubtedly numerous other areas involving advocacy for VA psychology at local and national levels, but the "ABPP bonus" and "Title 38" appear to have gotten most of the headlines during recent years, with prescription privileges emerging as a potential area of concern.

There are numerous issues that arise and play out at local levels such as extent of provision of mental health services, use of technicians, participation of psychologists in hospital administration, and limitations on time available for psychotherapy and psychological testing. It should be made clear that while the private practitioner has the option of using or not using technicians and may allocate time based on caseload and budgetary considerations, in institutional settings including the VA and other government agencies the decision to hire or not hire technicians is made by management, and time restrictions are established on a national or local basis, also by management. However, when local decision making is an option, management may seek advice from informed professional staff regarding issues that may arise. For example, time allocated to do a psychological assessment may be extended if necessary, or the number of psychotherapy visits may be increased. This provision of advice is perhaps the best way of doing advocacy work in local situations. It is quite possible for psychologists to encourage management to invest in a psychological assessment laboratory, fund training in some innovative treatment method, support establishment of a behavior therapy program, or do other things that improve the quality and comprehensiveness of psychological services in an institution. In offering such advice advocacy goals may be indirectly achieved through invocation of professional standards. For example, an instance occurred in which a neuropsychologist was asked to do a "neuropsychological assessment" in what was felt to be a substantially too brief period of time. The neuropsychologist replied by indicating that an assessment could be done but not a "neuropsychological assessment" because the time allocated was too brief to meet accepted professional standards for what constitutes a "neuropsychological assessment." The request was specifically for a "neuropsychological assessment" and the VA is obligated to abide by established professional standards issued by JCAHO and other accrediting agencies. The result was that the neuropsychologist was given enough time to do an adequate neuropsychological assessment. VA psychologists were greatly benefited here by the publication of practice guidelines by the American Academy of Clinical Neuropsychology (2007). Such interventions may often provide positive advocacy benefits because they have the capability of helping to establish precedents that may improve quality of care.

VA psychologists share public concerns regarding delivering state of the art healthcare to veterans. Even though VA psychologists are restricted from engaging in political advocacy, there are numerous ways they can express their concerns. For instance, VA psychologists can advocate to have the VA recognize and incorporate new developments in the profession. Reasonable successes have been achieved to have the VA incorporate the new specialties of health psychology, and clinical neuropsychology. While within the APA geropsychology is a proficiency rather than a specialty, the VA employs designated geropsychologists on the basis of their demonstrated expertise in providing services to the elderly (Graca & Ascheman, 1993). While continuing to appreciate the vital role of the generic clinical psychologist, the argument has been made that, similar to medical practice, there are specialized fields within general psychology that required advanced and specialized training for the individuals to practice competently. The advanced training is often the equivalent of a specialty residency or more in certain areas, notable among which are psychological aspects of physical illness, relationships between brain function and behavior, and particular problems of the elderly. The result has been that particularly in the larger VA facilities there are some specialized job positions for clinical health psychologists, neuropsychologists and geropsychologists. It is probably appropriate to compare these individuals to medical specialists like gastroenterologists, neurologists, and cardiologists. Efforts are now being made to formalize the training for these specialties in residencies or post-doctoral training programs. Advocacy efforts to support this specialization have involved a "working through" within psychology itself and in partnership with potential employers like VA. There was, in fact, extensive debate in the Council of Representatives of the APA taking place over a number of years regarding designation of new specialties, clinical neuropsychology being the first candidate specialty to undergo this process, obtaining designation as a specialty in 1996. Since that time, numerous new specialties have been proposed and approved by the Council of Representatives, such as forensic and family psychology. Advocates of a unitary clinical psychology profession have argued that specialization would fragment clinical psychology, and any competent clinical psychologist should be capable of working with medical and elderly patients, and of doing cognitive assessments of brain-damaged patients. However, the depth of knowledge, specific skills, and the complexity of focused healthcare in health psychology, geropsychology, and neuropsychology are becoming such that few clinical psychologists—however well trained—can credibly claim to move effectively among these realms at will. Be that as it may, within the APA there is strong sentiment for consideration of new specialties and proficiencies, and their designation as such.

Within the VA, one side of the argument contended that the VA should have a preference for hiring generalists who were capable of providing a range of psychological services, particularly in smaller facilities where it might not be feasible to hire multiple specialists. The other side, however, was advocating that for truly competent care, specialized positions were required for job positions that dealt with subject areas that necessarily rely on advanced training not sufficiently trained at the general psychologist level. This latter view appears to have prevailed, at least in the case of clinical neuropsychology.

Goals for clinical neuropsychology. The initial goal of clinical neuropsychology in the VA was to establish its status as a specialty within psychology but separate from clinical psychology. As background for this view, it is noted that neuropsychologists outside of the VA were not all clinical psychologists. Some of the leading figures of the field, such as Hans-Lukas Teuber, Edith Kaplan, Ward Halstead, and Allan Mirsky, are not clinical psychologists who graduated from APA approved programs. Neuropsychology as a science has developed as a multidisciplinary field that included not only psychologists but also physicians (generally characterized as behavioral neurologists), speech pathologists, and other rehabilitation specialists. The International Neuropsychological Society, the first neuropsychology organization to have a large membership in the United States, was always both international and interdisciplinary. Indeed several of its past presidents were speech pathologists or physicians, or were not North Americans. Thus, a model has developed for the field that would hold the view that a neuropsychologist need not be a clinical psychologist. Within the VA, the issue becomes particularly sensitive when the neuropsychologist is a psychologist but not a clinical psychologist graduating from APA University and internship approved programs. The matter is clearly debatable, but the VA has long adhered to a policy of only employing as clinicians APA approved clinical or counseling psychologists. The rationale has been that those rendering services in neuropsychology would have to be able to identify and simultaneously address mental health co-morbidities. Non-clinicians may be employed as consultants or research scientists, but are not eligible for clinical privileges.

Advocacy efforts, with the support of Division 40 of the APA, AVAPL, the American Academy of Neuropsychology (AACN), and the National Academy of Neuropsychology (NAN), have succeeded in establishing clinical neuropsychology as a specialty in the VA with psychologists in many hospitals designated specifically as clinical neuropsychologists. A listserv has recently been created which is administered through AVAPL and these neuropsychologists are now in daily contact with each other. Ruth Yoash-Gantz of the Hefner VA Medical Center in Salisbury, NC, who started this list and managed it before it was joined with the AVAPL list, deserves strong praise for accomplishing this important task. Some would consider a more advanced goal in this direction to have the VA employ graduates of doctoral training programs in neuropsychology that are not clinical psychology programs. APA approval would be desirable, but the degree would be specifically in clinical neuropsychology rather than clinical psychology. There are a number of University Ph.D. programs in North America that train highly competent clinical neuropsychologists which are not clinical psychology training programs. However, postdoctoral graduates of these programs must obtain APA approved doctoral degrees in clinical psychology as well as necessary competencies in clinical neuropsychology gained through coursework and approved internship experience in order to be hired by the VA.

Not all clinical neuropsychologists are sympathetic with this view, and the apparent division in the field has led the national neuropsychology organizations to do an evaluation of training design and standards that updates and possibly modifies the recommendations of the "Houston Conference" recommendations for training in clinical neuropsychology. In a detailed commentary on the Houston Conference extensive critiques were written concerning such matters as content of the proposed academic program, emphasis on patient care issues, basic science, and history (Ardila, 2002). Equally, responses have addressed these criticisms (Adams, 2002). The Houston Conference and activities of its type are of crucial significance to psychologists in the VA and the public sector in general because government agencies typically look to the various professional groups for guidance in determining their policies. The VA in particular abides by standards and policies of the American Psychological Association with regard to the definition of psychology. Only time will tell what will develop once the currently growing number of postdoctoral training programs that obtain APA approval acquires a sufficient size, thereby possibly gaining a modification of the VA's position.

Having been established in the VA as a specialty, achievement of additional goals becomes a possibility. Aside from the general goals for all psychologists discussed above, there are several other issues that pertain specifically to neuropsychologists. One potential goal is to increase the number of clinical neuropsychology Diplomates employed by the VA, achieved by hiring new psychologists who are already Diplomates or encouraging present employees to apply for and complete the diplomate examinations. An additional goal is increasing the opportunities for clinical neuropsychologists in the VA to employ technician support. The use of technicians in neuropsychological assessment has consistently proven to be of value in extending services and optimizing use of professional time (NAN, 2000).

An important advocacy issue in the VA regards time allotted for assessments and workload expectations. The VA, like most large hospital systems, has time limits assigned for particular procedures. A typical time limit for a neuropsychological assessment is 4 hours. Such limitations have changed the nature of testing over the years, particularly in regard to giving long, comprehensive batteries such as the Halstead-Reitan Battery or comprehensive flexible batteries. The use of longer comprehensive batteries appears limited to research applications when there is funding to support the additional time, or in specialized units (e.g., aphasia centers) in which there are strong scientific and academic influences. Limited time for assessment is a current issue, which many neuropsychologists are talking about. Availability of practice standards formulated by professional organizations including the American Psychological Association (2002) and the American Academy of Clinical Neuropsychology (2007) provide significant advocacy tools.

A key goal for times such as these, when prevalence of brain disorders is substantially increased because of war injuries and other disorders associated with deployment of military personnel, is that of achieving greater visibility for clinical neuropsychology. Such goal seeking needs to range from the level creating awareness that it exists to specific recommendations regarding its helpfulness in intervention and evaluation for various neurobehavioral conditions. In recent appeals for increased support by the military and the VA for war wounded soldiers and veterans, mention is generally made of the need for the services of more neurologists, neurosurgeons, nurses, speech pathologists, and rehabilitation specialists, with no mention of psychologists, let alone neuropsychologists. A united effort made by several organizations including the AVAPL, the National Academy of Neuropsychology, the American Academy of Clinical Neuropsychology, and the Divisions of Rehabilitation Psychology (22) and Clinical Neuropsychology of the American Psychological Association (40) have formed a TBI task force on the role of neuropsychology and rehabilitation psychology in the evaluation, management, and research of military veterans with traumatic brain injury, and have published a position paper (McCrea et al., 2008). There is now a growing recognition that clinical neuropsychologists, by virtue of the nature of their specialty, are ideally suited for important roles in programs for treatment of head trauma and other neurobehavioral disorders associated with engaging in warfare. At present there are several neuropsychologists in leadership positions in polytrauma centers established by the VA in association with the wars in Iraq and Afghanistan.

Future efforts

All of the goals discussed, including Title 38, the "ABPP Bonus," prescription privileges, and the establishment of clinical neuropsychology in the VA, have only been partially achieved. While Hybrid Title 38 status for practicing psychologists is now law, there have been difficulties in implementation. The law and its implementing regulations have been initially subject to interpretation that has varied from facility to facility, often related to differing views of local management. Implementation is the key issue now, and advocacy efforts need to be made to develop a fair and uniform implementation across the system. The impact of the "ABPP Bonus" appears to have been limited, and while positive things have happened, the VA could do more to recognize its Diplomates, and to make board certification comparable to what is the case for other health professions. Some advocacy efforts could be directed to the American Board of Professional Psychology (ABPP), which might make the general and professional public more aware that there is board certification in psychology. As a personal experience, I discovered some time ago that management at my VA facility was not aware that was the case. As a blatant example of this situation, when psychologists applied for clinical privileges the form they were given requested information about board certification, but in the case of psychologists that section had a stamp on it saying "Not Applicable." My advocacy effort was to cross out those words and fill in the information requested about my board certification status. Not all psychologists may agree with these views about board certification and it would be quite worthwhile to discuss the matter in various venues.

The status of clinical neuropsychology in the VA has improved substantially, and now clinical neuropsychologists are designated as such. Early advocacy efforts supportive of licensing may have marked the beginning of this improvement. The policy that they must be clinical psychologists is debatable and again is a matter that merits further discussion and study. Psychologists in the VA are viewed as belonging to the mental health and behavioral science specialty. In the central administrative organization of the VA they are under the jurisdiction of what is called the "Office of Mental Health Services" that represents a consolidation that took place between separate Psychology and Psychiatry Services. It is currently directed by a psychiatrist, with a psychologist serving as a chief consultant. Historically, the head of this organization has been a psychiatrist, although it is technically possible for a psychologist to fill the position. Some psychologists would advocate for a return to the independent services organization. In any event the leadership of the Office is the "boss" of all VA psychologists regardless of whether or not they are assigned at their local facilities to other services aside from Mental Health. Some clinical neuropsychologists do not view themselves as belonging in the mental health or psychiatric illness field, and tend to affiliate themselves with other medical services, notably Neurology, Neurosurgery, and Rehabilitation Medicine. Thus, in a local VA hospital, the clinical neuropsychologist is administratively part of Psychology or a consolidated Mental Health Service despite the fact that she, or he works on the Neurosurgery Service. This administrative structure is unlike what is often the case in private or university hospitals in which psychologists are administered by the service on which they work. In some cases a VA neuropsychologist may have a joint appointment with a medical school with the appointment being in the Psychology/Mental Health Service in the VA and the Department of Neurology in the medical school. This situation, while not generally atypical, is sometimes awkward for clinical neuropsychologists, and there may be some need to discuss advocacy directed at permitting psychologists to obtain appointments at VA hospitals outside of the mental health hierarchy.

A highly crucial and continuing aspect of advocacy in the public sector has to do with training. It is widely understood that the public sector has been the major supporter of professional education in the healthcare field for many years. The National Institutes of Health, the military, and the VA all have extensive medical education programs many of which include psychologists. The VA is particularly well known for its psychology internship program that has been in existence since 1946. This program continues to do well, but recently the VA began to support post-doctoral training for Ph.D.s, including training in neuropsychology. This effort is just at its beginnings and could benefit from support and advice. One issue that has arisen is that while the recommended length of a postdoctoral fellowship is 2 years, the VA has a policy of only funding Ph.D. post-doctoral fellowships for 1 year. However, within the constraints of a fixed budget, advocacy efforts appear to have resulted in a compromise in which the VA would permit the 2 years, but could only fund half the number of 1-year positions that would have been available. Thus, clinical neuropsychology Post-Doctoral Fellows can spend two years at the VA, but the possibility of obtaining such a position is substantially more competitive. Advocating for additional lines of funding for 2-year post-doctoral residencies in neuropsychology would be beneficial. A matter that has been an obstacle to supporting neuropsychology training in the VA has to do with APA accreditation. There are at my last count only 11 APA accredited post-doctoral training programs in neuropsychology. More are scheduled to come on line when the Fiscal 2008 new programs for VA (in six sites) come on line. The reason for this slow incremental growth is complex, involving funding, development of standards for post-doctoral accreditation by APA, and the intricacies of the accreditation procedure. Advocacy here would involve the APA negotiating with the VA, with the key players being VA neuropsychologists who are interested in developing training programs at their facilities. According to the list currently on the website of the Association of Post-Doctoral Programs in Clinical Neuropsychology (APPCN), the only VA sponsored programs are in Togus, ME, Memphis TN, and San Antonio TX. Another federal facility, Walter Reed Army Medical Center, also has a program. It can be assumed that the individuals who went through the substantial difficulties of developing this small number of programs are particularly strong advocates for neuropsychology in the VA.

HOW TO BECOME INVOLVED

Before beginning a discussion of how to become involved in advocacy for clinical neuropsychology in institutional settings there is a prior question of whether or not to get involved at all. As a general statement, it might be useful to say "Advocate, but do not advocate blindly or reflexively." Legal, regulatory, policy, and professional standard considerations may create situations in which inept advocacy efforts are counterproductive. Clinical neuropsychology is obviously not an area that is free of controversy, and advocacy efforts put forth as representing the consensus of the profession may not actually be the case. Becoming involved in advocacy should obligate the advocate to understand what is legal and appropriate, have knowledge of the degree of support for the views taken, and have pertinent information about the characteristics of the target audience. These considerations are of particular importance in VA hospitals and other government healthcare facilities because of the numerous restrictions present and sensitivities of federal officials to possible conflicts of interest. In planning and conducting advocacy activities, a distinction should be maintained on the one hand between "lobbying" and advocacy, and on the other between advocacy and "education," which is often a euphemism for sometimes-blatant persuasion to adopt some change. VA psychologists may not "lobby" and while they may be engaged in educating, they should not disguise advocacy efforts as educational or information-providing activity.

VA psychologists may, however, advocate in several ways. At a national level, advocacy efforts are focused on the AVAPL working in conjunction with the APA. The key components of the APA involved are the Practice Directorate and the Division of Psychologists in Public Service (18), which has a VA section. An absolutely essential step in getting involved in advocacy efforts would be to become a member of AVAPL and/or APA Division 18. Attendance at the annual meetings of these groups should provide reasonably comprehensive briefings on the present advocacy situation and identify places where new advocates can help for the common good. In addition, numerous listservs have neuropsychological followings that offer opportunities for networking. The APA Practice Directorate has acquired an intimate knowledge of the VA system components that relate to psychology and has had contact with the House Committee on Veterans Affairs and the Senate Committee on Veterans Affairs. The leadership of the Practice Directorate regularly attends the AVAPL meetings, at which they can receive advice about future activities. Thus attendance at an AVAPL meeting is a direct way of becoming involved in advocacy at a national level. Leaders of the Division 18 VA section also attend this meeting allowing for interaction among the groups that are most active at a national level regarding VA psychology. Several neuropsychologists also attend this meeting, giving them an opportunity to express their views. Most recently, the American Academy of Clinical Neuropsychology has formulated practice policies and participated in advocacy efforts for support of veterans with TBI that provide additional support for VA psychology. This group also holds an annual educational conference that should provide significant help for neuropsychologists who want to become ABCN/ABPP Diplomates.

The agenda at the local level is quite different. Local administrators have little if any control over systemic matters such as employment policies, salary, issues such as Hybrid Title 38 and the ABPP Bonus. These matters are all managed at a national level through the VA leadership working with Congress and various federal agencies. Advocacy efforts typically involve matters in which there is more local discretion. Thus, for example, the idea of employing a designated full-time clinical neuropsychologist with technicians and clinic facilities may be a local matter that can be advocated for by staff psychologists, sometimes supported by the affiliated medical school when there is one. To become involved, the individual psychologist should probably interface regularly and negotiate with the chief of the psychology or mental health service. The chief, if convinced, can seek the support of the Chief of Staff and Hospital Director who might be willing to allocate existing or requested resources needed to achieve the goal of the advocacy. As indicated, the individual neuropsychologist can make a case for such matters as adequate testing time, use of technicians, or purchase of needed test materials and related equipment. In the VA, and federal government in general, there are frequently obstacles to purchasing computers for testing, scoring, and data management purposes, and these can often be resolved at a local level.

There are advocates for VA psychology who do not work for the VA. Some of these people are not psychologists but individuals or groups who are supportive of veterans and become strong advocates for supporting their healthcare. Bridge building with these stakeholders can be very productive, but it must be coordinated with other efforts. They will support psychologists along with other healthcare providers who work with veterans. Regarding psychologists, as indicated, the APA has been very supportive of VA psychology, and it is clearly not the case that the Practice Directorate is preoccupied with psychologists in private practice. Another group is the psychologists at affiliated medical schools. These individuals often consult with their neighboring VA hospitals, and may provide services in teaching, supervision, and research collaboration. One learns that medical school people can open doors not available to VA staff. Thus, for example, a Department Chair can approach a Congressman directly, whereas a VA Service Chief cannot. Usually, if an advocacy situation exists, the VA staff member may approach a university faculty colleague and try to work out a strategy that is appropriate and effective in dealing with the advocacy matter. Throughout the VA system there are numerous instances of productive affiliations through which often major programs have emerged. The classic examples for neuropsychology are the Boston VA aphasia unit that was supported by collaboration between the Boston VA Hospital and Boston University, and more recently the impressive collaborative effort made by the San Diego VA hospital and the University of California in San Diego. In both of these programs VA staff members typically had university academic appointments, and university faculty were collaborators on research programs that took place entirely or in part at the VA facility. The names of Nelson Butters, Harold Goodglass, Laird Cermak, Edith Kaplan, and Dean Delis, known to all practicing neuropsychologists, were leaders of these programs. Thus the VA has made major contributions to our understanding of aphasia, amnesia, and other neurobehavioral disorders.

In getting involved, the writer has tried to point out that the best way to advocate is not necessarily writing letters to your Congressman or supporting the campaign of someone running for public office that supports what you are advocating. Indeed, in the VA these are probably highly ineffective ways and may be counterproductive. At a national level, if one is a VA psychologist, the best way to become involved in advocacy is through independent psychological and neuropsychological organizations, attending their meetings, and possibly serving on their committees. Within neuropsychology, NAN and AACN have participated actively in advocacy efforts. At a local level it is a matter of relating to hospital management through service chiefs in support of effecting changes. It is often very helpful to form a productive relationship with the affiliated medical school if there is one. If one looks at the major successes of VA psychology, they have occurred through these processes. Recently, the successes gained regarding Hybrid Title 38 and the ABPP bonus has come largely from the work of the APA and AVAPL. The major programs in neuropsychology at the Boston and San Diego VA hospital came about because of collaboration with affiliated universities.

Mention of these programs leads to a final thought that our research is one of the strongest forms of advocacy. It is quite likely that the successes of clinical neuropsychology in the VA came to a great extent from its extensive scientific base. The credibility of neuropsychology derives from its evidence base more clearly than for any other psychological specialty. When one considers the available literature in the field, it is hard to see how it could be ignored by the healthcare community. The publication of neuropsychology research that is particularly pertinent to veterans has clearly had an impact on clinical applications. The emergence of PTSD clinics, polytrauma centers, and neurorehabilitation programs probably could not have happened without emergence of the clinical conditions themselves along with peer-reviewed publication of the research needed to diagnose and treat them. Clinical neuropsychology has always been evidence based, and should continue to foster its research basis and hone its clinical tool derivatives. In this way it will continue to enjoy a remarkable degree of credibility in the healthcare community and strong acceptance even by skeptical observers.

The way in which advocacy efforts in the VA provide guidance for other psychologists in the public sector is general rather than specific. Agencies at different levels of government have different rules and policies. At a county or municipal level there may be no Hatch Act type restrictions, while at a federal level in the military or intelligence services the restrictions may be substantially more stringent than they are in the VA. However, some considerations should always be relevant. First, avoid any advocacy efforts that may appear to be illegal, inappropriate, or apparently self-serving. It is often counterproductive to act as an advocate in a way that is not consistent with the policies of one's organization, or that might appear to represent a conflict of interest. Take advantage of the right you have to join professional organizations that may engage in advocacy efforts. Within the VA, the AVAPL is such an organization. It is also important to maintain membership in the American Psychological Association and the appropriate Divisions. Membership in the national neuropsychological organizations, including NAN and AACN is also important. These organizations can advocate to or for your agency when you cannot. Psychologists in state, county, and municipal agencies may wish to join their local societies. Even as a federal employee, state associations may be of benefit in such matters as modification of the licensing laws, prescription privileges, and positive or negative plans, such as opening or closing a VA or military hospital.

ACKNOWLEDGMENT

This work was supported by the Medical Research Service, Department of Veterans Affairs.

REFERENCES

About VHA. http://www1.va.gov/health/aboutVHA.asp, accessed on May 30, 2009.

Adams, J. K. M. (2002). The Houston Conference: The road more traveled. *Neuropsychology Review*, *12*, 132–133.

Akaka, D. K. (2007). Psychologists: The backbone of the VA health care system. *Psychological Services*, *4*, 72–74.

American Academy of Clinical Neuropsychology (2007). American Academy of Clinical Neuropsychology (AACN) practice guidelines for neuropsychological assessment and consultation. *The Clinical Neuropsychologist*, *21*, 209–231.

American Psychological Association (2002). Criteria for practice guideline development and evaluation. *American Psychologist*, *57*, 1048–1051.

Ardila, A. (2002). Houston conference: Need for more fundamental knowledge in neuropsychology. *Neuropsychology Review*, *12*, 127–130.

Baker, R. B. (2007). *Stories from VA psychology*. Washington, DC: American Psychological Association.

Baker, R. B., & Pickren, W. E. (2007). *Psychology and the Department of Veterans Affairs*. Washington, DC: American Psychological Association.

Graca, J., & Ascheman, P. (1993). A survey of VA geropsychologists. *Clinical Gerontologist*, *12*, 19–30.

McCrea, M. (Chair), et al. (2008). Official position of the military TBI task force on the role of neuropsychology and rehabilitation psychology in the evaluation, management, and research of military veterans with traumatic brain injury. *The Clinical Neuropsychologist*, *22*, 10–26.

National Academy of Neuropsychology (2000). The use of neuropsychology test technicians in clinical practice. *Archives of Clinical Neuropsychology*, *15*, 381–382.

VHA Directive 2005–024. (2005). *Polytrauma Rehabilitation Centers*. Washington, DC: American Psychological Association.

WebsiteVetSuccess. http://www.vetsuccess.gov/resources/occupations/profile?id=82&PHPSESSID=082494a0a11410dd41f540f103578440, accessed on May 30, 2009.

The Clinical Neuropsychologist, 24: 417–428, 2010
http://www.psypress.com/tcn
ISSN: 1385-4046 print/1744-4144 online
DOI: 10.1080/13854040802482394

Psychology Press
Taylor & Francis Group

NEUROPSYCHOLOGICAL ADVOCACY AND EPILEPSY

David W. Loring[1], Bruce P. Hermann[2], and Morris J. Cohen[3]
[1]*Department of Neurology, Emory University, Atlanta, GA,* [2]*Department of Neurology, University of Wisconsin, WI, and* [3]*Department of Neurology, Medical College of Georgia, GA, USA*

Neuropsychologists are in a unique position to be active advocates for patients with epilepsy given their unique understanding of the behavioral and cognitive effects associated the disease, its progression, and its treatment. Neuropsychologists communicate the cognitive and behavioral consequences of epilepsy and its long-term implications to patients, family, school, and employers. In this article we review factors influencing the neuropsychological profile of patients with epilepsy, and discuss common behavioral comorbidities, as well as special issues associated with school placement and long-term planning. We also include a seizure action plan, which is designed to be both an educational tool for individuals with limited epilepsy knowledge, and a way to minimize stigma associated with an event should a seizure occur during school or work.

Keywords: Epilepsy; Cognition; Development; Seizures; School; Employment.

INTRODUCTION

Epilepsy is a prevalent disorder, affecting 1% of the population or approximately 3 million Americans (Annegers, 1996). Epilepsy can occur at any age, with a bimodal distribution of peak incidence occurring in childhood and older age, and a spectrum of severity ranging from mild and relatively benign to severe and incapacitating. In contrast to most other diseases, epilepsy is associated with an "active" lesion characterized by abnormal electrical discharges that may disrupt neuronal processing and affect cognition and behavior on an ongoing basis, independent of both other functional impairments associated with the disease (e.g., peri- or post-ictal seizure effects) and static brain lesions. The etiology of a patient's epilepsy may also affect neuropsychological function, and the very medications used for seizure control may also contribute abnormalities to the overall cognitive and behavioral profile. Thus, the challenge to neuropsychologists involved in epilepsy care and evaluation is to recognize the many ways in which epilepsy may affect neurobehavioral status, and be in a position to communicate how each of these factors may contribute to epilepsy's behavioral expression. Communication plays a critical role in epilepsy patient advocacy for patients of all ages since epilepsy

Address correspondence to: David W. Loring, Ph.D., Department of Neurology, Emory University, Woodruff Memorial Research Building, 101 Woodruff Circle, Suite 6000, Atlanta, GA 30322, USA. E-mail: dloring@emory.edu
Accepted for publication: September 12, 2008. First published online: February 10, 2009.

continues to be poorly understood, is often associated with varying degrees of stigma, and because even though there are a diversity of resources available that can minimize some of the negative consequences of epilepsy and its treatment, these resources are often underutilized. Therefore the neuropsychologist needs to be informed and able to educate the patient, families, hospital staff, school staff, and general public with regards to the effects of epilepsy and the available resources.

Epilepsy often begins during childhood, and how epilepsy and medical management interacts with normal cognitive and psychosocial development is often a reason for consultation with a neuropsychologist. Cognitive and behavioral difficulty is common in many epilepsy syndromes, and is often (but not invariably) related to clinical factors such as seizure frequency and severity, and age of seizure onset, as well as the underlying pathologic substrate giving rise to a patient's seizures. Although it is beyond the scope of this article to review the relationship between epilepsy syndromes and neuropsychological and psychiatric function, many patients with well-controlled epilepsy often display little or no cognitive difficulty. Many so-called "benign" epilepsy syndromes such as absence epilepsy are often outgrown; however, neurobehavioral comorbidities are increasingly recognized in patients with "benign" types of epilepsy (Camfield, Camfield, Gordon, Smith, & Dooley, 1993), and these patients may be left with life-long neuropsychological weaknesses, including working memory and attention, that often go unrecognized. The cognitive and behavioral changes associated with epilepsy may antedate a patient's first seizure and these difficulties are therefore apparent early on, providing an early window for assessment and intervention. There are many different seizure types and epilepsy syndromes, and there is great variability in how a patient's epilepsy may affect behavior.

When the epileptogenic lesion occurs during cognitive development it plays a critical role in the expression of neuropsychological impairment (Luria, 1973), with earlier age of onset of recurrent seizures associated with poorer cognitive function (Dikmen, Matthews, & Harley, 1975, 1977; Dodrill, 1992; Lennox & Lennox, 1960; O'Leary, Seidenberg, Berent, & Boll, 1981; Schoenfeld et al., 1999). Quantitative MR evidence has also shown an adverse impact of early-onset epilepsy on brain structure, with reductions in whole brain volume in patients with a history of complicated febrile convulsions (Theodore, DeCarli, & Gaillard, 2003), and with reduced callosal volume and decreased whole brain white or gray matter volumes associated with childhood seizure onset compared to patients whose epilepsy begins in adulthood (Hermann, Hansen, Seidenberg, Magnotta, & O'Leary, 2003; Weber et al., 2007).

Several studies have followed children with childhood-onset epilepsy into adulthood and beyond (30+ years), and difficulty in a number of areas including educational attainment, employment, independent living, and social function compared to either healthy controls or illness control groups is described (Britten, Morgan, Fenwick, & Britten, 1986; Harrison & Taylor, 1976; Jalava, Sillanpää, Camfield, & Camfield, 1997; Lindsay, Ounsted, & Richards, 1979a, 1979b; Shackleton, Kasteleijn-Nolst Trenite, de Craen, Vandenbroucke, & Westendorp, 2003). It is particularly noteworthzy that neurobehavioral comorbidities persist, even when epilepsy has remitted and medications have been discontinued (Sillanpää, Jalava, Kaleva, & Shinnar, 1998).

A significant problem faced is the lack of awareness of both the cognitive and behavioral consequences of epilepsy and its treatment. This lack of awareness is surprisingly widespread, and although the field has come a long way from simply counting seizure frequency as the only means of characterizing epilepsy and its severity, the fact that there is often comorbid psychiatric disturbance and cognitive difficulty suggests that continued education on multiple levels remains a primary unmet need that neuropsychology should aggressively address given its unique position in healthcare delivery. For example, it is now recognized that mood disorders in epilepsy are common, under-recognized, under-treated, and associated with increased general health care utilization. Specific brief screening measures have now been developed to screen efficiently for depression in epilepsy (e.g., Neurological Disorders Depression Inventory for Epilepsy, or NDDI-E) (Gilliam et al., 2006). Similar efforts are underway in pediatric epilepsy. The Epilepsy Foundation has specific information and activities ("Ask the Expert") regarding mood disorders in epilepsy.

FOCUSED GOALS

The focused goals for this issue are education and communication to increase awareness of the consequences of epilepsy, and provide information to connect interested psychologists and organizations with services. Practitioners need to learn the cognitive and psychological consequences of the various epilepsy syndromes, be familiar with available resources, and communicate this information in a usable format to individuals, families, schools, and workplaces. This will help reduce the stigma associated with epilepsy, reduce harm to patients, and aid patients with adjustment and reaching their goals. Specifically, steps can be taken to decrease additional psychosocial burden of experiencing a seizure in school or in the workplace by educating patients and families about possible effects on cognition and behavior, and the possible need for special education services that do not conform to current IDEA classification schemes. Additionally, educating patients and families about the need for long range planning and living wills and trusts should be helpful.

Previous and continuing efforts

Since education and communication are important aspects in successful advocacy, we will briefly review aspects of these important areas.

Cognition. Patients with generalized tonic-clonic seizures generally have more neuropsychological impairments than those with focal or localization-related epilepsy (Dikmen & Matthews, 1977; Dodrill, 1986). The most common localization-related epilepsies arise from temporal and frontal regions, with naming and word-finding difficulty common in patients with left temporal lobe epilepsy (TLE). Accompanying the naming impairment may be a material-specific difficulty with verbal memory, largely sparing other aspects of memory function. The pattern of deficits in patients with right TLE is less consistent and less well defined, although visual memory difficult is among the most commonly reported finding

(Barr et al., 1997; Helmstaedter, Pohl, & Elger, 1995; Helmstaedter, Pohl, Hufnagel, & Elger, 1991). Even though the area of seizure onset of focal epilepsy is quite limited, there may be neuropsychological impairment that extends well beyond the seizure onset zone (Hermann, Wyler, & Richey, 1988; Martin et al., 2000). These "frontal" deficits imply impaired functional connectivity that is disrupted with a temporal lobe focus, and may be considered to reflect negative "nociferous cortex" effects in which the negative effects associated with ongoing seizure discharge impair brain function at some distance away from the active seizure focus (Theodore, Fishbein, & Dubinsky, 1988). TLE patients with secondary generalized seizures are at higher risk of additional general neuropsychological impairment (Jokeit et al., 1997).

The age at which epilepsy develops is related to the expression of neuropsychological deficits. Children with TLE who develop epilepsy before they reach 5 years of age are at higher risk for having significant verbal *and* nonverbal memory impairment independent of their laterality of seizure onset (Lespinet et al., 2002). However, when epilepsy begins after age 10, the magnitude of memory impairment is smaller than when it develops early, with a pattern of material-specific asymmetry observed with poorer verbal memory impairment with left TLE and poorer nonverbal memory with right TLE (Lespinet et al., 2002). Several recent reviews that we have written may be consulted for readers interested in greater detail about neuropsychological patterns in epilepsy (Loring, Marino, & Meador, 2007; Loring, Barr, Hamberger, & Helmstaedter, 2008; Seidenberg, Pulsipher, & Hermann, 2007).

Psychiatry and behavior. Behavioral and psychiatric aspects of the disease are increasingly appreciated, and there is a spectrum of difficulties that may be seen in this population, ranging from mood disturbances that are thought to be biologically related to specific epilepsy syndromes, to treatment-related effects such as irritability occasionally associated with medical therapy.

In a large pediatric psychiatric epidemiological survey (Rutter, 1970), 7% of children in the general population had mental health issues. This compares to 12% of children with non-neurological physical disorders, 29% in children with uncomplicated epilepsy, and 58% in children with complicated epilepsy (i.e., structural brain abnormalities and seizures). Almost 30 years later, as part of the British Child and Adolescent Mental Health Survey, Davies, Heyman, and Goodman (2003) reported strikingly similar results.

Patients with TLE have a higher risk of developing depression and anxiety compared to patients with either other chronic medical conditions, or with epilepsy originating in non-temporal-lobe brain regions, with the extent of hippocampal dysfunction correlated with depression symptoms (Gilliam et al., 2007). Further, there is a potential contribution of the medications used to treat epilepsy. Although hyperactivity is a well-known behavioral side-effect associated with phenobarbital, it may also be seen with other medications in addition to depressed mood and irritability. However, some medications (such lamotrigine) may have a positive psychotropic effect. Thus, treatment of a patient's epilepsy might actually have a beneficial effect on the negative mood aspects of their clinical condition. Practitioners working with individuals with epilepsy need to be aware of these issues and carefully screen for primary and secondary mood disturbances. When found, they need to take steps to address these issues.

School and employment. Because seizures can be frightening to observe for individuals who have limited medical background or specific exposure to individuals with epilepsy, neuropsychologists should not only inform and educate appropriate parties about general expectations, but also provide specific guidelines to decrease the concerns that teachers or employers might have. This will in turn decrease the stigma associated with epilepsy.

One beneficial effect of being knowledgeable about epilepsy is that, in the presence of a patient who is experiencing a seizure, the practitioner can project a sense of calm, recognize the needs of the patients, and demonstrate an informed approach to patient care. Tonic-clonic seizures and complex partial seizures, although sharing a number of common features, will differ in presentation and post-ictal status.

Tonic-clonic seizures are commonly associated with a sudden cry or fall, with muscle rigidity, and muscle jerking. The seizures themselves may be associated with loss of bladder control and generally last for 30 seconds to several minutes. Generalized tonic-clonic seizures lasting more than 5 minutes should prompt a call for greater medical expertise. If a patient is seen for the first time after the seizure has ended, with the seizure not being witnessed, it may be believed that the patient has suffered a heart attack or a stroke. These patients should not be restrained, and should be placed on their side with a pillow (or something soft like a coat) under the head, after loosening neckwear and removing glasses.

Complex partial seizures are associated with a blank gaze, with patients appearing unaware of their surroundings and being non-responsive to questioning although, unlike tonic-clonic seizures, there is no sudden fall. The seizure may be accompanied by "psychomotor" activities such as chewing or lip smacking, picking at clothing, mumbling, handwriting, or undressing. These patients can be mistaken as having a variety of behavioral disorders such as substance abuse, mental illness, or conduct disorders. There should be no attempts to restrain the patient, and if the patient appears angry or aggressive, one should maintain a safe distance. As the patient recovers there should be no attempt to provide water, medications, or food until they are fully alert. This is also an important time to speak calmly and reassuringly to the patient, as well as reassuring bystanders that the situation is under control. However, if the seizure lasts longer than 5 minutes then there is cause for concern and medical personnel should be contacted.

One specific recommendation is the development of a seizure action plan (see Figure 1). This typically consists of a document containing not only standard medical information (e.g., physician contact information), but also specific epilepsy and seizures information including first aid (e.g., track duration of seizure, turn child on side, do not place anything in mouth), which can be referred to easily during a seizure should there be concern by the teacher or employer, as well as describing when a seizure may develop into a genuine medical emergency (e.g., convulsive seizure lasting more than 5 minutes). Helpful information should include a description of the typical post-ictal period (e.g., difficulty talking, headache, irritability, somnolence), and how long is usually necessary before recovery occurs

EPILEPSY FOUNDATION®

SEIZURE ACTION PLAN

Effective Date________

THIS STUDENT IS BEING TREATED FOR A SEIZURE DISORDER. THE INFORMATION BELOW SHOULD ASSIST YOU IF A SEIZURE OCCURS DURING SCHOOL HOURS.

Student's Name:______________________________ Date of Birth:________

Parent/Guardian:______________________________ Phone: ___________ Cell:___________

Treating Physician:______________________________ Phone: ___________

Significant medical history:______________________________

SEIZURE INFORMATION:

Seizure Type	*Length*	*Frequency*	*Description*

Seizure triggers or warning signs:______________________________

Student's reaction to seizure:______________________________

BASIC FIRST AID: CARE & COMFORT: *(Please describe basic first aid procedures)*

Does student need to leave the classroom after a seizure? YES NO

If YES, describe process for returning student to classroom

Basic Seizure First Aid:
- ✓ Stay calm & track time
- ✓ Keep child safe
- ✓ Do not restrain
- ✓ Do not put anything in mouth
- ✓ Stay with child until fully conscious
- ✓ Record seizure in log

For tonic-clonic (grand mal) seizure:
- ✓ Protect head
- ✓ Keep airway open/watch breathing
- ✓ Turn child on side

EMERGENCY RESPONSE:

A "seizure emergency" for this student is defined as:

Seizure Emergency Protocol: *(Check all that apply and clarify below)*
- ☐ Contact school nurse at ______________________
- ☐ Call 911 for transport to ______________________
- ☐ Notify parent or emergency contact
- ☐ Notify doctor
- ☐ Administer emergency medications as indicated below
- ☐ Other______________________

A Seizure is generally considered an Emergency when:
- ✓ A convulsive (tonic-clonic) seizure lasts longer than 5 minutes
- ✓ Student has repeated seizures without regaining consciousness
- ✓ Student has a first time seizure
- ✓ Student is injured or has diabetes
- ✓ Student has breathing difficulties
- ✓ Student has a seizure in water

TREATMENT PROTOCOL DURING SCHOOL HOURS: (include daily and emergency medications)

Daily Medication	Dosage & Time of Day Given	Common Side Effects & Special Instructions

Emergency/Rescue Medication

____

Does student have a **Vagus Nerve Stimulator (VNS)**? YES NO

If YES, Describe magnet use______________________________

SPECIAL CONSIDERATIONS & SAFETY PRECAUTIONS: *(regarding school activities, sports, trips, etc.)*

Physician Signature:______________________________ **Date:**____________

Parent Signature:______________________________ **Date:**____________

Figure 1 Epilepsy action plan (courtesy of the Epilepsy Foundation).

(although full recovery may take 24 hours or more). If necessary, details about rescue medication such as Diastat® can be described, although most often patients in whom Diastat® has been prescribed will have made arrangements for its use independently.

Being aware of the condition has the potential to stave off additional and unnecessary negative attention, both in the schoolroom and in the workplace. For example, if a child has a spell during a class, the child could be permitted to let the seizure run its course safely, rather than an ambulance being called for immediately. In addition to avoiding the attention of a "medical emergency," in many cases the child could avoid missing the remainder of the school day and possibly return to the classroom. Similarly, greater awareness of the specifics of an adult patient's seizure can similarly avoid an unnecessary trip to the Emergency Department.

Learning disabilities. The primary skill and expertise of the neuropsychologist in assessments of pediatric epilepsy patients involves school performance issues. There are several practical ways a neuropsychologist can help in this area. First, the neuropsychologist can work with the school psychologist to explain the differences between declarative memory deficits that may be associated with various epilepsy syndromes and learning disabilities, which may also be comorbid with epilepsy, and differ both in their diagnosis and implications for school placement.

Second, when a child with epilepsy does not meet formal criteria for a learning disability, an intellectual disability, or emotional/behavior disorder, the child may still receive special educational services through the "other health impaired" category under IDEA (Individuals with Disabilities Educational Act) criteria. Neuropsychologists may educate families and schools on how children with epilepsy may qualify for special education services under the "other health impaired" category and what services may be indicated. Unfortunately, qualification under this category does not mandate a neuropsychological or even psychoeducational evaluation. In those cases where assessment is indicated but not performed as part of the other health impaired qualification, neuropsychologists may assist families in documenting the need and utility of appropriate testing in order to increase the likelihood that correct diagnosis and services can be provided to the student. Children with traumatic brain injury, in contrast, are treated as a separate category of Special Education students in which neuropsychological evaluation is suggested and psychoeducational evaluation is considered to be a mandatory component for placement in Special Education.

The failure to require a neuropsychological evaluation, or at a minimum psychoeducational evaluation, of students with epilepsy is a serious oversight by the Department of Education, reflecting a general lack of awareness of the cognitive and emotional/behavioral difficulties that can be directly associated with epilepsy and its management. Thus, neuropsychologists as a profession should continue to work with appropriate organizations to have epilepsy, like traumatic brain injury, recognized by IDEA as a condition requiring neuropsychological and psychoeducational evaluation, and should lobby for appropriate change at the federal level. If successful, this change in characterization will be among the most potent ways of educating students with epilepsy and their families about the cognitive and behavioral risks associated with this disease.

In addition to IDEA, the Americans with Disabilities Act prevents discrimination against individuals on the basis of a handicapping condition that impairs one or more major life activities. Thus, any technical school or college/ university receiving federal support must abide by these guidelines and provide appropriate assistance and accommodations to qualified students with disabilities.

Finally, neuropsychological evaluations provide valuable evidence needed to substantiate why particular students should take reduced course loads and why requiring typical course loads would be unduly burdensome to specific individuals. This is particularly important because some college students receive their health insurance by remaining on their parents' policies. However, students with cognitive difficulties associated with their epilepsy may not be able to successfully complete a full-time credit load required by many insurance carries to verify enrollment status. Consequently, the neuropsychologist can comment on various definitions of "full time" student status in which decreased cognitive efficiency and learning requires a greater time for preparation for each class. In these cases, a traditional full-time load exceeds the capacity of a patient and will be associated with a high likelihood of failure. If the neuropsychologist is able to appropriately intervene with specific neuropsychological results and recommendations, then appropriate accommodation may be made with respect to continued health insurance eligibility for students on their parent's policy.

Long-term planning. Finally, the neuropsychologist is in a unique position to encourage families to begin the process of long-term planning for their child with epilepsy, who may not be able to function independently as a young adult. For example, this could involve recommending to the parents that they consult with an attorney and/or an investment advisor about establishing a living will and or a trust for the child. Typically, this involves the identification of an individual or family member who is willing to act as the legal guardian for the child, along with someone who acts as the executor of the will in the event of the unforeseen demise of both parents. Parents often find it difficult to sit down with the appropriate professionals and proactively address this possibility.

SUPPORT GROUPS

Like many other clinical conditions, there are often local support groups for patients with epilepsy. Since epilepsy is not a diagnosis in which neuropsychological consultation is always considered, presentations at state and local professional meetings and with various civic groups not only educates about how epilepsy and its treatment may affect cognition and behavior, but also provides the opportunity to demonstrate the unique contribution that neuropsychology may provide to patient care and management. Issues such as those described above are generally warmly received by the audience, particularly by patients and families in whom epilepsy care is provided outside the context of a specialized epilepsy program.

Table 1 Resources relevant to advocacy and epilepsy

- **Epilepsy Foundation** (www.epilepsyfoundation.org). The Epilepsy Foundation is the national voluntary agency solely dedicated to the welfare of the 3 million people with epilepsy in the U.S. and their families. The organization works to ensure that people with seizures are able to participate in all life experiences; and to prevent, control, and cure epilepsy through research, education, advocacy, and services. In addition to programs conducted at the national level, epilepsy clients throughout the United States are served by local Epilepsy Foundation offices in nearly 100 communities, and links to the affiliate network can be obtained at the EF website.
- **International League Against Epilepsy** (www.ilae-epilepsy.org). Founded in 1909, the International League Against Epilepsy (ILAE) is the world's pre-eminent association of physicians and other health professionals working towards a world where no person's life is limited by epilepsy. Its mission is to provide the highest quality of care and well-being for those afflicted with the condition and other related seizure disorders.
- **International Bureau for Epilepsy** (www.ibe-epilepsy.org). The International Bureau for Epilepsy (IBE) was established in 1961 as an organization of laypersons and professionals interested in the medical and non-medical aspects of epilepsy. The IBE addresses such social problems as education, employment, insurance, driving license restrictions, and public awareness.
- **Epilepsy.com** is another educational web-based resource for both patients and providers. This site provides a wealth of information regarding the medical, social, and behavioral complications of epilepsy, and provides considerable information regarding available resources.
- **The Center for Disease and Prevention (CDC)** has an extensive website devoted to epilepsy (www.cdc.gov/Epilepsy). In addition to authoritative information about epilepsy, epilepsy research, and epilepsy programs, this site contains a valuable toolkit directed toward parents with teenaged children with epilepsy. Materials include a "Reach Out" brochure that describes how the presence of a teenager with epilepsy may affect all members of the family. There are also stationery sheets that can be downloaded, which contain first aid information at the bottom as well as quotes from parents advocating for the teen that are designed to educate the reader. The site also has links to streaming audio files in which parents can listen to several typical parent–teen conversations, and then also hear the conversations again from the perspective of the teen. This site also has a link to a documentary-style video featuring families that have survived the teen years.
- **NIH and the National Institute of Neurologic Disorders and Stroke** (www.ninds.nih.gov/disorders/epilepsy/epilepsy.htm). Although this site contains less practical information about epilepsy from the patient's perspective, it offers a wealth of authoritative information about the nature of epilepsy and its treatment. In addition, there is information in Spanish that will be of great benefit for appropriate families. A number of NINDS publications on various epilepsy syndromes are included, as well as information about ongoing clinic trials. Finally, links to a large number of epilepsy organizations and to the North American Antiepilepsy Drug Pregnancy Registry are included.

FUTURE EFFORTS

Great strides have been made in raising the level of awareness regarding the behavioral and cognitive risks often associated with epilepsy. Most current careers in the neuropsychology of epilepsy involve epilepsy surgery and related activities. There is, however, a greater need for involvement of neuropsychology in more traditional pediatric neuropsychology contexts, in which areas of strengths and weakness not traditionally evaluated or addressed in school psychology evaluation are identified to maximize individual long-term outcomes (i.e., quality of life, employment, compensatory strategies), and we anticipate increasing interest in pediatric epilepsy outside the context of epilepsy surgery. In addition, many strategies successfully employed in rehabilitation psychology likely will be increasingly implemented in order to achieve the above long-term outcome objectives.

For neuropsychologists in training, research careers in epilepsy should be considered. Neuropsychological outcomes are increasingly being used as endpoints in clinical trials, and imaging skills are being acquired and used to further understand the biologic substrates of persons with epilepsy. This would increase the wealth of knowledge in the area of epilepsy.

HOW TO BECOME INVOLVED

Joining and participating in patient-related societies, such as the Epilepsy Foundation (previously known as the Epilepsy Foundation of America, or EFA), and contacting school systems for teacher education are among the best ways to become involved. Relevant resources are listed in Table 1. Also, be aware of the current cognitive and psychological impacts of epilepsy and communicate this information to those individuals with whom you work.

For neuropsychologists who are more politically active, there are always important advocacy initiatives that can benefit from added participation. At the time of this writing, for example, there are multiple areas on the federal level that are attempting to lessen the burden associated with epilepsy, some of which include the ADA Restoration Act, State Children's Health Insurance Program (SCHIP), reauthorization of the Workforce Investment Act and Vocational Rehabilitation Act, as well as general promotion of policies that provide ready access to all epilepsy mediation and treatment to persons with epilepsy. Greater information regarding advocacy at the federal level can be found at http://www.epilepsyfoundation.org/advocacy/.

REFERENCES

Annegers, J. F. (1996). The epidemiology of epilepsy. In E. Wyllie (Ed.), *The treatment of epilepsy: Principles and practice* (2nd ed., pp. 165–172). Baltimore: Williams & Wilkins.

Barr, W. B., Chelune, G. J., Hermann, B. P., Loring, D. W., Perrine, K., Strauss, E., et al. (1997). The use of figural reproduction tests as measures of nonverbal memory in epilepsy surgery candidates. *Journal of the International Neuropsychological Society*, *3*(5), 435–443.

Britten, N., Morgan, K., Fenwick, P. B., & Britten, H. (1986). Epilepsy and handicap from birth to age 36. *Developmental Medicine & Child Neurology*, *28*(6), 719–728.

Camfield, C., Camfield, P., Gordon, K., Smith, B., & Dooley, J. (1993). Outcome of childhood epilepsy: A population-based study with a simple predictive scoring system for those treated with medication. *Journal of Pediatrics*, *122*(6), 861–868.

Davies, S., Heyman, I., & Goodman, R. (2003). A population survey of mental health problems in children with epilepsy. *Developmental Medicine & Child Neurology*, *45*(5), 292–295.

Dikmen, S., & Matthews, C. G. (1977). Effect of major motor seizure frequency upon cognitive-intellectual functions in adults. *Epilepsia*, *18*(1), 21–29.

Dikmen, S., Matthews, C. G., & Harley, J. P. (1975). The effect of early versus late onset of major motor epilepsy upon cognitive-intellectual performance. *Epilepsia*, *16*(1), 73–81.

Dikmen, S., Matthews, C. G., & Harley, J. P. (1977). Effect of early versus late onset of major motor epilepsy on cognitive-intellectual performance: Further considerations. *Epilepsia, 18*(1), 31–36.

Dodrill, C. B. (1986). Correlates of generalized tonic-clonic seizures with intellectual, neuropsychological, emotional, and social function in patients with epilepsy. *Epilepsia, 27*(4), 399–411.

Dodrill, C. B. (1992). The relationship of neuropsychological abilities to seizure factors and to surgery for epilepsy. Acta Neurologica Scandinavica. *Supplementum, 140*, 106–110.

Gilliam, F. G., Barry, J. J., Hermann, B. P., Meador, K. J., Vahle, V., & Kanner, A. M. (2006). Rapid detection of major depression in epilepsy: A multicentre study. *The Lancet Neurology, 5*(5), 399–405.

Gilliam, F. G., Maton, B. M., Martin, R. C., Sawrie, S. M., Faught, R. E., Hugg, J. W., et al. (2007). Hippocampal 1H-MRSI correlates with severity of depression symptoms in temporal lobe epilepsy. *Neurology, 68*(5), 364–368.

Harrison, R. M., & Taylor, D. C. (1976). Childhood seizures: A 25-year follow up. Social and medical prognosis. *Lancet, 1*(7966), 948–951.

Helmstaedter, C., Pohl, C., & Elger, C. E. (1995). Relations between verbal and nonverbal memory performance: Evidence of confounding effects particularly in patients with right temporal lobe epilepsy. *Cortex, 31*(2), 345–355.

Helmstaedter, C., Pohl, C., Hufnagel, A., & Elger, C. E. (1991). Visual learning deficits in nonresected patients with right temporal lobe epilepsy. *Cortex, 27*(4), 547–555.

Hermann, B., Hansen, R., Seidenberg, M., Magnotta, V., & O'Leary, D. (2003). Neurodevelopmental vulnerability of the corpus callosum to childhood onset localization-related epilepsy. *Neuroimage, 18*(2), 284–292.

Hermann, B. P., Wyler, A. R., & Richey, E. T. (1988). Wisconsin Card Sorting Test performance in patients with complex partial seizures of temporal-lobe origin. *Journal of Clinical & Experimental Neuropsychology, 10*(4), 467–476.

Jalava, M., Sillanpää, M., Camfield, C., & Camfield, P. (1997). Social adjustment and competence 35 years after onset of childhood epilepsy: A prospective controlled study. *Epilepsia, 38*(6), 708–715.

Jokeit, H., Seitz, R., Markowitsch, H., Neumann, N., Witte, O., & Ebner, A. (1997). Prefrontal asymmetric interictal glucose hypometabolism and cognitive impairment in patients with temporal lobe epilepsy. *Brain, 120*(12), 2283–2294.

Lennox, W. G., & Lennox, M. (1960). *Epilepsy and related disorders.* Boston: Little Brown & Co.

Lespinet, V., Bresson, C., N'Kaoua, B., Rougier, A., & Claverie, B. (2002). Effect of age of onset of temporal lobe epilepsy on the severity and the nature of preoperative memory deficits. *Neuropsychologia, 40*(9), 1591–1600.

Lindsay, J., Ounsted, C., & Richards, P. (1979a). Long-term outcome in children with temporal lobe seizures. I: Social outcome and childhood factors. *Developmental Medicine & Child Neurology, 21*(3), 285–298.

Lindsay, J., Ounsted, C., & Richards, P. (1979b). Long-term outcome in children with temporal lobe seizures. III: Psychiatric aspects in childhood and adult life. *Developmental Medicine & Child Neurology, 21*(5), 630–636.

Loring, D., Marino, S., & Meador, K. (2007). Neuropsychological and behavioral effects of antiepilepsy drugs. *Neuropsychology Review, 17*(4), 413–425.

Loring, D. W., Barr, W. B., Hamberger, M. J., & Helmstaedter, C. (2008). Neuropsychological evaluation – Adults. In J. Engel Jr & T. A. Pedley (Eds.), *Epilepsy: A comprehensive textbook,* (2nd ed., pp. 1057–1065). Philadelphia: Lippincott Williams & Wilkins.

Luria, A. R. (1973). The working brain: An introduction to neuropsychology [trans. B. Haigh]. New York: Basic Books.

Martin, R. C., Sawrie, S. M., Gilliam, F. G., Palmer, C. A., Faught, E., Morawetz, R. B., et al. (2000). Wisconsin Card Sorting performance in patients with temporal lobe epilepsy: Clinical and neuroanatomical correlates. *Epilepsia, 41*(12), 1626–1632.

O'Leary, D. S., Seidenberg, M., Berent, S., & Boll, T. J. (1981). Effects of age of onset of tonic-clonic seizures on neuropsychological performance in children. *Epilepsia, 22*(2), 197–204.

Rutter, M. L. (1970). Psycho-social disorders in childhood, and their outcome in adult life. *Journal of the Royal College of Physicians London, 4*(3), 211–218.

Schoenfeld, J., Seidenberg, M., Woodard, A., Hecox, K., Inglese, C., Mack, K., et al. (1999). Neuropsychological and behavioral status of children with complex partial seizures. *Developmental Medicine & Child Neurology, 41*(11), 724–731.

Seidenberg, M., Pulsipher, D., & Hermann, B. (2007). Cognitive progression in epilepsy. *Neuropsychology Review, 17*(4), 445–454.

Shackleton, D. P., Kasteleijn-Nolst Trenite, D. G. A., de Craen, A. J. M., Vandenbroucke, J. P., & Westendorp, R. G. J. (2003). Living with epilepsy: Long-term prognosis and psychosocial outcomes. *Neurology, 61*(1), 64–70.

Sillanpää, M., Jalava, M., Kaleva, O., & Shinnar, S. (1998). Long-term prognosis of seizures with onset in childhood. *New England Journal of Medicine, 338*(24), 1715–1722.

Theodore, W. H., DeCarli, C., & Gaillard, W. D. (2003). Total cerebral volume is reduced in patients with localization-related epilepsy and a history of complex febrile seizures. *Archives of Neurology, 60*(2), 250–252.

Theodore, W. H., Fishbein, D., & Dubinsky, R. (1988). Patterns of cerebral glucose metabolism in patients with partial seizures. *Neurology, 38*(8), 1201–1206.

Weber, B., Luders, E., Faber, J., Richter, S., Quesada, C. M., Urbach, H., et al. (2007). Distinct regional atrophy in the corpus callosum of patients with temporal lobe epilepsy. *Brain, 130*(12), 3149–3154.

The Clinical Neuropsychologist, 24: 429–453, 2010
http://www.psypress.com/tcn
ISSN: 1385-4046 print/1744-4144 online
DOI: 10.1080/13854040903058960

Psychology Press
Taylor & Francis Group

INCREASING CULTURALLY COMPETENT NEUROPSYCHOLOGICAL SERVICES FOR ETHNIC MINORITY POPULATIONS: A CALL TO ACTION

Monica Rivera Mindt[1,2,3], Desiree Byrd[2,3], Pedro Saez[1], and Jennifer Manly[4]

[1]*Department of Psychology, Fordham University, New York,* [2]*Department of Pathology, The Mount Sinai School of Medicine, New York,* [3]*Department of Psychiatry, The Mount Sinai School of Medicine, New York, and* [4]*Taub Institute for Research on Alzheimer's Disease and the Aging Brain and the Department of Neurology, Columbia University College of Physicians and Surgeons, New York, NY, USA*

US demographic and sociopolitical shifts have resulted in a rapidly growing need for culturally competent neuropsychological services. However, clinical neuropsychology as a field has not kept pace with the needs of ethnic minority clients. In this discussion we review: historical precedents and the limits of universalism in neuropsychology; ethical/professional guidelines pertinent to neuropsychological practice with ethnic minority clients; critical cultural considerations in neuropsychology; current disparities germane to practice; and challenges to the provision of services to racial/ethnic minority clients. We provide a call to action for neuropsychologists and related organizations to advance multiculturalism and diversity within the field by increasing multicultural awareness and knowledge, multicultural education and training, multicultural neuropsychological research, and the provision of culturally competent neuropsychological services to racial/ethnic minority clients. Lastly, we discuss strategies for increasing the provision of culturally competent neuropsychological services, and offer several resources to meet these goals.

Keywords: Ethnic minority; Cultural competence; Diversity; Neuropsychology.

INTRODUCTION

In the span of just over 100 years the US has shifted from a country in which one in eight residents was of ethnic minority status to a country in which approximately one in three residents is of ethnic minority status (US Census Bureau, 2002, 2007a). In roughly the same time frame, clinical neuropsychology has emerged as a discipline. However, despite the rapid rate of expansion of ethnic minority populations, the field of clinical neuropsychology has been slow to respond to the clinical needs of ethnic minority clients. In this discussion we provide an overview of critical cultural considerations in clinical neuropsychology and current disparities in neuropsychological practice. We also set out specific goals and a road map for

Address correspondence to: Monica Rivera Mindt, Ph.D., Department of Psychology, Fordham University, New York, NY, USA. E-mail: monica.mindt@mssm.edu
Accepted for publication: May 21, 2009.

increasing the provision of neuropsychological services for ethnic minority patient populations. Finally, we suggest resources for increasing cultural competence in neuropsychological practice.

According to the American Psychological Association's (APA) *Guidelines on Multicultural Education, Training, Research, Practice, and Organizational Change for Psychologists* (APA, 2003), "*all* individuals are cultural beings who possess a cultural, racial, and ethnic heritage" (p. 380). Working from these guidelines, *culture* is defined as the quintessence of a worldview born of learned and transmitted belief systems and value orientations that influence customs, norms, practices, and social institutions, including psychological processes (cognition, behavior, etc.) and organizations (educational systems, media, etc.) and that is transmitted from one generation to the next.

For the purposes of this discussion we will refer to persons of culturally, racially, and/or ethnically diverse backgrounds (e.g., African Americans, Hispanics/Latinos, Asians/Asian Americans, Native Hawaiians and other Pacific Islanders, American Indians and Alaska Natives) as *ethnic minorities*—consistent with previous authors and current US Census Bureau nomenclature (APA, 2003; US Census Bureau, 2007a). Likewise, we adopt the conceptualization of *cultural competence* set forth by Sue et al. (Sue, Arredondo, & McDavis, 1992; Sue et al., 1998) and Sue (2001) as we consider its application to neuropsychology at the individual and organizational levels:

(1) Awareness of one's own assumptions, values, biases, and stereotypes about ethnic minorities; how such beliefs and attitudes could negatively impact the provision of *neuropsychological services*; and the development of a positive stance towards multiculturalism.
(2) Knowledge and understanding regarding one's own worldview and that of one's clients; specific knowledge regarding the culture of one's clients; and understanding of sociopolitical influences.
(3) Acquisition of specific, culturally appropriate *assessment*, intervention, and communication skills necessary to effectively work with ethnic minority groups.
(4) Development of core cultural competencies, at the organizational level, based on new theories, practices, policies, and organizational structures that are more responsive to all groups.

HISTORICAL PRECEDENT AND LIMITS OF UNIVERSALISM

Vygotsky (1978) and Luria (1976) conceived of cognition as the result of a dynamic interplay of biological, socioeconomic, and cultural determinants (i.e., *radical environmentalism*; Nell, 2000). In contrast, the theory of *universalism* holds that cognitive processes are fundamentally similar across humankind, irrespective of the cultural milieu in which they arise (Nell, 2000). The field of neuropsychology, at least here in the US, has largely held a universalist presupposition of both cognition and the manner in which cognitive processes are assessed, emphasizing "a direct, unencumbered link between the neurobiological brain, cognitive processes, and behavior" (Perez-Arce, 1999, p. 582).

A potential advantage of a universalist view of cognition is that it frees neuropsychology from the need to examine construct validity and related issues. If cognitive processes are similar across cultural groups, then neuropsychological assessment instruments may be considered universally applicable. Thus, evaluation of culturally diverse clients becomes easier and less time consuming if neuropsychologists do not have to tailor each test (or construct) to the sample to be tested, and comparisons across cultures are drastically simplified if the same tests are used. In contrast, a potential disadvantage of the universalist view is that it can lead directly to nativism, because when ethnic groups differ on neuropsychological test performances, those differences can be attributed to genetic endowment rather than culture and environment (Nell, 2000). Further, Cole (1996) proposed that a universalist view of cognition underlies the concept of "culture-free" tests. He argued that cognitive tests are inevitably cultural devices that assess abilities valued by the culture wherein the test was developed, and therefore have questionable construct validity when applied outside of that culture (Cole, 1996). Several investigators have further argued that sensitivity to cultural and ethnic differences has generally been lacking within neuropsychology (Ardila, 2005; Cole, 1996; Cuellar, 1998; Nell, 2000; Perez-Arce, 1999; Uzzell, Pontón, & Ardila, 2006). Consequently, several potential disadvantages may result from a universalist view of cognition, including: (1) inaccurate and harmful racial/ethnic generalizations, (2) inadequate science (not examining construct validity), and (3) inappropriate use of tests in the assessment of racial/ethnic minority populations. In the end, neuropsychology has largely ascribed to a universalist approach of cognition with a lack of research to either support it or definitely dispute it.

INCREASING NEUROPSYCHOLOGICAL SERVICES FOR ETHNIC MINORITIES

Three major factors argue for neuropsychology as a field to increase the provision of culturally competent neuropsychological services for ethnic minorities. These factors include: (1) demographic shifts in the US population, (2) the ethics and ethos of the broader discipline of psychology, and (3) construct validity requirements in neuropsychological evaluation.

Demographics

The US Census Bureau recently announced that the US ethnic minority population reached 100.7 million (34%; US Census Bureau, 2007a). In several states, ethnic minority groups already outnumber non-Hispanic whites (US Census Bureau, 2007a). By the year 2050, approximately 50% of all US residents will belong to an ethnic minority group. Regardless of the urgency that current and future demographic shifts create by increasing demand for neuropsychological services among ethnic minority individuals, there is an ethical imperative for the competent provision of services to these individuals.

Ethics and ethos

The ethical standards set forth in APA's *Ethical Principles of Psychologists and Code of Conduct* (EPPCC; APA, 2002) provide clear directives regarding the provision of culturally competent neuropsychological services. For instance, Standard 9.06 (Interpreting Assessment Results) of the code states that when psychologists interpret assessment results, they should "... take into account the various test factors, test-taking abilities, and other characteristics of the person being assessed, such as situational, personal, linguistic, and cultural differences, that might affect psychologists' judgments or reduce the accuracy of their interpretations." Ethical Standard 2.01 (APA, 2002; Boundaries of Competence) states that, "cultural expertise or competence at the individual level is essential for the clinician who is working with cross-cultural populations." It is clear that neuropsychologists, similar to all psychologists, have an ethical mandate to provide culturally competent neuropsychological services to ethnic minority clients. Moreover, operating under the universalist approach in neuropsychology is not only a barrier to accurate science and best practice, it is also contrary to the ethos of the broader discipline of psychology.

Construct validity

Finally, fundamental to valid neuropsychological evaluation is the use of valid instruments. APA Ethical Standard 9.02b (APA, 2002) states that "Psychologists use assessment instruments whose validity and reliability have been established for use with members of the population tested." However, as Helms (1992) has cogently argued, by and large researchers (and test publishers) have failed to investigate the cultural equivalence of neuropsychological instruments; that is, whether the constructs being measured (e.g., intelligence processing speed, learning, executive functioning, etc.) have a similar meaning within and across cultural groups. As Luria (1976) observed, tests developed and validated for use in one culture frequently resulted in experimental failures and were invalid for use with other cultural groups. Thus, neuropsychological instruments designed to measure constructs in one culture may not be readily applied to individuals of other cultures with the expectation that they will be equally measuring the same construct.

Fortunately, emerging research offers promising models for empirically investigating the construct validity of neuropsychological instruments across groups. For instance, a recent Canadian study (Tuokko et al., 2009) elegantly addressed the issue of cross-linguistic construct validity in a sample of English- and French-speaking older adults. In this study factor-analytic techniques were used to examine whether or not the latent variables underlying the *Canadian Study of Health and Aging* (CSHA) neuropsychological test battery administered in English or French were the same (i.e., invariant). The results revealed that the best-fitting baseline model, which was established in the English-speaking *Exploratory* sample

($n = 716$), demonstrated invariance among the English-speaking ($n = 715$) and the French-speaking ($n = 446$) *Validation* samples in terms of long-term retrieval and visuospatial speed and partial invariance for verbal ability (possibly due to differences in translation or other cultural effects). Thus, Tuokko et al. (2009) were able to provide some empirical support for the cross-linguistic construct validity of the CSHA neuropsychological battery utilizing a relatively straightforward multi-group confirmatory factor analysis (CFA) framework. This approach represents one promising methodology for examining the construct validity (via measurement invariance) of neuropsychological instruments across a variety of ethnic and linguistic groups (Bowden, Cook, Bardenhagen, Shores, & Carstairs, 2004; Teresi, 2006; Tuokko et al., 2009).

CURRENT DISPARITIES IN NEUROPSYCHOLOGICAL PRACTICE

Health disparities

US ethnic minority populations are disproportionately impacted by a myriad of sociocultural factors, each of which may play a role in the increased rates and possibly virulence, of particular medical disorders within these groups (Cargill & Stone, 2005). Such factors include: lower education/literacy, higher rates of poverty, and limited access to and/or use of health care services (Cargill & Stone, 2005; Fiscella, Franks, Gold, & Clancy, 2000; US Census Bureau, 2007b). Further, many ethnic minority groups (most notably African Americans, Hispanics/Latinos, and American Indians) are disproportionately suffering from medical conditions (e.g., hypertension, HIV/AIDS, hepatitis, diabetes, etc.) that may increase/heighten their need for neuropsychological services than the general population (Centers for Disease Control, 2007a, 2007b).

Diagnostic disparities

While sensitivity for neuropsychological tests appears equitable across ethnic groups, specificity is compromised for ethnic minorities (Heaton, Taylor, & Manly, 2003; Lichtenberg, Ross, & Christensen, 1994; Manly et al., 1998a, 1998b; Norman, Evans, Miller, & Heaton, 2000; Roberts & Hamsher, 1984). Numerous studies report the disproportionate rate of false-positive errors for neuropsychological disorders in African American and Latino communities (Adams, Boake, & Crain, 1982; Diehr, Heaton, Miller, & Grant, 1998; Gladsjo et al., 1999; Klusman, Moulton, Hornbostel, Picano, & Beattie, 1992; Manly et al., 1998a; Norman et al., 2000; Taylor & Heaton, 2001). This finding is most remarkable when reported from data collected on carefully evaluated, neurologically normal samples (Heaton et al., 2003). Thus, while neuropsychologists are able to provide meaningful contributions to the diagnosis and treatment planning for their non-Hispanic white clients, the lack of specificity of neuropsychological measures leaves neuropsychologists less readily able to provide parity in the standard of care for their minority clients.

Disparities in use/availability of neuropsychological services

The need for neuropsychological services for ethnic minority populations is growing, but there appears to be underutilization of services by these groups. Anecdotal evidence suggests that awareness of neuropsychological services is decreased among ethnic minorities relative to non-Hispanic whites. Decreased awareness may be related to the restrictive costs of neuropsychological evaluations, limited number of neuropsychologists at medical facilities frequented by ethnic minorities, and fewer referrals for ethnic minority patients by physicians. Even in patients who are aware of neuropsychological service options, cultural mistrust may be an additional barrier (Terrell & Terrell, 1983). A legacy of cultural mistrust of assessment of "intellectual" abilities exists for many ethnic minorities due to a history of racist misinterpretations of test differences by behavioral scientists (Gould, 1996). Access to health insurance that covers neuropsychological services is another barrier that could limit neuropsychological service utilization by ethnic minorities. Ethnic minorities are un- or underinsured in the US at a far greater rate than non-Hispanic whites (Cargill & Stone, 2005; Fiscella et al., 2000). Finally, the number of neuropsychologists who believe that they are competent to work with ethnic minorities and/or possess proficiency in non-English languages is severely limited. Multiple cultural, institutional, and financial barriers may impede neuropsychological service utilization among ethnic minorities.

The only comprehensive research of which we are aware that has examined US neuropsychologists' current practice with ethnic minorities was conducted by Echemendia, Harris, Congett, Diaz, and Puente (1997). Of the neuropsychologists surveyed ($N = 911$) who provided neuropsychological services to Latinos, approximately 82% of respondents self-rated their ability to treat Latinos as "somewhat competent" or "not at all competent." One of the most striking outcomes of this study is the finding that perceived competence to work with an ethnically diverse patient population appears to make a big difference in provision of neuropsychological services. Those respondents who rated themselves as "extremely competent" to work with Latinos also reported the largest (37%) Latino caseloads, and as level of neuropsychologists' self-rated competence to work with Latinos increased, so did the number of Latino clients served by these neuropsychologists. Overall, the authors of the survey concluded that US neuropsychologists are not adequately prepared to provide services to Latinos, nor do they have the appropriate tools to do so (Echemendia et al., 1997). No other studies have examined similar practice issues with other ethnic minority populations to our knowledge.

In sum, neuropsychologists are faced with several disparities. Current health disparities and continued growth of ethnic minority populations suggest that neuropsychologists will be increasingly called to provide services to ethnically diverse clients. Current diagnostic disparities due to a lack of appropriate training and instrumentation put ethnic minority clients at risk of not receiving appropriate diagnoses and the standard of care. Finally, current disparities in the availability and/or use of neuropsychological services put ethnic minorities at further risk of not receiving appropriate diagnosis and care. Given these disparities, some of the most pressing challenges currently facing neuropsychologists in practice are discussed below.

CURRENT CHALLENGES TO CULTURALLY COMPETENT NEUROPSYCHOLOGICAL SERVICES

Standards of training in multicultural neuropsychology at graduate and postgraduate levels

Clinicians often lack in-depth training in assessment of ethnic minorities. In 2000, van Gorp and colleagues (van Gorp, Myers, & Drake, 2000, p. 24) stated that a growth in scientific sophistication regarding cross-cultural psychology and the role of social status in behavior "have occurred independent of and with little impact on the developments in the field of clinical neuropsychology" and that "Neuropsychology curricula evidence too little course content that would increase their trainee's appreciation of the potential impact these social status factors can have on the selection and interpretation of neuropsychological assessment measures, on the context of the assessments conducted, on the samples included in neuropsychological research, and on the conclusions drawn from research with limited or inadequately characterized study samples." We have quoted so extensively from this publication because these statements are an accurate description of the current environment for most neuropsychologists-in-training. The fact that the referenced chapter was written more than 9 years ago is a striking observation about the lack of progress in multicultural training within our field.

The Houston Conference guidelines (The Houston conference on specialty education and training in clinical neuropsychology, 1998) mention that trainees should gain knowledge about "cultural and individual differences and diversity" from their core of knowledge of general psychology, and the ability to recognize "multicultural issues" from their training in assessment skills (p. 162). However, little detail was provided in the proceedings about the level of multicultural knowledge and skills required to function as a clinical neuropsychologist, or how this was to be achieved. In addition, APA-approved neuropsychology training programs must abide by Domain D of the Guidelines and principles for accreditation of programs in professional psychology (*Guidelines and principles for accreditation of programs in professional psychology*; APA, 1996), "Cultural and Individual Differences and Diversity." Essentially, Domain D requires that training programs implement a coherent plan to provide students with relevant knowledge and experience regarding how cultural and individual diversity relate to psychological research and practice. However, it is unclear that neuropsychology training programs have taken the initiative to formally integrate multicultural issues to foster cultural competence into their curricula, didactics, or training.

Broken pipeline for neuropsychologists from diverse backgrounds

Ethnic minorities are sorely under-represented as professionals within the field of neuropsychology. In 1997, ethnic minorities comprised approximately 26% of the US population, but only comprised 5.4% of neuropsychologists in the field according to APA's Division 40 (clinical neuropsychology) membership (0.9% African American, 2.5% Latino, 1.4% Asian, and 0.6% American Indian). Unfortunately, this gap in representation has widened since then. In 2006, ethnic minorities comprised approximately 34% of the US population, but still only made up 6% of neuropsychologists in the field (1.1% African American, 3.1% Latino, 1.4% Asian, and 0.4% Native American; APA Division 40, 2006). While membership in professional organizations is not a precise marker of ethnic minority presence in the field, it is consistent with anecdotal evidence and serves as an indicator of the status of the profession.

The lack of concerted, national leadership to cultivate ethnic minority neuropsychologists at early stages of professional development is a major barrier for the diversification of neuropsychology. As compared to other psychology specialty programs, such as counseling and school psychology, ethnic minorities are disproportionately underrepresented within neuropsychology training programs (Rivera Mindt, 2007). Previous efforts have largely failed as they have been too few and too circumscribed. Few minority students are applying to graduate programs that offer specific training in neuropsychology. Even in clinical psychology graduate programs where the overall proportion of ethnic minority applicants is relatively high, fewer minorities apply to the neuropsychology track within those programs. Feedback from training directors indicates that many ethnic minority applicants to neuropsychology programs have not completed the basic undergraduate requirements for graduate study in neuropsychology and/or have Graduate Record Examination (GRE) scores that fail to meet program's set (GRE) score criterion.

We believe that one of the primary reasons that few ethnic minority students apply for, or accept positions in, many of the highly selective graduate programs that include extensive neuropsychology training is due to the lack of diversity within faculty, the student bodies, and/or the communities surrounding these universities. Research suggests that minority student representation in psychology doctoral programs is significantly associated with ethnic minority faculty representation and research opportunities with ethnic minority issues (Cole & Barber, 2003a, 2003b; Muñoz-Dunbar & Stanton, 1999). Very few graduate programs with neuropsychology specialty tracks have minority faculty who can serve as role models/mentors for ethnic minority students. Equally challenging, many programs do not have access to ethnically or linguistically diverse populations who can participate in research or provide trainees with clinical experience with ethnic minorities.

Domain D (*Guidelines and principles for accreditation of programs in professional psychology*; APA, 2008, p. 14) states APA-accredited programs will make "systematic, coherent, and long-term efforts to attract and retain students and faculty from differing ethnic, racial, and personal backgrounds into the program," that they will "ensure a supportive and encouraging learning environment appropriate for the training of diverse individuals and the provision of training opportunities for a broad spectrum of individuals," and avoid "any actions that would restrict program access on grounds that are irrelevant to success in graduate training." This principle has not been enforced in many neuropsychology training programs. Increasing ethnic minority faculty in neuropsychology training programs, and avoiding the common trend of ethnic minority faculty being more likely to occupy adjunct or instruction-only positions would be one way for neuropsychology programs to encourage diversification within the student body.

FOCUSED GOALS

The focused goals for this issue are to advocate for and demonstrate practical ways in which the field of clinical neuropsychology and individual practitioners can increase multicultural awareness and knowledge, increase multicultural education and training, increase multicultural research, and increase the provision of culturally competent neuropsychological services to ethnic minorities. We will review some of the obstacles to obtaining these goals and suggest ways to overcome the barriers.

PREVIOUS AND CONTINUING EFFORTS

Research

Empirical research. Ethnic minorities are significantly under-represented in clinical research (National Institute of Mental Health, 2001), including neuropsychology. It is unclear if many of the neurocognitive models utilized in neuropsychology are valid in ethnic minority populations. Previous research has gone far in beginning to contextualize neuropsychological test performance by offering normative data that provide comprehensive demographic corrections for certain racial/ethnic and linguistic groups (i.e., African Americans and Spanish-speaking Latinos of primarily Mexican/Mexican-American origin; Artiola i Fortuni, Heaton, & Hermosillo, 1999; Heaton, Grant, & Matthews, 1991; Heaton, Miller, Taylor, & Grant, 2004; Pontón et al., 1996; Sano et al., 1997). While this work improves diagnostic accuracy and specificity for particular ethnic minority groups, there are also limits to this work.

First, no comprehensive norms exist for adequately characterized English-speaking Latinos, Spanish-speaking Latinos of non-Mexican/Mexican-American origin, bilinguals, Asian Americans, Native Hawaiians and Pacific Islanders, American Indians, or Alaska Natives. While the Wechsler Adult Intelligence Scale – 3rd Edition and Wechsler Memory Scale – 3rd Edition provide the only demographic corrections for English-speaking Latinos of which we are aware, these norms do not provide information regarding exactly what region of the country the Latino participants were from nor how they were recruited (Lange, Chelune, Taylor, Woodward, & Heaton, 2006; Wechsler, 1997a, 1997b). This is problematic as US Latino subgroups tend to exhibit nonrandom, preferential geographical affinity (i.e., Mexicans in the southwest, Puerto Ricans in the northeast, etc.) that could interact with other demographic characteristics (e.g., education, acculturation, language, etc.) to create specific patterns of behavior and/or cognition that could potentially impact neuropsychological test performance (Llorente, 2008). Second, race/ethnicity-based norms do not address the potential performance differences associated with bilingualism, and there is a dearth of research in this area (Ardila, 2002; Bialystok, 2007; Gasquione, Croyle, Cavazos-Gonzalez, & Sandoval, 2007). Third, and most importantly, race/ethnicity-based norms do not *explain* performance differences between groups. Such research may inadvertently leave unexplained racial/ethnic differences in neuropsychological test performance open to harmful misinterpretation (Manly, 2005; Nell, 2000).

Practice research. As we discussed previously, the only comprehensive research of which we are aware that has specifically examined neuropsychological practice as it pertains to ethic minorities is Echemendia et al.'s study (1997) examining neuropsychological training and practice with Latino clients. While Echemendia and Harris (2004); Echemendia et al. (1997) have made a significant contribution to the field of neuropsychology by conducting this critical research on neuropsychological practice with Latino clients, additional research on neuropsychological practice with other ethnically diverse populations and broad research on neuropsychological service utilization among ethnically diverse populations is still needed.

Practice

Practice guidelines. Little exists in the way of formalized guidelines for neuropsychological practice with ethnically diverse clients. The American Academy of Clinical Neuropsychology (AACN) dedicated approximately one page (pp. 216–217) of their *Practice Guidelines for Neuropsychological Assessment and Consultation* (AACN, 2007) toward neuropsychological practice with "underserved populations/cultural issues." These guidelines are meant to augment APA's ethical standards, and readers are encouraged to read these guidelines directly—in their entirety.

The AACN guidelines state that "neuropsychologists who agree to evaluate members of special populations are specifically educated about issues and have experience in administering and interpreting procedures relevant to the patient in question" (2007, p. 217). The guidelines offer recommendations on alternate courses of action should neuropsychologists not have requisite education and/or experience to effectively work with "special" populations. The AACN guidelines also offer brief statements regarding the crafting of appropriate neuropsychological reports for "special" populations, the use of interpreters, the threats to validity of translated/adapted neuropsychological instruments, and related strategies to cope with instruments that have not been standardized or normed with the population with which one is working.

The AACN guidelines for working with underserved populations/cultural issues are an important first step for the field of neuropsychology, but there are several limitations to the guidelines as well. These guidelines are: (1) brief; (2) offer little in the way of providing practical suggestions for creating a pathway for neuropsychologists to gain appropriate training/experience; and (3) do not provide minimum competency levels as part of the standard of practice for working with ethnically diverse clients.

Linguistic issues. Approximately one in five US residents (47 million) speak a language other than English at home (US Census Bureau, 2003). This great linguistic diversity poses great challenges to the provision of culturally competent neuropsychological services to non-English-speaking clients, and the tremendous linguistic heterogeneity *within* certain linguistic groups further complicates the issue (Harris, Tulsky, & Schultheis, 2003). For instance, as a group, Latinos and Asian Americans vary greatly with respect to linguistic skill and language maintenance (Sattler, 2001; Wong & Fujii, 2004). Determination of language proficiency is a complex issue in bilinguals as some bilinguals may be more proficient in their native language, as opposed to their second language, or vice versa. Balanced bilinguals (i.e., equal mastery of both languages) are typically the exception (Rivera Mindt et al., 2009).

The paucity of bilingual neuropsychologists and psychometrists has led many well-intentioned clinical neuropsychologists of varying levels of fluency to administer neuropsychological evaluations in languages other than English. Echemendia et al. (1997) reported that only 11% of neuropsychologists reported Spanish language fluency in the "adequate" to "fluent" range. When respondents were asked if they used translators with monolingual Spanish-speakers, over 50% said "yes" and 19% responded "sometimes". Eighty percent of these reported that the translators had no formal psychological or neuropsychological training. Further exacerbating this problem is the use of existing neuropsychological instruments in non-standardized applications. Examples include the reliance on nonverbal neuropsychological instruments and literal translations of English instruments for use with examinees with limited English proficiency. Although it is often mistakenly assumed otherwise, multicultural assessment practices do not advocate deviations from standard procedures with ethnic minorities, and such use of tests is not empirically supported (Cuellar, 1998).

Future efforts

The potential for effective advocacy within neuropsychology comes from variations of our current practice and knowledge skill set. Small, yet consistent, changes in the way we conduct neuropsychological training, research, and practice will produce a significant shift in the provision of services to ethnic minority communities. Primary targets for future efforts include neuropsychological education/training, research, and practice. We propose the following specific recommendations as a call to action for all neuropsychologists to increase the provision of culturally competent neuropsychological services. These recommendations are based on our review of the literature and the field, as well as APA's *Multicultural Guidelines* (2003).

Goal 1: Increase multicultural awareness and knowledge. We recommend that all neuropsychologists, regardless of training level, actively follow APA's *Multicultural Guidelines* (2003) on cultivating cultural awareness, knowledge of self and others, and recognition of the importance of multicultural sensitivity/ responsiveness. The recommended actions are necessary, though not sufficient, first steps towards transforming the field of neuropsychology into one that is ready and able to effectively work with ethnically diverse populations. Specific strategies towards these ends will be discussed in the following sections (*Getting Involved & Tools/Resources*).

APA Multicultural Guideline 1: "Neuropsychologists are encouraged to recognize that, as cultural beings, they may hold attitudes and beliefs that can detrimentally influence their perceptions of individuals who are [ethnically] different from themselves" (p. 382). A "color-blind" or "intuitive" approach to the provision of neuropsychological services is unlikely to lead to equitable assessment and treatment across ethnic groups (APA, 2003). Instead, past evidence suggests that neuropsychologists' efforts to change their attitudes and biases will go far to thwart such attitudes from negatively impacting their relationships with clients, students, and research participants (APA, 2003).

APA Multicultural Guideline 2: "Neuropsychologists are encouraged to recognize the importance of multicultural sensitivity/responsiveness to, knowledge of, *ethnically* different individuals" (p. 385). As neuropsychologists strive to become culturally competent, we must understand the sociocultural context that our clients, students, and research participants come from. Experiences with prejudice, racism, and the realities of being a member of a stigmatized group can all have a substantive impact on both utilization of neuropsychological services and actual test performance (e.g., stereotype threat; APA, 2003; Steele & Aronson, 1995). By incorporating knowledge of other cultures and minority identity development, as well as specific sociocultural information from those we work with, neuropsychologists will improve the standard of care and elevate the standard of practice for all clients (APA, 2003).

Goal 2: Increase multicultural education and training. In this section we provide three overarching recommendations aimed at increasing cultural competence of neuropsychologists and neuropsychology organizations, developing and implementing standards for multicultural neuropsychology, and mending the broken pipeline in neuropsychology. All of these recommendations are grounded in the following principle:

APA Multicultural Guideline 3: "As educators, neuropsychologists are encouraged to employ the constructs of multiculturalism and diversity in neuropsychological education [and training]" (p. 386). Despite the pioneering work of Vygotsky, Luria, and others, the field of neuropsychology has been historically reticent to move away from a purely biologically deterministic perspective towards one that also incorporates cultural, historical, and sociopolitical factors (APA, 2003). Consequently, neuropsychological education and training curricula reflect this reticence (if not outright rejection), and as a result fail to achieve the standards set forth in *APA Multicultural Guideline* 3 (Rivera Mindt, 2007). The cost of this reticence is manifest in our utter lack of preparation and competency for providing appropriate services to a full one-third of our US population. Such collateral damage is simply unacceptable. Below we provide our recommendations for moving the field forward through education and training.

- **Increase cultural competence of individual neuropsychologists and neuropsychology organizations.** As a discipline, one of the first and most effective acts of advocacy is to commit to the provision of the best possible services to ethnic minorities. This orientation to service delivery includes assessment of the cultural orientation of the client, culturally specific styles of interaction and provision of feedback, and the use of appropriate assessment measures and methodology (Dana, 1996). Cultural competence can be achieved through enhanced education and training, reliance on evidence-based practice, and increased research on the psychometric properties of neuropsychological tests in ethnic minority populations.

Doctoral, internship, postdoctoral fellowship and continuing education programs are primary targets for the development of cultural competence in neuropsychology. Each level of the neuropsychologist's training should be completed with a standard for mastery of cultural considerations in the administration and interpretation of neuropsychological measures based on the growing empirical literature. Additional mechanisms to ensure competency include: proficiency exam questions specific to culture and neuropsychology, and provision of clinical opportunities in diverse settings. For a more detailed discussion of efforts to enhance multicultural neuropsychology training, see Fastenau, Evans, Johnson, and Bond (2002).

We further advocate an empirical approach to neuropsychological cultural competence via the application of evidence-based practice (EBP): integrating the best research evidence with clinical expertise and patient values (Sackett, Straus, Richardson, Rosenberg, & Haynes, 2000). Ways to implement EBP are discussed in another article in this issue (Chelune, 2008). Readers are encouraged to apply the principles of EBP to work with ethnically diverse populations.

- **Develop and implement comprehensive multicultural neuropsychology training standards.** Clinicians and researchers lack in-depth training in the culturally competent evaluation and treatment of ethnic minorities. We recommend that neuropsychology training programs actively take up this challenge in earnest, and become leaders among APA accredited programs in enforcing Domain D of the *Guidelines and principles for accreditation of programs in professional psychology* (APA, 1996).

It is important to note that efforts to increase cultural competence through multicultural and diversity training result in increasing students' self-awareness and therapeutic competence (APA, 2003), which Echemendia et al. (1997) have shown to be critical for increasing the provision of services to ethnic minorities. Moreover, culture-centered education and training has been shown to provide benefits at the individual (i.e., greater commitment towards racial/ethnic understanding), institutional (i.e., a workforce better prepared to engage with diverse colleagues and clients), and societal levels (i.e., promotion of multicultural research; American Council on Education & American Association of University Professors, 2000). However, comprehensive multicultural training standards in neuropsychology are sorely lacking.

The Houston Guidelines are among the most influential training guidelines in the field, outlining training standards and minimum competencies. Since the Houston Guidelines are to be updated in the near future, this is an ideal opportunity to expand the guiding principles for neuropsychology training programs with respect to training in multicultural neuropsychology. We recommend that the future delegates take up this topic with full comprehension of how current research, practice, and ethical multicultural concerns can be integrated into neuropsychological training at graduate and postdoctoral levels.

Close attention must also be paid to developing *cohesive* multicultural training curricula for neuropsychologists already in the profession. We recommend that professional organizations (Division 40, INS, NAN, and AACN, etc.) focus on providing continuing education in cultural competence training at conferences and/or other venues. Instead of ad hoc culture-related presentations, symposia, or workshops, organizations are encouraged to put together specific task forces charged with working with program committee members to provide coherent and useful cultural competency training for its membership.

- **Mend the broken pipeline in neuropsychology.** Efforts to mend the broken pipeline for ethnic minority neuropsychologists will require a concerted and organized approach on the part of neuropsychology training programs utilizing several strategies. First, this effort must clearly start with outreach and mentoring of ethnic minority students at the undergraduate level. We recommend the use of creative solutions that can be implemented to recruit and retain students to existing programs, such as offering practical and research opportunities that would provide experiences with ethnically diverse individuals, even if these opportunities involve long-distance collaborations.

Our second recommendation relates to financial support of students/trainees, from the undergraduate to postdoctoral levels. Programs should set aside training and travel monies for ethnic minority students/trainees. Such funds could cover tuition, stipends, and professional development to allow for students/trainees to attend national conferences, since these students may derive particular benefit from connecting with ethnic minority students in other programs and from connecting with a nationwide network of ethnic minority neuropsychologists present at these meetings.

Our third recommendation to mend the broken pipeline in neuropsychology is a call for a task force of faculty and directors of neuropsychology training programs (from all levels of training), as well as independent advisors, to develop a model/s of training to foster cultural competence in neuropsychology. Individuals who have had success with specific aspects of training in multicultural neuropsychology, and those that may be able to provide specific examples and templates that will help programs implement these standards, would be ideal candidates for this task force. The ultimate goal for this task force would be to help neuropsychology training programs live up to the commitment of Domain D of the *Guidelines and principles for accreditation of programs in professional psychology* (APA, 2008).

Our fourth and final recommendation to mend the broken pipeline is for neuropsychology programs to actively recruit and retain ethnic minority faculty, and avoid the trend of hiring minority faculty in "adjunct" or instruction-only positions. Increased presence of ethnic minority neuropsychology faculty will provide students/trainees with role models and mentors of diverse backgrounds. This will also likely support the recruitment and retention of ethnic minority students/trainees and the overarching mission of implementing multicultural guidelines more broadly. Moreover, such hiring practices reinforce to students/trainees the program's commitment to the diversification of neuropsychology and further their development of cultural competence by having ethnically diverse supervisors—a critical aspect of developing perceived cultural competence according to Echemendia et al. (1997).

Goal 3: Increase multicultural neuropsychological research. The following recommendations are geared towards increasing empirical and practice research to develop evidence-based practice and better target-improved service utilization by ethnic minorities. These recommendations are grounded in APA's *Multicultural Guideline 4*: "Culturally sensitive *neuro*psychological researchers are encouraged to recognize the importance of conducting culture-centered and ethical neuropsychological research among persons from ethnic, linguistic, and racial minority backgrounds" (APA, 2003, p. 388).

- **Increase empirical research on multicultural issues in neuropsychology to better inform evidence based practice.** Our first recommendation in this area is to increase ethnic minority representation in neuropsychological research, and provide adequate characterization of ethnic minorities within the study (i.e., geographic region of residence, country of origin if applicable, immigration information, acculturation, quality of education, etc.). We encourage investigators and grant-funding agencies alike to prioritize the inclusion of ethnic minority participants in neuropsychological research to better understand how existing neurocognitive models apply to ethnic minorities, and improve the external validity of this research.

Our second recommendation is to increase research dedicated to examining the psychometric integrity of neuropsychological measures in ethnic minority cohorts. In spite of the overwhelming evidence of the impact of culture on neuropsychological test performance, the discipline has lagged in the demonstration of sound psychometric properties of neuropsychological instruments. We cannot assume that neuropsychological instruments test the same (or different) constructs in different cultural groups or that these measures are equally reliable, sensitive, or specific. Rigorous empirical investigation into the reliability, as well as construct and diagnostic validity of neuropsychological instruments across different ethnic and linguistic groups is paramount to moving the field forward. Editors of major neuropsychological journals can consider invited issues in which such research is welcomed and encouraged.

Consideration of base rates of conditions and symptoms, (e.g., the relative frequency of an event within a population) can help decrease neuropsychological-related misdiagnoses by providing the clinician/researcher with a valuable diagnostic tool. The use of base rates is especially relevant in practice with ethnic minority populations given the demonstrated health disparities that impact the relative prevalence of neurocognitive conditions in these groups. Not only can base rate information assist in diagnostic accuracy, it can lessen the chance of obtaining false-positive errors. The more accurate base rate estimates are for ethnic minorities, the less likely the chance of erroneous findings.

Our third recommendation aimed at fostering evidence-based practice is the development of norms for those groups for whom high-quality comprehensive norms do not yet exist, including English-speaking Latinos, bilinguals, Asian Americans, Native Hawaiians and Pacific Islanders, and American Indians and Alaska Natives. Such norms must include information on the geographic region from which the sample is drawn and sociocultural characterization (acculturation, quality of education, country of origin, etc.), as well recruitment strategies. While improved norms are important, we clearly recognize and have discussed the limitations of ethnic-specific norms.

Our fourth and final recommendation is for an increase in research to better understand the effects of education, language, and other sociocultural factors on neuropsychological test performance. This issue is critical for informing evidence-based practice. The field must move away from handling such variables as either invisible or as posthoc issues to be controlled for—this impedes our progress as a field. Instead, even if researchers are not primarily focused upon such factors in their research, these issues may still be examined in a thoughtful and a priori manner as secondary or exploratory hypotheses.

Implementation of these recommendations will require effort at the individual and organizational levels. At the individual level, neuropsychologists can be mindful of including and appropriately characterizing ethnic minorities in their research. In addition, they can follow the suggestion of Echemendia et al. (1997), and organize at the national level in order to collaboratively and systematically collect normative data on the commonly used tests within the field. At the organizational level, our call to action includes: encouraging professional organizations and grant funding agencies to provide leadership in prioritizing research and organizational efforts to support multicultural research and development of appropriate normative data for ethnically diverse populations.

- **Increase practice research on multicultural issues and service utilization in neuropsychology.** We recommend that investigators and professional organizations (Division 40, INS, NAN, AACN, etc.) actively pursue research on neuropsychological practice with other ethnically diverse populations and broad research on neuropsychological service utilization among ethnically diverse populations. Such research is critical to getting a more accurate picture of disparities in neuropsychological service provision and will help guide efforts to increase services to underserved patient populations.

Goal 4: Increase provision of culturally competent neuropsychological services to ethnic minorities. In providing this set of practice recommendations, we are guided by APA *Multicultural Guideline* 5: "Psychologists are encouraged to apply culturally appropriate skills in clinical and other applied *neuro*psychological practice" (APA, 2003, p. 390).

- **Develop and implement professional standards for the provision of neuropsychological services to ethnically diverse clients.** We recommend that organizations that provide board certification in clinical neuropsychology, such as AACN, extend their brief guidelines on practice with underserved populations and cultural issues to develop and implement a set of minimum cultural competencies required in order to obtain board certification. Meeting such competencies would require specific types of education and training, as well as evaluation of such competencies. Thus, this effort should be coordinated with delegates of the Houston Guidelines in order to establish clear expected minimum cultural competencies in neuropsychology as a requisite for board certification, that would cover both knowledge and training based, experiential skills.
- **Increase appropriate services to linguistic minorities.** Careful examination of linguistic fluency is necessary in the context of neuropsychological evaluations in order to ensure accurate and fair results. Linguistic fluency determinations

are most preferably done through the use of validated assessment instruments, as individuals may have difficulty in accurately self-assessing language dominance/proficiency. Evaluating linguistic fluency and bilingualism by and large have not been part of standard neuropsychological training or discourse, and there has been a lack of clarity in the field regarding parameters for valid evaluation of linguistic minorities (Rivera Mindt et al., 2009).

We recommend that a task force be created to develop professional standards for the provision of neuropsychological services to linguistic minorities. Such a task force should be derived from leaders in neuropsychological research and practice with linguistic minorities, and should work closely with delegates of the Houston Guideline revisions and other professional organizations. Key points for discussion within such a task force would include valid instruments for evaluating linguistic fluency and bilingualism, appropriate measures for use with linguistic minorities, and training and competency levels for bilingual/multilingual neuropsychologists and psychometrists, as well as guidelines for the training and use of interpreters within this context. It is recommended that the training and minimum competency guidelines put forth by such a task force be made an integral part of training and board certification requirements.

Finally, it is recommended that special recruitment efforts be made by graduate programs to attract trainees who speak more than one language. Financial support for such trainees can be developed through special fellowships aimed at increasing linguistic diversity among neuropsychological trainees.

- **Increase availability utilization, and outreach for ethnic minorities.** We believe that all of the above-mentioned recommendations will go far to increase the availability and use of neuropsychological services to ethnic minorities. While such efforts are necessary, they are not likely to be sufficient, however. Increasing the availability of neuropsychological services to ethnic minorities will also require innovation and creativity, at both the administrative and practitioner levels. Based on preliminary work by Shpungin (2007), we recommend that practicing neuropsychologists take mindful stock of how their practice might impact ethnic minority clients in the following ways:

  (1) *First impressions*: Does your practice contain images of diverse people via brochures, websites, or fliers; anti-discrimination statements; diversity intentions; and/or related services? Is your facility accessible and convenient for clients (i.e., parking or close to public transport)?
  (2) *Waiting area*: Is your waiting area a welcoming place for ethnic and/or linguistic minorities (i.e., written signs, symbols, magazines, art, decorations, play materials, greetings, staff)?
  (3) *Intake interview*: Is your intake interview culturally appropriate for the various ethnic minority clients you may encounter? Do you, and if so, how do you ask about race/ethnicity, culture, quality of education, etc.?
  (4) *Clinician match*: Do you explicitly ask about a patient's preference regarding ethnic or linguistic match?
  (5) *Clinical services and treatment planning*: Do you—and if so, how do you—incorporate your client's ethnicity and sociocultural background into your

choice of neuropsychological batteries, recommendations, and treatment planning?

We also recommend that neuropsychologists become involved in and reach out to ethnic minority communities. We can increase neuropsychological awareness among ethnic minorities by: (1) offering educational talks *in the community* regarding the utility of neuropsychological services; (2) distributing descriptive pamphlets in clinics that serve ethnic minorities; and (3) offering some pro bono or reduced fee evaluations for the community. Increasing awareness also has a secondary benefit of helping clients and their family members advocate for themselves by requesting neuropsychological referrals when not offered by their physician.

WHAT TO DO "IN THE MEANTIME"

While many of the above-mentioned future goals for neuropsychological best practice with ethnic minority individuals will clearly take time to realize, clinicians and researchers remain faced with the challenge of what to do "in the meantime." For example, some might read the current critiques of the field, and come away with the (inaccurate) impression that it is better *not* to use normative corrections at all when evaluating individuals of a different race and/or ethnicity or that it is better *not* to provide services to patients of different cultures (even if there are no other accessible and better qualified practitioners in the area). However, this is far from our intent. Instead, it is recommended that some "middle-ground" approaches be utilized in order to best evaluate ethnically diverse individuals at present, including: (1) utilizing the best available neuropsychological instruments and norms possible *and* acknowledging the potential limitations of these instruments and norms in the interpretation of your findings (say in a neuropsychological report or manuscript); (2) gathering as much sociocultural information as possible (i.e., acculturation, quality of education, linguistic information, etc.) in order to best contextualize the neuropsychological findings of an ethnically diverse client or research participant; (3) referring out to a neuropsychologist who has expertise with the population in question when this is feasible or consulting with such a neuropsychologist/s when referring out is not feasible; and (4) becoming actively involved in advancing your own cultural competence, as well as that of our field (please see the following sections for resources).

HOW TO BECOME INVOLVED

Readers can become involved in advancing their own cultural competence and that of the field more broadly in a myriad ways that go beyond the recommendations discussed above. Below we provide a list of ways to get involved:

(1) *Professional organizations*: Become involved in issues and/or workgroups dedicated to multiculturalism and cultural competence within your local, state, and national professional organizations. There may be ready activities to become engaged in or the opportunity to help advance these issues within your organizations. For instance, APA Division 40 and NAN have active ethnic

minority committees involved in a number of activities, including advocacy, training, mentoring, and networking efforts. These committees also regularly sponsor workshops and presentations germane to the issues at hand.

(2) *Community*: As we mentioned above, it is imperative for neuropsychologists to become involved in ethnic minority communities in order to increase awareness and access to neuropsychological services. At the same time, neuropsychologists stand to learn much from the ethnic minority communities around them. Becoming involved in community based events, provider networks, and non-profit agencies who work with the communities of interest are all excellent ways to learn more about your ethnic minority communities and cultivate dialogues with these communities.

(3) *Work*: Find out about and participate in the multicultural and diversity training opportunities within your institution. If your institution does not offer such opportunities, request them! For those in private practice, we recommend that you provide such opportunities for your staff.

(4) *Get connected*: Find a colleague, mentor, or network where you can go when you have questions about issues of multiculturalism and diversity in neuropsychological practice. For instance, APA's Division 40 has demonstrated great leadership on this front by offering the Division 40 Ethnic Minority Affairs (EMA) Committee email list-serve.

(5) *Promote organizational change through multiculturalism and diversity*: Become an agent of change in your professional organizations, community, and work. Figure out how you can help via contributing to policies and practices, curriculum, resource availability, community relations, professional development, support, and mentoring (APA, 2003).

TOOLS AND RESOURCES

Readers are strongly encouraged to refer directly to APA's *Multicultural Guidelines* (2003) for a more comprehensive review of multicultural and cultural competency issues in psychological education, research, and practice. In addition, we recommend the following resources:

Reading resources

- *The Issues of Diversity in Clinical Neuropsychology* Series (Springer Press; Series Editor: E. Fletcher-Janzen), which includes an exceptional volume by Llorente (2008) on neuropsychological evaluation with Latinos.
- Wong and Fujji (2004) for an excellent overview on evaluation with Asian Americans, including demographic and cultural considerations, as well as practical guidelines.
- Wong, Strickland, Fletcher-Janzen, Ardial, and Reynolds (2000) and Paniagua (2005) for broader overviews and useful suggestions for working with ethnically diverse clients.

- *American Psychologist* (2002; Volume 57 [2]) for discussion on poverty, culture, and learning in psychology.
- AACN *Practice Guidelines for Neuropsychological Assessment and Consultation* (2007)
- Additional useful texts include: Nell (2000), Pontón and Ardila (1999), Fletcher-Janzen, Strickland, and Reynolds (2000), Pontón and Leon-Carron (2001), and the work of Janet Helms, D.W. Sue, and D. S. Sue.

To join the Division 40 Ethnic Minority Affairs (EMA) Email list-serve, visit: http://div40.org/Committee_Activities_Pages/Advisory_Committee/ethnic_min_affair_com.htm

Visit the US Census Bureau for additional information on current demographic characteristics of ethnic minority populations in the US: http://www.census.gov/pubinfo/www/hotlinks.html

Additional links to societies and professional organizations include:

- Hispanic Neuropsychological Society: http://www.hnps.org-a.googlepages.com/
- APA Division 45 (Society for the Psychological Study of Ethnic Minority Issues): http://www.apa.org/divisions/div45/
- APA's Office of Ethnic Minority Affairs: http://www.apa.org/pi/oema/
- Association of Black Psychologists: http://www.abpsi.org/
- National Latino/a Psychological Association: http://www.nlpa.ws/
- Society of Indian Psychologists: http://www.geocities.com/indianpsych/
- Asian American Psychological Association: http://www.aapaonline.org
- International Association for Cross Cultural Psychology: http://www.iaccp.org/
- Society for the Psychological Study of Social Issues: http://www.spssi.org

Additional links to educational and research resources include:

- Center for Cross-Cultural Research: http://www.ac.wwu.edu/~culture/
- Cross-Cultural Library: http://latino.sscnet.ucla.edu/Cross-Cultural-Library.html
- Indian Health Service and Links to American Indian/Alaska Native Affairs: http://www.ihs.gov/misc/links_gateway/Links_Main.cfm
- Asian Studies WWW Virtual Library: http://coombs.anu.edu.au/WWWVL-AsianStudies.html

ACKNOWLEDGEMENTS

The authors wish to thank Dr. Laura Howe for her guidance and editorial assistance with this manuscript. This work was in part supported by grant 1K23MH07 971 801 (PI: M. Rivera Mindt) from the National Institutes of Health and an Early Career Development Award (to MRM) from the Northeast Consortium for Minority Faculty Development.

REFERENCES

Adams, R. L., Boake, C., & Crain, C. (1982). Bias in a neuropsychological test classification related to education, age, and ethnicity. *Journal of Consulting and Clinical Psychology*, *50*, 143–145.

American Academy of Clinical Neuropsychology (AACN) Board of Directors (2007). AACN Practice Guidelines for Neuropsychological Assessment and Consultation. *The Clinical Neuropsychologist*, *21*, 209–231.

American Psychological Association (1997). *Demographic characteristics of Division 40 members, 1997*. Washington, DC: APA.

American Psychological Association (2002). Ethical principles of psychologists and code of conduct. *American Psychologist*, *57*(12), 1060–1073.

American Psychological Association (2003). Guidelines on multicultural education, training, research, practice, and organizational change for psychologists. *American Psychologist*, *58*, 377–402.

American Psychological Association (2006). *Demographic characteristics of Division 40 members, 2006*. Washington, DC: APA.

American Psychological Association. (2008). *Guidelines and principles for accreditation of programs in professional psychology*. Washington, DC: American Psychological Association Office of Program Consultation and Accreditation and Education Directorates.

Ardila, A. (2002). The impact of culture on neuropsychological test performance. In B. Uzzell, B. Ponton, & A. Ardila (Eds.), *International handbook of cross-cultural neuropsychology*. Mahwah, NJ: Lawrence Erlbaum Associates, Inc.

Ardila, A. (2005). Cultural values underlying psychometric cognitive testing. *Neuropsychology Review*, *15*, 185–195.

Artiola i Fortuny, L., Heaton, R. K., & Hermosillo, D. (1999). Neuropsychological comparisons of Spanish-speaking participants from the US-Mexico border region versus Spain. *Journal of the International Neuropsychological Society*, *4*, 363–379.

Bialystok, E. (2007). Neurocognitive effects of bilingualism: How linguistic experience leads to neurocognitive changes. *International Journal of Bilingual Education and Bilingualism*, *10*, 210–223.

Bowden, S. C., Cook, M. J., Bardenhagen, F. J., Shores, E. A., & Carstairs, J. R. (2004). Measurement invariance of core cognitive abilities in heterogeneous neurological and community samples. *Intelligence*, *33*, 363–389.

Cargill, V. A., & Stone, V. E. (2005). HIV/AIDS: A minority health issue. *The Medical Clinics of North America*, *89*, 895–912.

Centers for Disease Control (2007a). *About minority health*. Retrieved January 11, 2007, from: http://www.cdc.gov/omhd/AMH/AMH.htm

Centers for Disease Control (2007b). *Highlights in minority health and health disparities*. Retrieved January 11, 2007, from: http://www.cdc.gov/omhd/Highlights/Highlight.htm

Cole, M. (1996). *Cultural psychology: A once and future discipline*. Cambridge, MA: Harvard University Press.

Cole, S., & Barber, E. (2003a). The problem. *Increasing faculty diversity: The occupational choices of high-achieving minority students* (pp. 1–38). Cambridge, MA: Harvard University Press.

Cole, S., & Barber, E. (2003b). Role models, interaction with faculty, and career aspirations. *Increasing faculty diversity: The occupational choices of high-achieving minority students* (pp. 163–186). Cambridge, MA: Harvard University Press.

Cuellar, I. (1998). Cross cultural clinical psychological assessment of Hispanic Americans. *Journal of Personality Assessment*, *70*, 71–86.

Dana, R. H. (1996). Culturally competent assessment practice in the United States. *Journal of Personality Assessment*, *66*(3), 472–487.

Diehr, M. C., Cherner, M., Wolfson, T. J., Miller, S. W., Grant, I., & Heaton, R. K. (2003). The 50 and 100-item short forms of the Paced Auditory Serial Addition Task (PASAT): Demographically corrected norms and comparisons with the full PASAT in normal and clinical samples. *Journal of Clinical and Experimental Neuropsychology*, *25*, 571–585.

Diehr, M. C., Heaton, R. K., Miller, W., & Grant, I. (1998). The Paced Auditory Serial Addition Task (PASAT): Norms for age, education, and ethnicity. *Assessment*, *5*, 375–387.

Echemendia, R. J., & Harris, J. G. (2004). Neuropsychological test use with Hispanic/Latino populations in the United States: Part II of a national survey. *Applied Neuropsychology*, *11*, 4–12.

Echemendia, R. J., Harris, J. G., Congett, S. M., Diaz, M. L., & Puente, A. E. (1997). Neuropsychological training and practices with Hispanics: A national survey. *The Clinical Neuropsychologist*, *11*, 229–243.

Fastenau, P. S., Evans, J. D., Johnson, K. E., & Bond, G. R. (2002). Multicultural training in clinical neuropsychology. In F. R. Ferraro (Ed.), *Minority and cross-cultural aspects of neuropsychological assessment* (pp. 345–373). Lisse, Netherlands: Swets & Zeitlinger.

Fiscella, K., Franks, P., Gold, M. R., & Clancy (2000). Inequality in quality: Addressing socioeconomic, racial, and ethnic disparities in health care. *Journal of the American Medical Association*, *283*, 2579–2584.

Fletcher-Jansen, E., Strickland, T., & Reynolds, C. (Eds.) (2000). *Handbook of cross-cultural neuropsychology*. New York: Kluwer Academic.

Gasquione, P. G., Croyle, K. L., Cavazos-Gonzalez, C., & Sandoval, C. (2007). Language of administration and neuropsychological test performance in neurologically intact Hispanic American bilingual adults. *Archives of Clinical Neuropsychology*, *22*, 991–1001.

Gladsjo, J. A., Schuman, C. C., Evans, J. D., Peavey, G. M., Miller, S. W., & Heaton, R. K. (1999). Norms for letter and category fluency: Demographic corrections for age, education, and ethnicity. *Assessment*, *6*, 147–178.

Gould, S.J. (1996). *The mismeasure of man (Rev. ed.)*. New York: W.W. Norton & Co.

Harris, J. G., Tulsky, D. S., & Schultheis, M. T. (2003). Assessment of the non-native English speaker: Assimilating history and research findings to guide clinical practice. In S.D. Tulsky, D. H. Saklofske, G. J. Chelune, R. K. Heaton, R. J. Ivnik, R. Bornstein, et al. (Eds.), *Clinical interpretation of the WAIS-III and WMS-III* (pp. 343–390). San Diego, CA: Academic Press.

Heaton, R. K., Taylor, M. J., & Manly, J. J. (2003). Demographic effects and use of demographically corrected norms with the WAIS-III and WMS-III. In S. D. Tulsky, D. H. Saklofske, G. J. Chelune, R. K. Heaton, R. J. Ivnik, R. Bornstein, et al. (Eds.), *Clinical interpretation of the WAIS-III and WMS-III* (pp. 181–210). San Diego, CA: Academic Press.

Heaton, R. K., Grant, I., & Matthews, C. G. (1991). *Comprehensive norms for an expanded Halstead-Reitan Battery: Demographic corrections, research findings, and clinical applications*. Odessa, FL: Psychological Assessment Resources, Inc.

Heaton, R. K., Miller, W., Taylor, M., & Grant, I. (2004). *Revised comprehensive norms for an Expanded Halstead-Reitan Battery: Demographically adjusted neuropsychological norms for African Americans and Caucasian adults*. Lutz, FL: Psychological Assessment Resources, Inc.

Helms, J. E. (1992). Why is there no study of cultural equivalence in standardized cognitive ability testing? *American Psychologist*, *47*, 1083–1101.

Klusman, L. E., Moulton, J. M., Hornbostel, L. K., Picano, J. J., & Beattie (1992). Neuropsychological abnormalities in asymptomatic HIV seropositive military personnel. *Journal of Neuropsychiatry and Clinical Neurosciences, 3*, 422–428.

Lange, R. T., Chelune, G. J., Taylor, M. J., Heaton, R. K., & Woodward, T. S. (2006). Development of demographic norms for four new WAIS-III/WMS-III indexes. *Psychological Assessment, 18*(2), 174–181.

Lichtenberg, P. A., Ross, T., & Christensen, B. (1994). Preliminary normative data on the Boston Naming Test for an older adult population. *The Clinical Neuropsychologist, 8*, 109–111.

Llorente, A. M. (2008). *Principles of neuropsychological assessment with Hispanics: Theoretical foundations and clinical practice*. New York: Springer Science+Business Media, LLC.

Luria, A. R. (1976). *Cognitive development: Its cultural and social foundations*. Cambridge, MA: Harvard University Press.

Manly, J. J. (2005). Advantages and disadvantages of separate norms for African Americans. *The Clinical Neuropsychologist, 2*, 270–275.

Manly, J. J., Jacobs, D. M., Sano, M., Bell, K., Merchant, C. A., Small, S. A., et al. (1998a). Neurocognitive test performance among non-demented elderly African Americans and Whites. *Neurology, 50*, 1238–1245.

Manly, J. J., Jacobs, D. M., Sano, M., Bell, K., Merchant, C. A., Small, S. A., et al. (1998b). Cross-cultural comparison of neuropsychological test performance and diagnosis of dementia. *Neurology, 50*, 91.

Muñoz-Dunbar, R., & Stanton, A.L. (1999). Ethnic diversity in clinical psychology: Recruitment and admission practices among doctoral programs. *Teaching in Psychology, 26*, 259–263.

National Institute of Mental Health Council Workgroup on Racial/Ethnic Diversity in Research Training and Health Disparities Research (2001). *An investment in America's future: Racial/Ethnic diversity in mental health research careers*. Washington, DC: Author.

Nell, V. (2000). *Cross-cultural neuropsychological assessment: Theory and practice*. Mahwah, NJ: Lawrence Erlbaum Associates Inc.

Norman, M. A., Evans, J. D., Miller, W. S., & Heaton, R. K. (2000). Demographically corrected norms for the California Verbal Learning Test. *Journal of Clinical and Experimental Neuropsychology, 22*, 80–94.

Paniagua, F. A. (2005). *Assessing and treating culturally diverse clients: Practical guide* (3rd ed.). Thousand Oaks, CA: Sage.

Perez-Arce, P. (1999). The influence of culture on cognition. *Archives of Clinical Neuropsychology, 14*, 581–592.

Pontón, M. O., & Ardila, A. (1999). The future of neuropsychology with Hispanic populations in the United States. *Archives of Clinical Neuropsychology, 14*, 565–580.

Pontón,, M. O., & Leon-Carrion, J. (Eds.). (2001). *Neuropsychology and the Hispanic patient*. Mahwah, NJ: Lawrence Erlbaum Associates, Inc..

Pontón, M. O., Satz, P., Herrera, L., Ortiz, F., Urrutia, C. P., Young, R., et al. (1996). Normative data stratified by age and education for the Neuropsychological Screening Battery for Latinos (NeSBHIS): Initial report. *Journal of the International Neuropsychological Society, 2*, 906–917.

Rivera Mindt, M. (2007, August). *Development of cultural competence in didactics and clinical training of graduate students in clinical neuropsychology*. Paper presented at the American Psychological Association 115th Annual Meeting, San Francisco, CA.

Rivera Mindt, M., Arentoft, A., Kubo Germano, K., D'Aquila, E., Scheiner, D., Pizzirusso, M., et al. (2008). Neuropsychological, cognitive, and theoretical considerations for evaluation of bilingual individuals. *Neuropsychology Review, 18*, 255–268.

Roberts, R. J., & Hamsher, K. D. (1984). Effects of minority status on facial recognition and naming performance. *Journal of Clinical Psychology*, *40*, 539–545.

Sackett, D. L., Straus, S., Richardson, S., Rosenberg, W., & Haynes, R.B. (2000). *Evidence-based medicine: How to practice and teach EBM* (2nd ed.). London: Churchill Livingstone.

Sano, M., Mackell, J. A., Pontón, M., Ferreira, P., Wilson, J., Pawluczyk, S., et al. (1997). The Spanish Instrument Protocol: Design and implementation of a study to evaluate treatment efficacy instruments for Spanish-speaking clients with Alzheimer's disease. The Alzheimer's Disease Cooperative Study. *Alzheimer's Disease and Associated Disorders*, *11*(suppl 2), 57–64.

Sattler, J. M. (2001). *Assessment of children: Cognitive applications* (4th ed.). La Mesa, CA: Jerome M. Sattler.

Shpungin, E. (2007, August). *Psychology training clinics diversity survey: Preliminary results.* Paper presented at the American Psychological Association 115th Annual Meeting, San Francisco, CA.

Steele, C., & Aronson, J. (1995). Stereotype threat and the intellectual test performance of African Americans. *Journal of Personality and Social Psychology*, *69*, 678–709.

Sue, D. W. (2001). Multidimensional facets of cultural competence. *The Counseling Psychologist*, *29*, 790–821.

Sue, D. W., Arredondo, P., & McDavis, R. J. (1992). Multicultural competencies/standards: A pressing need. *Journal of Counseling and Development*, *70*, 477–486.

Sue, D. W., Carter, R. T., Casas, J. M., Fouad, N. A., Ivey, A. E., Jensen, M., et al. (1998). *Multicultural counseling competencies: Individual and organizational development.* Thousand Oaks, CA: Sage.

Taylor, M. J., & Heaton, R. K. (2001). Sensitivity and specificity of WAIS-III/WMS-III demographically corrected factor scores in neuropsychological assessment. *Journal of the International Neuropsychological Society*, *7*, 867–874.

Teresi, J. A. (2006). Overview of quantitative measurement methods: Equivalence, invariance, and differential item functioning in health applications. *Medical Care*, *44*, S39–S49.

Terrell, F., & Terrell, S. (1983). The relationship between race of examiner, cultural mistrust, and the intelligence test performance of black children. *Psychology in the Schools*, *20*, 367–69.

The Houston conference on specialty education and training in clinical neuropsychology (1998). *Archives of Clinical Neuropsychology*, 13*(2), 160–166.*

Tuokko, H. A., Chou, P. H. B., Bowden, S. C., Simartd, M., Ska, B., & Crossley, M. (2009). Partial measurement equivalence of French and English versions of the Canadian Study of Health and Aging neuropsychological battery. *Journal of the International Neuropsychological Society*, *15*, 416–425.

US Census Bureau (2002). *Census analysis tracks* 100 *years of change.* Press release CB02-CN.173 issued December 17, 2002.

US Census Bureau (2003). *Nearly 1-in-5 speak a foreign language at home; Most also speak English 'very well,' Census Bureau reports.* Press release CB03-157 issued October 8, 2003.

US Census Bureau (2007a). *Minority population tops 100 million.* Press release CB07-70 issued May 17, 2007.

US Census Bureau (2007b). *Facts for features: Hispanic Heritage Month 2007: Sept. 15 – Oct. 15.* Press release CB07-FF.14 issued July 16, 2007.

Uzzell, B., Pontón, M., & Ardila, A. (Eds.) (2006). *International handbook of cross-cultural neuropsychology.* Hillsdale, NJ: Lawrence Erlbaum Associates Inc.

van Gorp, W., Myers, H., & Drake, E. (2000). Neuropsychological training: Ethnocultural considerations in the context of general competency training. In E. Fletcher-Jansen,

T. Strickland, & C. Reynolds (Eds.), *Handbook of cross-cultural neuropsychology*. New York: Kluwer Academic.

Vygotsky, L. S. (1978). *Mind in society*. Cambridge, MA: Harvard University Press.

Wechsler, D. (1997a). *Wechsler Adult Intelligence Scale-Third Edition*. New York: Psychological Corporation.

Wechsler, D. (1997b). *Wechsler Memory Scale-Third Edition*. New York: Psychological Corporation.

Wong, T. M., & Fujii, D. F. (2004). Neuropsychological assessment of Asian Americans: Demographic factors, cultural diversity, and practical guidelines. *Applied Neuropsychology*, *11*, 23–36.

Wong, T. M., Strickland, T. L., Fletcher-Janzen, E., Ardila, A., & Reynolds, C. R. (2000). Theoretical and practical issues in the neuropsychological assessment and treatment of culturally dissimilar clients. In C. R. Reynolds, E. Fletcher-Janzen, & T. L. Strickland (Eds.), *Handbook of cross-cultural neuropsychology* (pp. 3–18). Dordrecht, The Netherlands: Kluwer Academic Publishers.

The Clinical Neuropsychologist, 24: 454–467, 2010
http://www.psypress.com/tcn
ISSN: 1385-4046 print/1744-4144 online
DOI: 10.1080/13854040802360574

Psychology Press
Taylor & Francis Group

EVIDENCE-BASED RESEARCH AND PRACTICE IN CLINICAL NEUROPSYCHOLOGY

Gordon J. Chelune
Center for Alzheimer's Care, Imaging and Research, Department of Neurology, University of Utah School of Medicine, Salt Lake City, UT, USA

While a definition for evidence-based clinical neuropsychological practice (EBCNP) has yet to emerge, it is likely to integrate the same core features as evidence-based medicine; namely, best research evidence, clinical expertise, and individual patient needs. Given the nascent stage of EBCNP, suggestions are made to advance evidence-based approaches in both research and practice. The common elements are: recognition that clinical outcomes are recorded at the level of the individual; and to be useful, outcomes research must be presented in a way that can be directly applied on a case-by-case basis. Tracking the outcomes of our clinical services in an evidence-based manner that is publicly verifiable will demonstrate the value of neuropsychological services to our patients, our referral sources, and ultimately to payers.

Keywords: Evidence-based practice; Outcomes research; Advocacy.

INTRODUCTION

The term "evidence-based practice" has become almost ubiquitous in today's health care environment, yet it remains poorly understood and seldom practiced in clinical neuropsychology. The impetus for evidence-based practice in medicine has its roots in the outcomes movement of the 1980s when it became increasingly apparent to payers and many practitioners that a significant portion of health care expenditures in the United States was being wasted on unproven or ineffective tests and treatments (Horwitz, 1996). As a result, a more value-driven, evidence-based health care system began to emerge in which procedures and treatments were seen as having "value" (i.e., were reimbursable) only if they could be objectively demonstrated to have a positive impact on a patient's condition in a cost-effective manner. Outcomes accountability and the management of individual patients on the basis of epidemiologic information regarding outcomes became increasingly critical to the practice of medicine (Johnson, 1997). The term "outcomes" here is used in a broad sense to refer to discrete, measurable events that impact a patient's condition and that can be tracked both in the aggregate on a group level but also, importantly, at the level of the specific individual.

Address correspondence to: Gordon J. Chelune, Ph.D., Center for Alzheimer's Care, Imaging and Research, 650 Komas Drive, Suite 106A, Salt Lake City, UT 84108-1225, USA. E-mail: Gordon.chelune@hsc.utah.edu
Accepted for publication: July 8, 2008. First published online: September 25, 2008.

The term "evidence-based medicine" (EBM) was introduced in 1992 (Evidence-Based Medicine Working Group, 1992) and is defined by Sackett and colleagues (Sackett, Straus, Richardson, Rosenberg, & Haynes, 2000) as simply "the integration of best research evidence with clinical expertise and patient values" (p. 1) with the goal to maximize clinical outcomes and quality of life for the patient. According to Sackett et al. (2000) the practice of EBM requires clinicians to focus their assessments by first translating their need for information regarding the management and treatment of a given patient into answerable questions, and then finding the best empirical evidence to answer those questions through a critical appraisal of existing evidence for its validity, impact, and applicability. This appraisal of information must be integrated with the clinician's expertise within the context of the patient's unique characteristics and needs.

The American Psychological Association (APA Presidential Task Force on Evidence-Based Practice, 2006) has also adopted a similar definition for evidence-based psychological practice (EBPP), and suggests that "clinical decisions be made in collaboration with the patient, based on the best clinically relevant evidence, and with consideration for the probable costs, benefits, and available resources and options" (p. 285). EBPP is generating considerable interest (see the 2007 special issue of the *Journal of Clinical Psychology*, *63*, 607–707), and is believed to have the potential to improve psychological care through increased accountability and quality improvement, enhance financial reimbursement for services, and advance education, training and research (Hunsley, 2007; Kazdin, 2008).

A definition of evidence-based clinical neuropsychological practice (EBCNP) has not yet emerged, but is likely to contain many of the key elements found in EBM and EBPP, namely the integration of clinical expertise, best outcomes research, and the unique characteristics of the patient. However, EBCNP is also likely to involve additional considerations and requirements. Because neuropsychological assessment services are often rendered as consultative services to other professionals who have the primary responsibility for managing the patient's care, the special concerns and needs of these referral sources must also be integrated into EBCNP. For example, a college student who has undergone a temporal lobectomy for intractable seizures may be referred by his/her epileptologist to determine whether s/he has incurred any significant memory loss as a result of surgery. The same patient may be referred by a guidance counselor at the college to determine whether the patient is capable of successfully returning to school. While the clinician may feel that the patient might benefit from a comprehensive assessment that includes academic achievement testing, EBCNP would suggest that such comprehensive testing would be superfluous and inappropriate for addressing the epileptologist's concerns, yet be entirely appropriate for answering the guidance counselor's question. To practice in a cost-effective manner, EBCNP will require practitioners to do only what is necessary to answer the specific questions asked while continuing to use their clinical judgment and expertise to know when to clarify or expand the referral question to explore alternative hypotheses and to meet the needs of the patient.

Embedded in both situations is the need for clinicians to: (1) evaluate presenting problems and complaints and convert these into answerable questions (i.e., "Has the patient incurred a memory deficit as the result of surgery?" or "Is the patient able to successfully return to his/her academic program?"); (2) gather relevant background information from the patient's history and integrate this with the best available outcomes research specific to these questions; (3) choose a relevant test protocol that will generate meaningful data for the given patient and specific questions; (4) analyze these data within the context of the individual patient; and (5) objectively monitor the outcomes of the evaluation. Indeed, EBCNP is clinical outcomes research in practice; i.e., the scientific method applied at the level of the individual—hypothesis formation, literature review, study design and data collection, analysis, and conclusion. By tracking the outcomes of our EBCNP across patients in a manner that is publicly verifiable, we can demonstrate our "value" to our patients, our referral sources, and to payers (see Prigatano & Morrone-Stupinsky, 2010 this issue). To make EBCNP the standard of practice in neuropsychology, clinicians and researchers will need to change how they routinely carry out their activities and develop methods of increasing the interactions between research and practice.

FOCUSED GOALS

To advance evidence-based research and practice in neuropsychology, it is this writer's opinion that researchers and clinicians alike need to embrace two simple tenets: (1) clinical outcomes are individual events that are characterized by a change in status, performance, or other objectively defined endpoint; and (2) to be useful in the care of patients, data from outcomes research must be analyzed and packaged in such a way that they can be directly evaluated and "used" by the end-user, namely the clinician (Chelune, 2002b). In the sections to follow, I will offer some suggestions and examples on how investigators can transform "research" into "outcomes research" by augmenting traditional data analyses that are designed for making group inferences with simple base-rate analyses that permit individual case inferences. Next, I will offer several ways in which the EBCNP-minded clinician can better integrate outcomes research into practice and report writing. Although presented sequentially, I believe there is a marriage between clinical practice and outcomes research such that clinical questions should drive outcomes research as much as the latter informs practice.

FUTURE EFFORTS

The research perspective

Several years ago Glenn Smith (2002) posed an intriguing question for outcome researchers: "is the outcome of interest how many or how much?" (p. 432). Essentially, what is the goal of our clinical research—to compare groups on the basis of how much they differ on a given variable or how frequently they differ? To be maximally informative for clinicians, research results must be applicable in the case of the individual patient. Historically, neuropsychological research has focused on "how much," and has employed group designs with null hypothesis significance testing (NHST) methods. While it is useful to test whether the mean performance of a patient group with a condition of interest (COI) reliably differs from a contrast group (normal controls or other relevant patient groups) on some performance parameter, reports that solely present mean group differences with associated *p*-values are not particularly useful in clinical practice. At a minimum, the American Psychological Association (Wilkinson & Task Force on Statistical Inference, 1999) and others (Zakzanis, 2001) have urged researchers to present effect sizes for primary outcomes as well as overlap statistics (i.e., amount of test measure overlap between groups) to better characterize the magnitude of the group differences. While statistically savvy EBCNP clinicians may be able to use these data to derive individual effect sizes for their patients' performances, such data still are difficult to apply to the individual patient being evaluated.

It is argued that researchers could easily supplement their primary NHST analyses with additional base-rate data for their groups and perhaps incorporate simple epidemiological tests such as the odds ratio (Bieliauskas, Fastenau, Lacy, & Roper, 1997) to translate neuropsychological test scores into outcomes data that can be applied at the level of the individual and better inform the clinical process. For example, it may be of interest to know that patients with intractable seizures who have high baseline memory performances show greater decrements on average on repeat memory testing following left temporal lobectomies than those with lower baseline scores (Chelune, Naugle, Luders, & Awad, 1991). However, this information is difficult to apply at the level of the individual prospective surgical candidate with a given memory score of 96. Rather, it is far more useful for the neuropsychologist and the referring epileptologist when counseling this prospective surgical candidate to know there is outcomes research suggesting patients with memory scores ≥ 90 at baseline have an estimated relative risk of an acquired post-surgical memory deficit that is 4.9 times higher than those with scores below 90 (Chelune & Najm, 2001). To advance EBCNP research and practice, investigators are encouraged to consider the following three suggestions.

(1) *Define neuropsychological outcomes in a manner that can be applied.* Most neuropsychological studies report mean performance differences between groups or associations between cognitive variables and other measures of interest (e.g., biomarkers). Since clinical outcomes are recorded as individual events (Chelune, 2002b), such group data are difficult to interpret at the level of the individual without converting the findings into operational terms. For example, it has been reported that patients with Alzheimer's disease (AD) can be distinguished from patients with frontal-temporal dementia (FTD) by greater discrepancies between letter and semantic fluency (Rascovsky, Salmon, Hansen, Thal, & Galasko, 2007). To be most useful in clinical practice, the end-user of this information would need to know the "size" of the discrepancy that best distinguishes the two groups; that is, the investigators would need to determine a "magnitude" of discrepancy that represents a positive versus negative outcome or indicator of AD. The choice of cutoff is somewhat arbitrary and could be adjusted to be maximally sensitive and/or specific to AD (see Sackett et al., 2000, for a discussion of SpIn and SnOut cutoffs). Nonetheless, conversion of research findings into such discrete outcomes would allow the EBCNP practitioner to directly apply the information when evaluating the individual patient. Converting group data into discrete outcomes also provides the

basis for reporting base-rate information; that is, moving from "how much" to "how many" (Smith, 2002).
(2) *Report base-rate information.* If researchers are willing to supplement their reports by defining discrete "outcomes," it becomes a simple matter of then reporting base-rate information about the groups of interest. In the example above (Rascovsky et al., 2007), it would be helpful to the clinician to know what percentage of cases in the AD and FTD groups had positive discrepancy findings as this information could be combined with other relevant research (e.g., data concerning differences in executive functions, discrepancies between recall and retrieval in these groups, etc.) to increase the accuracy of the EBCNP practitioner's evidence-based inferences on a case-by-case basis. As discussed in the next section, base-rate data also provide the basis for some simple, but powerful, statistical tests often used in evidence-based medicine.
(3) *Provide contingency table analyses.* Conventional NHST results can be supplemented by information about outcomes and their base rates by casting outcomes data into a simple 2 × 2 contingency table similar to the one depicted in Figure 1. Additional clinically useful information about the patient groups and test operating characteristics can be derived using this contingency table format for analyses and ultimately used by clinicians to inform the individual decision-making process (Ivnik et al., 2001; Sackett et al., 2000). Table 1 summarizes a number of these statistics, and provides the reader with their simple calculation formulas that can be computed by hand or with a calculator (no computer is necessary).

Of the various statistics listed, several deserve special attention for their ability to inform clinical practice. *Sensitivity* and *Specificity* provide the clinician with important information about how sensitive the cutoff is for accurately identifying "true positive" cases with the condition of interest (COI) and how specific it is for identifying "true negative" cases without the COI. Most studies attempt to maximize both sensitivity and specificity, although clinically this may not be the most useful approach. For example, Sackett et al. (2000) suggest that in some instances we may want cutoff scores that are highly sensitive to the COI even though some false positives (normals) may be included such that a negative result almost always rules the case out (SnOut: high sensitivity and negative result, rules case out). In other situations we may want a cutoff that maximizes specificity even if some

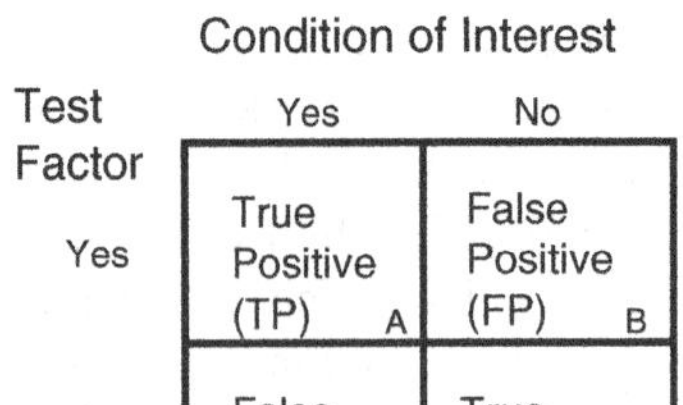

Figure 1 Contingency table layout depicting the outcomes for the condition of interest and the results of the test factor.

patients with the COI are included (false negatives) such that an abnormal test finding almost always rules the case in (SpIn: high specificity plus positive result, rules case in).

In retrospective studies, the *Odds Ratio* (OR) provides an estimate of *relative risk* by comparing the odds of having the COI when the test factor is positive to the odds of having the COI when the test factor is negative. For example, in studies of patients with lung cancer (the COI), a history of smoking (the test factor) is associated with a higher relative risk of the disease. The odds ratio is sample specific, but provides useful information when sample is large and/or when the clinician's patient appears to be drawn from a sample similar to that described in the research. The *Likelihood Ratio* (LR) is related to the odds ratio but describes the likelihood of having the COI given the specific sensitivity and specificity of the cutoff score. By varying the cutoff score and the associated sensitivity and specificity values, the researcher can provide estimates of likelihood of having the COI for different test values.

Information about the *Pre- and Post-Test Odds* is likely to be extremely valuable for EBCNP practice, as a comparison of the two describes the efficacy of the test measure in the diagnostic process. For example, if prior to any testing a patient has a pre-test odds of having the COI of .20 (a one in five chance), but after testing the post-test odds is now .60 (three in five), our ability to correctly identify the COI has increased threefold. Data such as these are not only important for practitioners, but also provide a basis for cost-effectiveness analyses important for third party payers.

Example application. To illustrate how contingency table analyses can supplement traditional NHST approaches, data are presented from a study (Chelune & Stone, 2005) designed to examine processing speed deficits among patients with relapsing remitting (RRMS) and secondary progressive (SPMS)

Table 1 Contingency table statistics, calculation formulas, and results from the application example

Contingency table statistic	Calculation formula	Example
Prevalence of the condition of interest (COI)	Cells (A + C)/N	20.8%
Percentage of impaired test results	(A + B)/N	58.7%
Percentage of normal test results	(C + D)/N	41.3%
Overall correct hit rate	A + D/N	56.4%
Sensitivity (% of true positives)	A/(A + C)	86.1%
Specificity (% of true negatives)	D/(B + D)	48.5%
Positive predictive power	A/(A + B)	30.5%
Negative predictive power	D/(C + D)	93.0%
Odds ratio (estimated relative risk)	(A*D)/(B*C)	5.8
Likelihood ratio (LR)	Sensitivity/(1–Specificity)	1.67
Pre-test odds	Prevalence/(1–Prevalence)	.26
Post-test odds	Pre-test Odds*LR	.43

Letters A, B, C, D refer to the cells in the contingency table (see Figure 1) starting in upper left-hand corner (i.e., true positives identified by a positive test factor) and proceeding in a clockwise fashion. *N* = Cells A + B + C + D.

multiple sclerosis. The impetus for this study came from referring physicians' clinical need to determine when the course of their patients with RRMS had progressed into a SPMS stage, which would signal a need to adjust the patients' medication regimes. For a given patient the referral question was frequently posed as "my patient with RRMS is complaining of increased cognitive problems, but has a stable physical exam–has the patient's course become secondary progressive?" Review of the literature suggests that cognitive processing speed deficits are common in multiple sclerosis, but particularly frequent in SPMS (Chelune, Stott, & Pinkston, 2008; Rao, Leo, Bernardin, & Unverzagt, 1991). Operationally, the hypothesis became "Do deficits in processing speed help distinguish patients with RRMS from those with SPMS?"

To empirically answer this question we retrospectively examined the performances of 274 patients with RRMS and 72 SPMS on the Wechsler Adult Intelligence Scale-III (The Psychological Corporation, 2002) Processing Speed Index (PSI), Trails B, and the Rao version of the Paced Auditory Serial Addition Test (PASAT) (Strauss, Sherman, & Spreen, 2006). While all three measures were moderately intercorrelated, they were entered into a series of stepwise discriminate function analyses (DFA) to identify which test or combination of tests best discriminated the patient groups. Results indicated that all three tests were significant independent predictors (canonical correlations from .304 to .383), but the PSI variable had the highest canonical correlation (.383) and was the only variable retained in the multivariate DFA. When a linear group contrast was performed, the RRMS group was found to have significantly higher ($p < .0001$) demographically corrected PSI T-scores ($M = 39.7$; $SD = 10.8$) than the SPMS group ($M = 29.0$; $SD = 9.5$). The amount of variance (η^2) accounted for by the group effect was .146, and Cohen's d was 1.02 reflecting a large effect size but still associated with a .46 overlap (OL%) between the distributions of the two groups.

From the above analyses it is clear that the RRMS group performed better than the SPMS group on measures of processing speed and that the PSI index clearly differentiated the two groups. However, these group findings are difficult to apply when the clinician must answer "Does *my* patient have SPMS?" To transform these findings into results that can be applied at the level of the individual, we cast our data into the 2 × 2 table depicted in Figure 2, and

Test Factor	Condition of Interest: SPMS	Condition of Interest: RRMS
Tc ≤ 40	62 (A)	141 (B)
Tc > 40	10 (C)	133 (D)

Figure 2 Contingency table showing the frequency of patients with secondary progressive multiple sclerosis (SPMSS) and relapsing remitting multiple sclerosis (RRMS) who had Processing Speed Index (PSI) scores above and below a demographically corrected T-score (Tc) of 40.

performed a series of contingency table analyses, with the results summarized in the "Example" column of Table 1. The first step was to choose a PSI cutoff score to define our Test Factor. Following the guidelines suggested by Heaton and colleagues (Heaton, Taylor, & Manly, 2003), we chose demographically corrected T-scores (Tc) one standard deviation or greater below the mean ($Tc \leq 40$; approximately the bottom 15th percentile) to reflect *impairment*. The resulting sensitivity of this cutoff was 86.1%, whereas the specificity was 48.5%. Thus, PSI scores $\leq$Tc 40 were able to identify most of the patients with SPMS in this sample but also misclassified many RRMS cases. Nonetheless, the OR for this cutoff was 5.8, indicating that patients with PSI scores $\leq$Tc 40 were nearly six times more likely to have SPMS than RRMS. Comparing the pre- (.26) and post-test odds (.43), we see that using PSI scores $\leq$Tc 40 to classify patients as having SPMS nearly doubled our chances of correctly identifying these patients. Finally, if we compute a *Receiver Operating Curve* (ROC) to plot the sensitivities and specificities for predicting SPMS group membership associated with different PSI scores, we can derive likelihood ratios (LR) for each level of PSI performance. For example, the LR associated with a Tc of 40 is about 1.7, whereas Tc scores of 36 yield an LR of 2.2, and Tc scores of 30 have an LR of 3.4 in this sample. Thus, while the post-test odds using a cutoff of $Tc \leq 40$ is .43, they are .88 when using a cutoff of $Tc \leq 30$. Plotting LR values against different test values is likely to be particularly helpful to the clinician in EBNP practice.

In summary, supplementary contingency table analyses can enhance our group findings by providing us information that can be directly applied at the level of the individual to address the question "Does my patient have SPMS?" For example, we can now say that a patient with MS who obtains a PSI score of $Tc = 36$ within the context of the referral question of "Does s/he have SPMS?" is nearly six times more likely to have SPMS than RRMS. Further, the individual risk of SPMS associated with a PSI Tc-score of 36 is more than twice that of those scoring above this level.

THE CLINICAL PERSPECTIVE

Just as investigators need to provide more information about individual outcomes in their studies to facilitate EBCNP, it is incumbent on practitioners to use this information in their evaluations of the individual patient to make EBCNP the standard of care and a financially viable service within today's value-drive health care system. All too often neuropsychological reports provide lengthy descriptions of a patient's test results and then, as if magically, come to a conclusion that the "overall test results are consistent with ..." a post-lobectomy memory deficit, traumatic brain-injury, secondary progressive multiple sclerosis, et cetera. But are these conclusions based on objective evidence, and if so, on what basis? Except perhaps in forensic cases or complex cases where multiple hypotheses are being considered, practitioners are seldom prepared to answer these questions. If we are to practice EBCNP, we must understand and begin to use outcomes research and base-rate information to guide our practice and shape our reports for consumers. This can be accomplished by following three basic practice guidelines inherent in all evidence-based practice (Sackett et al., 2000).

(1) *Convert referral questions into answerable questions.* As noted by Sackett and colleagues (2000), the first step in evidence-based practice is to convert our "need to know" into answerable questions. Rarely are we asked to simply describe a patient's cognitive skills. Rather, our consumers typically want to know "Does this patient have a memory deficit?" "Has this patient suffered a traumatic brain injury?" "Can this patient return to work?" "Has this patient's MS become secondary progressive?" "Has this patient's dementia progressed?" and the like. To answer these questions the clinician must define a priori what will constitute a positive ("yes") or negative ("no") outcome. This will, in part, be based on the patient's unique history and circumstances and the clinician's expertise, but also will require knowledge of the relevant outcomes literature related to the question, the choice assessment tools best suited to answering the question, and the specific pattern or magnitude of test findings needed to constitute a positive versus negative decision. Only by operationalizing the criteria for our conclusions and making these publicly verifiable (i.e., explicit in our reports) can we examine and track their accuracy and their potential benefit to the patient in an evidence-based manner.
(2) *Use base-rate information when reporting test results.* One way to objectively define an outcome is to place it within the context of base-rate expectations. A base rate simply refers to how frequently an event, condition, or test finding occurs in a specified population, which may be the general population, a carefully screened "normal" population, or a patient population with a documented disease or disorder. It is important for the clinician to know the characteristics of the population from which the base-rate data are derived. It is also important to recognize that some base rates are derived from data that are normally distributed, such as the IQ and factor scores on the Wechsler Adult Intelligence Scale, where the scores reflect standardized deviations from the population mean. Other test measures, such as the recognition scores on the Wechsler Memory Scale-III, are asymmetric and not normally distributed, and base rates are best reported as a cumulative percentage (Tulsky, Chiaravalloti, Palmer, & Chelune, 2003). There is nothing about the base rates themselves that defines a given score as "abnormal" or "impaired," merely whether it is a common or rare finding in the reference population. However, if a patient's specific test result is rare in the general population (or reference group) but outcomes research demonstrates that it occurs frequently in a target population of interest, we can infer with some level of probability that the patient more likely belongs to the target population. In the absence of outcomes research to guide us, we can still identify the finding as unusual (i.e., rare), if not impaired.

Most contemporary neuropsychological tests have normative information about the base rates of various test performances in a "normal" population, and in some cases for small patient samples. Also, increasingly these normative data are adjusted for relevant demographic factors so that an individual comparison standard is generated. Assuming that the test scores are normally distributed, we can describe a patient's performances in terms of how far they deviate from demographic expectations (Busch, Chelune, & Suchy, 2006). For example, an 81-year-old woman with 14 years of education who obtains a PSI of 91 on the WAIS-III falls in the "average" range for the general population in her age group, but is 1.5 standard deviations (T-score of 35) below expectations for her demographic cohort. The clinical significance of this test result will depend on the patient's history and the referral question at hand. If the patient has been bed-ridden and in the hospital for 3 weeks for a hip fracture and is now being considered for discharge home in a wheelchair, the finding may not be considered abnormal or a contradiction to discharge. However, if the patient is referred to a dementia clinic for work-up and has a history of diabetes and hypertension, this finding in the context of other results might help distinguish vascular cognitive impairment versus Alzheimer's disease (Levy & Chelune, 2007).

Using the discrepancy between various factor scores derived from the Third Edition of the Wechsler Adult Intelligence and Memory Scales and the direction of these discrepancies, Hawkins and Tulsky (2003) describe how the base rates of discrepancy scores can inform the clinical decision-making process and be helpful in classifying patients with lateralized brain lesions, traumatic brain injuries and neurodegenerative conditions. However, the test user should be mindful and note whether the base rates for the discrepancy scores are one-tailed or two-tailed (Tulsky, Rolfhus, & Zhu, 2000); that is, whether the base rates represent the cumulative percentage of the absolute values of the discrepancy regardless of the direction or whether the base rates are for directional values. The base rates of test–retest reliable change scores are also increasingly used to monitor meaningful change in cognitive status as a function of disease progression, treatment response, surgical or pharmacological intervention, and recovery of function (Busch et al., 2006; Chelune, 2002a; Collie, Darby, Falleti, Silbert, & Maruff, 2002; Strauss et al., 2006). Whether the clinician is looking at a single score or the discrepancy between scores, at a basic level simply reporting the base-rate information for the test findings that we interpret as meaningful for our conclusions allows others to follow our logic and objectively evaluate our work. This is the beginning of EBCNP practice—making our inferences and opinions publicly verifiable.

(3) *Incorporate and use outcomes research to guide our assessments.* It is incumbent on the clinician in EBCNP to use the best available information to guide and inform the evaluation of the patient. This begins with selecting published test instruments and normative data most relevant to the clinical questions being posed. Test measures with poor reliability are likely to yield spurious findings, and those with poor sensitivity to the COI will yield overly conservative results (Strauss et al., 2006). If base-rate information is to be derived from normative samples, the clinician must know the characteristics of the reference sample to which the patient is to be compared, how it was obtained, and what inclusion and exclusion criteria were used in composing the sample (Busch et al., 2006; Ritchie, Frerichs, & Tuokko, 2007; Strauss et al., 2006).

Once the referral question has been converted into an answerable question and we have selected the most appropriate tests and norms to evaluate our patient, we can begin to seek relevant outcomes studies in the literature to further guide our evaluation and interpretation of the patient's test data. Textbooks would seem to be an obvious source of relevant information, but often the information contained is dated and presented in broad strokes, making it difficult to use at the level of the individual patient. Journals, especially electronic journals specifically devoted to evidence-based practice such as the *Cochrane Report*, *Journal of Evidence-Based*

Medicine, and *Evidence-Based Mental Health*, are the best sources of current outcomes data.

Unfortunately there is no specific repository for neuropsychological outcomes research as yet, and the EBCNP clinician will most likely need to conduct a search of the research literature. Fortunately, the Internet offers ready access to a wide array of journals and databases through public gateways such as *PubMed* (www.ncbi.nlm.hih.gov/PubMed) or more specialized databases such as *PsycArticles* or *PsycINFO* that may be available through university libraries, and finding patient-relevant studies is relatively easy if the clinician has clearly defined questions.

Sorting through the "hits" from electronic searches for the best empirical evidence may be challenging. For single studies, the clinician should look for well-designed studies that follow the recommendations of the American Psychological Association's Task Force on Statistical Inference (Wilkinson & Task Force on Statistical Inference, 1999); namely, studies that have clear designs, a specified population that the study is designed to reflect, and sampling procedures that characterize the inclusion and exclusion criteria for selecting participants, well-defined variables that are explicitly assessed, sample sizes that are appropriately powered to test the hypotheses, appropriate analyses, reporting of effect sizes for the primary outcomes measures, and interpretations that are credible, robust, and generalizable to other patients that mirror the characteristics of the sample studied. Well-designed studies that report base-rate analyses such as ORs, pre- and post-test odds, and LRs deserve special attention. However, it is rare that a single study will be definitive. Therefore, clinicians should also look for systematic reviews that summarize the research literature on the topic of interest, specify the methods used to generate the systematic search, and critically appraise and synthesize the results of the studies reviewed. Systematic reviews based on meta-analyses of the literature are especially useful as they are based on an empirical method for statistically integrating the results of many studies involving large numbers of patients by emphasizing the effect sizes of the group differences and the factors that moderate these differences. By carefully specifying the criteria for their searches, researchers make explicit any biases that may be inherent in their reviews. For example, Belanger and colleagues (Belanger, Curtiss, Demery, Lebowitz, & Vanderploeg, 2005) performed a meta-analysis of the literature on the neuropsychological effects of mild traumatic brain injury based on 39 studies involving 1463 patients and 1191 controls. They report an overall moderate effect size ($d = .54$), with the findings moderated by such factors as time since injury, cognitive domain, sampling methods, and patient characteristics. In their review they report that the acute effects of injury were most apparent for delayed memory and fluency ($d = 1.03$ and .89, respectively). These findings are derived across a large number of patients and different sampling approaches, and are likely to be quite robust and generalizable, making the information useful in EBCNP practice.

Neuropsychological research is published in an ever-growing list of neuropsychology and medical journals. At some point there may be a journal or service that culls this literature for outcomes-related findings and makes it available to clinical neuropsychologists who have specific patient-related questions.

Until then, clinicians should learn to develop search strategies for identifying the "best available research" to assist them in evaluating individual patients, and apply this information in a routine manner. If EBCNP truly becomes the standard of care, practitioners themselves will eventually need to become outcomes researchers, monitoring and tracking the outcomes of their own practices. This will require clinicians to work prospectively, set up automated and continuous data collection systems that provide access to archival data in a comfortable and easy to use manner, ask answerable questions of their patient data, and be willing to make their findings available to others (Dodrill, 1999). Such practice-based databases of individual clinicians will, of course, be subject to the same types of sampling and selection biases that researchers face, limiting generalizability but providing publicly verifiable information about the clinician's practice that can be shared with consumers, patients and payers. These individual practice-based monitoring systems also offer the opportunity for clinicians to pool their data sets to answer broader questions, provide within study replication, and identify between-site variables that affect outcomes (Costa, 1983).

ADVOCATING FOR EBCNP: THE MARRIAGE OF SCIENCE AND PRACTICE

Advocacy for neuropsychology is not necessarily limited to efforts directed at changing policies or laws. As noted by Howe and colleagues (Howe, Sweet, & Bauer, 2010 this issue), advocacy can also involve efforts to change the views and practices of individuals and organizations. The proposition advanced here is that engaging in EBCNP practice and research is to "advocate" for neuropsychology. If our goal is to advance the science and practice of neuropsychology in a manner that is publicly verifiable by our consumers, our patients, and payers, then our research and our clinical work products should be the "best" arguments for why neuropsychological services demonstrably provide "added value" for individual patient care. Within the proposed EBCNP framework, we are all potentially advocates by virtue of our day-to-day efforts.

Outcomes-based clinical neuropsychological research and practice are only beginning to emerge, and a definition for EBCNP has yet to be clearly formulated. What I have offered here are only suggestions for what I see as potentially relevant steps that can simultaneously advance evidence-based practice and research, while providing a basis for advocating the value of the profession. I believe we need to think of outcomes in terms of discrete events and findings, and we should be prepared to make explicit the criteria for our decisions regarding these outcomes. Making EBCNP the standard of care in our field and a financially viable service will require the combined "advocacy" efforts of both outcomes researchers and clinical practitioners. If researchers would supplement their data analyses with simple contingency table analyses that provide additional information on the validity (sensitivity and specificity) and potential impact and value of cognitive assessment (odds ratios, likelihood ratios, and changes in pre- to post-test odds), it will clearly advance both the science and potentially the practice of neuropsychology. However, this information will only have an impact on EBCNP if it used and applied by practitioners in a way that payers can determine the value of neuropsychological services.

REFERENCES

APA Presidential Task Force on Evidence-Based Practice (2006). Evidence-based practice in psychology. *American Psychologist*, *61*(4), 271–285.

Belanger, H. G., Curtiss, G., Demery, J. A., Lebowitz, B. K., & Vanderploeg, R. D. (2005). Factors moderating neuropsychological outcomes following mild traumatic brain injury: A meta-analysis. *Journal of the International Neuropsychological Society*, *11*, 215–227.

Bieliauskas, L. A., Fastenau, P. S., Lacy, M. A., & Roper, B. L. (1997). Use of the odds ratio to translate neuropsychological test scores into real-world outcomes: From statistical significance to clinical significance. *Journal of Clinical and Experimental Neuropsychology*, *19*(6), 889–896.

Busch, R. M., Chelune, G. J., & Suchy, Y. (2006). Using norms in neuropsychological assessment of the elderly. In D. K. Attix, & K. A. Welsh-Bohmer (Eds.), *Geriatric neuropsychology: Assessment and intervention* (pp. 133–157). New York: Guilford Press.

Chelune, G. J. (2002a). Assessing reliable neuropsychological change. In R. Franklin (Ed.), *Prediction in forensic and neuropsychology: New approaches to psychometrically sound assessment* (pp. 123–148). Mahwah, NJ: Lawrence Erlbaum Associates Inc.

Chelune, G. J., (2002b). Making neuropsychological outcomes research consumer friendly: A commentary on Keith et al., (2002). *Neuropsychology*, *16*(3), 422–425.

Chelune, G. J., & Najm, I. (2001). Risk factors associated with postsurgical decrements in memory. In H. O. Lüders, & Y. Comair (Eds.), *Epilepsy surgery* (2nd ed., pp. 497–504). New York, Lippincott: Williams & Wilkins.

Chelune, G. J., Naugle, R. I., Luders, H., & Awad, I. A. (1991). Prediction of cognitive change as a function of preoperative ability status among temporal lobectomy patients seen at 6-month follow-up. *Neurology*, *41*(3), 399–404.

Chelune, G. J., & Stone, L. (2005). Risk of processing speed deficits among patients with relapsing and remitting and secondary progressive multiple sclerosis. *Journal of Clinical and Experimental Neuropsychology*, *11*, 52.

Chelune, G. J., Stott, H., & Pinkston, J. (2008). Multiple sclerosis. In J. E. Morgan, & J. H. Ricker (Eds.), *Textbook of clinical neuropsychology* (pp. 599–615). New York: Taylor & Francis.

Collie, A., Darby, D. G., Falleti, M. G., Silbert, B. S., & Maruff, P. (2002). Determining the extent of cognitive change after coronary surgery: A review of statistical procedures. *Annals of Thoracic Surgery*, *73*(6), 2005–2011.

Costa, L. (1983). Clinical neuropsychology: A discipline in evolution. *Journal of Clinical Neuropsychology*, *5*(1), 1–11.

Dodrill, C. B. (1999). Myths of neuropsychology: Further considerations. *The Clinical Neuropsychologist*, *13*(4), 562–572.

Evidence-Based Medicine Working Group (1992). Evidence-based medicine. A new approach to teaching the practice of medicine. *Journal of the American Medical Association*, *268*(17), 2420–2425.

Hawkins, K. A., & Tulsky, D. S. (2003). WAIS-III WMS-III discrepancy analysis: Six-factor model index discrepancy base rates, implications, and a preliminary consideration of utility. In D. S. Tulsky, D. H. Saklofske, G. J. Chelune, R. K. Heaton, R. J. Ivnik, R. Bornstein, et al. (Eds.), *Clinical interpretation of the WAIS-III and WMS-III* (pp. 211–272). New York: Academic Press.

Heaton, R. K., Taylor, M. J., & Manly, J. (2003). Demographic effects and use of demographically corrected norms with the WAIS-III and WMS-III. In D. S. Tulsky, D. H. Saklofske, G. J. Chelune, R. K. Heaton, R. J. Ivnik, R. Bornstein, et al. (Eds.), *Clinical interpretation of the WAIS-III and WMS-III*. New York: Academic Press.

Horwitz, R. I. (1996). The dark side of evidence-based medicine. *Cleveland Clinic Journal of Medicine*, *63*(6), 320–323.

Howe, L., Sweet, J., & Bauer, R. (2010). Advocacy 101: A step beyond just complaining: How the individual practitioner can become involved and make a difference. *The Clinical Neuropsychologist*, *24*(3), 373–390.

Hunsley, J. (2007). Addressing key challenges in evidence-based practice in psychology. *Professional Psychology: Research and Practice*, *38*, 113–121.

Ivnik, R. J., Smith, G. E., Cerhan, J. H., Boeve, B. F., Tangalos, E. G., & Petersen, R. C. (2001). Understanding the diagnostic capabilities of cognitive tests. *The Clinical Neuropsychologist*, *15*(1), 114–124.

Johnson, L. A. (1997). Outcomes management a decade out: An interview with Paul Ellwood. *Group Practice Journal*, *46*, 12–15.

Kazdin, A. E. (2008). Evidence-based treatment and practice: New opportunities to bridge clinical research and practice, enhance the knowledge base, and improve patient care. *American Psychologist*, *63*(3), 146–159.

Levy, J. A., & Chelune, G. J. (2007). Cognitive-behavioral profiles of neurodegenerative dementias: Beyond Alzheimer's disease. *Journal of Geriatric Psychiatry and Neurology*, *20*(4), 227–238.

Prigatano, G. P., & Morrone-Stupinsky, J. (2010). Advancing the profession of clinical neuropsychology with appropriate outcome studies and demonstrated clinical skills. *The Clinical Neuropsychologist*, *24*(3), 468–480.

Rao, S. M., Leo, G. J., Bernardin, L., & Unverzagt, F. (1991). Cognitive dysfunction in multiple sclerosis: Frequency, patterns, and prediction. *Neurology*, *41*, 685–691.

Rascovsky, K., Salmon, D. P., Hansen, L. A., Thal, L. J., & Galasko, D. (2007). Disparate letter and semantic category fluency deficits in autopsy-confirmed frontotemporal dementia and Alzheimer's disease. *Neuropsychology*, *21*(1), 20–30.

Ritchie, L. J., Frerichs, R. J., & Tuokko, H. (2007). Effective normative samples for the detection of cognitive impairment in older adults. *The Clinical Neuropsychologist*, *21*, 863–874.

Sackett, D. L., Straus, S. E., Richardson, W. S., Rosenberg, W., & Haynes, R. B. (2000). *Evidence-based medicine: How to practice and teach EBM* (2nd ed.). New York: Churchill Livingston.

Smith, G. E. (2002). What is the outcome we seek? A commentary on Keith et al. (2002). *Neuropsychology*, *16*(3), 432–433.

Strauss, E., Sherman, M. S., & Spreen, O. (2006). *A compendium of neuropsychological tests* (3rd ed.). New York: Oxford University Press.

The Psychological Corporation. (2002). *WAIS-III–WMS-III–WIAT-II scoring assistant (rev.)*. San Antonio, TX: The Psychological Corporation.

Tulsky, D. S., Chiaravalloti, N. D., Palmer, B. W., & Chelune, G. J. (2003). The Wechsler Memory Scale: A new perspective. In D. S. Tulsky, D. H. Saklofske, G. J. Chelune, R. K. Heaton, R. J. Ivnik, R. Bornstein, et al. (Eds.), *Clinical interpretation of the WAIS-III and WMS-III* (3rd ed., pp. 93–137). New York: Academic Press.

Tulsky, D. S., Rolfhus, E. L., & Zhu, J. (2000). Two-tailed versus one-tailed base rates of discrepancy scores in the WAIS-III. *The Clinical Neuropsychologist*, *14*, 451–460.

Wilkinson, L., & Task Force on Statistical Inference. (1999). Statistical methods in psychology journals. *American Psychologist*, *54*, 594–604.

Zakzanis, K. K. (2001). Statistics to tell the truth, the whole truth, and nothing but the truth: Formulae, illustrative numerical examples, and heuristic interpretation of effect size analyses for neuropsychological researchers. *Archives of Clinical Neuropsychology*, *16*(7), 653–667.

The Clinical Neuropsychologist, 24: 468–480, 2010
http://www.psypress.com/tcn
ISSN: 1385-4046 print/1744-4144 online
DOI: 10.1080/13854040802585048

Psychology Press
Taylor & Francis Group

ADVANCING THE PROFESSION OF CLINICAL NEUROPSYCHOLOGY WITH APPROPRIATE OUTCOME STUDIES AND DEMONSTRATED CLINICAL SKILLS

George P. Prigatano and Jeannine Morrone-Strupinsky
Barrow Neurological Institute, St. Joseph's Hospital and Medical Center, Phoenix, AZ, USA

Healthcare economics and politics require clinical neuropsychologists to clearly document the value of their services. Therefore, advancing clinical neuropsychology as an economically viable profession requires carefully designed outcome studies and clear demonstration of the value of neuropsychologists' judgment in various patient care matters. In this paper we propose steps for achieving these two goals.

Keywords: Value; Training; Outcome studies.

INTRODUCTION

A major issue facing clinical neuropsychologists is getting financially reimbursed for the services they provide. The "gate-keepers" of financial reimbursement often have professional and economic reasons for why they will or will not pay for neuropsychological services. For clinical neuropsychology to flourish as a profession, two types of "data" or "evidence" are needed. One type of data comes from well-designed, "evidence-based" outcome studies that demonstrate the efficacy and the cost-effectiveness of our procedures and interventions (Prigatano & Pliskin, 2003). Another crucial type of "data" needed is for individual practicing clinicians to demonstrate clearly to the referring physicians the value of their clinical judgment in patient care. Neuropsychologists possess unique clinical and professional skills that can add meaningful information to case conceptualization and impact patient care, which can make a real difference for physicians. These skills and our profession's unique ability to add information to case conceptualization need to be clearly taught to residents through a mentoring model so that they can understand and communicate this information to providers.

If we do not take seriously the need for these two different sources of "evidence" our profession will lose economic footing in an already struggling healthcare economy. The end result will be two-fold. First, clients or patients will be seen only on a "fee for service" basis, which only some families can afford. The result would be that some patients in need of neuropsychological services

Address correspondence to: George P. Prigatano, Ph.D., Clinical Neuropsychology, Barrow Neurological Institute, St. Joseph's Hospital and Medical Center, 222 West Thomas Rd., Suite 315, Phoenix, AZ 85013, USA. E-mail: george.prigatano@chw.edu
Accepted for publication: October 26, 2008. First published online: January 29, 2009.

would not obtain them, which could lead to postponement of proper diagnosis, lack of proper treatment interventions, or other negative outcomes that could have been avoided if neuropsychological assessment was part of the clinical and diagnostic workup. The other impact will be an expanding trend of neuropsychologists to do more "medical-legal" work to survive economically. Although this is not negative in and of itself, neuropsychology began as a clinical science, and for our profession to grow, clinical neuropsychologists need to remain active in providing both patient care and conducting research relevant to our field. It is for this reason that we need to seriously evaluate what we do, how good we are at it, and what is the value of our work.

Professional identity of neuropsychologists

Harold Goodglass (1994) noted that the "clinical application of neuropsychology is as close as or closer to its scientific roots than any other specialty within psychology" (p. 5). Neuropsychologists have flourished because they have been able to relate their discipline to a growing database in the neurosciences. This technical knowledge is indispensable to our work, but it is an insufficient condition for the successful practice of clinical neuropsychology. We must also be good at taking this integrated information and presenting it in a way that helps reduce patients' suffering and allows the referring physician to recognize that our contributions have improved patient care.

The value of our work is ultimately judged by four individuals: the patient, a relevant family member, the referral source, and the payor for the services we provide. Outcome studies can demonstrate that neuropsychological tests are reliable and valid instruments for helping answer diagnostic questions. However, if we apply that knowledge in a way that is insensitive to the patient's experience when receiving our services, it is highly likely that patients and their families will not come back to see us (Prigatano, 2000) or follow our recommendations (Westervelt, Brown, Tremont, Javorsky, & Stern, 2007). Our goal, therefore, is not only to demonstrate the efficacy and cost-effectiveness of our work, but also to develop and train neuropsychologists to be scientist-practitioners who are able to blend our science with patient and family needs and concerns. Patient satisfaction is often directly related to the perception that the clinical neuropsychologist took adequate time to carefully listen to his or her concerns and then acted on those concerns in a way that helped the patient (Prigatano, 1999).

Scope of practice of clinical neuropsychologists

The scope of practice for clinical neuropsychologists is indeed a broad one (Sweet, Nelson, & Moberg, 2006). Numerous papers document that clinical neuropsychologists are actively involved in the examination and assessment of individuals from infancy through the elderly years (see Lezak, Howieson, & Loring, 2003; Morgan & Ricker, 2008). A casual review of existing journals shows that neuropsychologists are progressively becoming more interested in applying this information to the successful management of neuropsychological disturbances in different patient populations (see *The Clinical Neuropsychologist*, *Journal of Clinical and Experimental Neuropsychology*, *Archives of Clinical Neuropsychology*) and trying to remediate or reverse the effects of neuropsychological disturbances (e.g., Stuss, Winocur, & Robertson, 1999). When the disturbances cannot be successfully remediated, helping the person and family adjust to the permanent neuropsychological disturbances and return to a productive lifestyle when possible becomes a major focus of clinical neuropsychologists (Prigatano, 1999).

Outcome studies provide objective evaluation of our diagnostic and interventional skills. Such studies must demonstrate the efficacy of our work and the costs associated with those benefits. Collaborative work with healthcare economists and professional managers of health maintenance (cost containment) organizations is vital to this cause.

In practice, clinical neuropsychologists must demonstrate to physicians the logic behind what they say concerning a patient, and how their knowledge contributes to patient care. This will result in avoiding marginalization of neuropsychology departments in medical centers (see Howe, Sweet, & Bauer, 2010 this issue). To do this, clinical neuropsychologists must share a similar language and terminology as physicians, but never lose their identity as psychologists or their insight as to the underlying nature of the psychological disturbance of a patient. They must articulate in a clear and concise way what is "wrong" with the patient, but at the same time indicate what are the next practical steps in caring for that patient.

FOCUSED GOALS

The focused goals of this paper include the following:

(1) To clarify for neuropsychologists the two types of data needed for the field of neuropsychology to flourish.
(2) To describe types of outcome studies that continue to form the foundation of the scientific basis of our practice.
(3) To explicitly identify the clinical and professional skills that need to be developed by practicing clinicians and should be integrated into training programs.

PREVIOUS AND CONTINUING EFFORTS

Advancing the profession of clinical neuropsychology requires carefully designed outcome studies, which unequivocally demonstrate the "objective" (i.e., economic and scientific) value of our work, as well as its "subjective" value to the patient, family, and physician (i.e., the degree to which they are personally satisfied with our work and are willing to pay for it) (Prigatano, Zigler, & Rosenstein, 2003).

Outcome research refers to research that produces some measurable change in a functional system as a direct (or indirect) effect of a planned intervention or service. Randomized controlled trials (RCT) are often considered the "gold standard" for documenting scientific evidence of a treatment or intervention effect. When considering an economic effect, one typically refers to "cost-outcome" studies. There are four basic types of cost analysis used in outcome research: cost-efficiency or minimization, cost-benefit, cost-effectiveness, and cost-utilization (see Prigatano & Pliskin, 2003). Healthcare economic studies often deal with cost-effectiveness issues. These studies measure the relative healthcare benefit of at least two different treatments, and relate the degree of benefit relative to the costs involved. However, any form of cost-outcome research is welcome in today's healthcare market. It has been difficult for neuropsychologists to enter into this line of research because of our training and professional background. However, if we do not do this research, others will do it for us and may not consider all the relevant factors. It is for this reason that Prigatano and Pliskin (2003) indicated that their text was simply: "A Beginning."

Intrinsic to cost-outcome research is the concept of value. Value refers to the "worth" of the service, and this can be measured both objectively and subjectively. Economic value is one objective marker. If the service is worth more than what is paid for it, then healthcare economists would consider it to have "good value," and vice versa. The goal of neuropsychologists is to obtain "fair value" for their services. Value can also be measured in non-economic terms, such as the quality of life of the person. This implies a relative state of good health and reduction of symptoms, including psychiatric symptoms.

FUTURE EFFORTS

Outcome studies

It is beyond the scope of this brief paper to discuss the various methodological approaches to cost-outcome research. However, we will attempt to provide some specific examples of how this can be done and what types of methodological skills are required.

> Neuropsychologists should conduct outcome studies that demonstrate neuropsychological testing/evaluations lead to practical decisions for patients (and their families).

Clinical neuropsychologists are frequently asked to help neurologists determine if a patient's subjective complaints correlate with objective measures of brain functioning. The differential diagnostic question of neurological versus psychiatric disorders persists, despite advances in neuroimaging. Many patients with anxiety and/or depression are evaluated each year by neurologists because of memory complaints. Proper identification of these patients via neuropsychological evaluations can lead to appropriate diagnosis and psychiatric treatments (see case reports by Prigatano & Caples, 2003; Prigatano & Gagliardi, 2005). The economic benefit of proper diagnosis, not to mention the subjective value for the patient, can be staggering. Clinical neuropsychologists need to collaborate with healthcare economists when conducting this type of work. They are skilled in monitoring the costs of medication, hospital visits, and outpatient visits, which can be reduced when depression is properly diagnosed and treated (Hargreaves, Shumway, Hu, & Cuffel, 1998).

Similarly, identifying patients who have epileptic versus nonepileptic seizures could potentially save the healthcare system several million dollars per year. The cost of treating persons who have nonepileptic seizures as if they had epilepsy has been estimated to be approximately $100,000.00 per patient over their lifetime

(Martin, Bell, Hermann, & Mennemayer, 2003). Clinical neuropsychologists are in a position to aid in this differential diagnosis. Studies have appeared which demonstrate that how the patient reports his/her subjective symptoms can be studied in relationship to his/her level of performance on neuropsychological tests (Fargo et al., 2004). Such information can aid in the differential diagnosis of these patients. Drummond, O'Brien, Stoddart, and Torrance (1997) provide examples of how various healthcare research methodologies may be applied to this problem.

Additionally, neuropsychologists sometimes conduct presurgical evaluations of patients with Parkinson's disease who are being considered for a deep brain stimulator to determine whether they are demented and/or severely depressed (Pillon, 2002). Both variables have been shown to be related to significant morbidity following surgery. Identification of these patients can aid physicians' decision making, which might avoid future needless economic expenses for inappropriate patients.

Another area where neuropsychologists impact medical decision making includes when neurosurgeons request objective information about change and neuropsychological functioning after surgery (Dodrill & Ojemann, 2007). Neurosurgeons may also ask if abnormal findings observed on neuroimaging are paralleled by neuropsychological impairments. For example, recently a 45-year-old woman was referred for a neuropsychological examination because she had a complaint of memory disturbance. Blood flow studies showed hyperperfusion in the left hemisphere. Her treating psychiatrist and neurologist, however, suspected that her subjective complaints represented a longstanding personality disorder. The neurosurgeon specifically wanted to know whether neuropsychological test findings suggested that those functions mediated by the left hemisphere were in fact inferior to those by the right hemisphere. This would help him make a decision as to whether or not he would intervene surgically.

Rehabilitation is another area where neuropsychology plays an important role and our impact could be measured and quantified. Physiatrists, as well as other physicians, may refer patients to neuropsychologists to document disturbances in higher cerebral functioning after known brain disorders that have relevance for rehabilitation planning and patient management. Comparing rehabilitation programs that utilize neuropsychologists to plan various forms of intervention versus programs that do not is one practical place to begin. To do this, however, requires knowledge of how to conduct basic clinical trials (Anonymous, 1983). Embodied in the rehabilitation setting are several other research studies that neuropsychologists could conduct. One area is the ability of neuropsychologists simply to predict the time that is needed for patients to achieve certain rehabilitation goals (Prigatano & Wong, 1997, 1999). Also, neuropsychologists play an important role in educating family members in order to manage a person with known neurological disturbances (e.g., Attix & Welsh-Bohmer, 2006). Measuring the amount of distress family members experience when receiving this form of training versus not is another natural place to begin outcome studies in this area.

Attorneys also request neuropsychological evaluations in a variety of medical-legal cases. Questions range from whether or not a patient is legally competent to make economic decisions to whether or not the individual in fact has suffered a brain disorder and can return to previous life activities. Since neuropsychological test findings are objective, they are valuable to the legal system. No outcome studies have been requested by attorneys.

Neuropsychological test findings can lead to some practical decisions regarding patient care. Common questions center around whether the patient is safe to return home after medical treatment or care, whether the patient is safe to operate a motor vehicle, and whether s/he has recovered adequately to return to part-time or full-time work following the onset of a brain disorder. One example will be given to highlight the potential value of such evaluations. It has been noted that the cost of falls in the elderly population is substantial for the Medicare population (Rizzo et al., 1998). Studies have examined whether neuropsychological evaluations can predict likelihood for falls, which account for 10% of emergency room visits. Dementia is a significant risk factor for falls, as are disturbances in executive functioning and impairments of attention in a non-demented sample (Holtzer et al., 2007). These findings should encourage neuropsychologists to develop efficient assessment techniques that would allow for the screening of elderly patients who are at risk for falls. To accomplish this goal, neuropsychologists should work closely with gerontologists. Within the context of a given geriatric clinic, they could attempt to identify a priori those individuals who are likely to have a fall versus those who are not. One can use actuarial methods to determine whether or not the neuropsychologists' predictions exceed those of base rates that exist in a given population. If this could be done, it would result in Medicare authorizing neuropsychological services for the elderly at risk for falls.

> Neuropsychologists need to conduct outcome studies to demonstrate that neuropsychological testing/evaluations lead to the development of new knowledge relevant to patient diagnosis and care.

Levin et al. (1990) demonstrated that the two most common neuropsychological consequences of traumatic brain injury (TBI) were decreases in speed of information processing and memory. Dikmen, Machamer, Winn, and Temkin (1995) later demonstrated a dose–response relationship between simple speed of performance and severity of TBI. This led to recognition that disturbances of white matter tracts following traumatic brain injury may be the basis of many neuropsychological impairments. Johnson, Bigler, Burr, and Blatter (1994) showed a relationship between the ventricle to brain ratio and performance on the Digit Symbol-Coding subtest of the Wechsler Scales (a measure of processing speed) for males. Collectively, these studies show that the use of standardized neuropsychological tests helped neuropsychologists better understand the predictable neuropsychological problems of TBI patients and what are the important neuroanatomical correlates of these disturbances. These observations guide new research questions. This type of new knowledge becomes important in cases of differential diagnosis, particularly when evaluating patients with a history of mild TBI who are involved in litigation and/or are complaining of residual disturbances several months or years post trauma.

> Neuropsychologists need to conduct outcome studies to demonstrate that neuropsychological knowledge/tests can be combined with neuroimaging to improve patient care.

Håberg, Kvistad, Unsgård, and Haraldseth (2004) have demonstrated the clinical application of functional magnetic resonance imaging (fMRI) to map language functions as a part of presurgical evaluation for patients who have primary brain tumors. This procedure has been helpful to neurosurgeons and replicated by many investigators (Bookheimer, 2007). In a similar vein, Marla Hamberger and colleagues have performed pre-resection language mapping in patients with dominant hemisphere nonlesional and lesional temporal lobe epilepsy, with the goal of preserving postoperative language abilities (Hamberger, McClelland, McKhann, Williams, & Goodman, 2007; Hamberger, Seidel, Goodman, Perrine, & McKhann, 2003; Hamberger, Seidel, McKhann, Perrine, & Goodman, 2005). Outcome studies are needed to demonstrate that patients have less morbidity as a result of surgeons having this knowledge and/or that they require much less speech and language therapy following their operations.

> Neuropsychologists need to conduct outcome studies to demonstrate that intervention programs, based on neuropsychological and psychological principles, result in important cognitive and behavioral changes for the patient, and these changes are mirrored in brain structure and activation pattern changes.

While this class of study has yet to be carried out by neuropsychologists, the recent work by Als et al. (2004) provides an excellent example of how this research could be conducted. These individuals conducted a randomized clinical trial in which 30 premature infants were randomized to one of two treatment groups. The experimental group had behavioral interventions aimed at reducing the individual child's distress level during the first 72 hours in intensive care. The intervention was continued to the age of 2 weeks. The treated group not only showed improved behavioral and cognitive functioning, but for some of these infants there was also in vivo evidence of enhanced brain structure and function. Demonstrating such effects would be crucial for future studies in neuropsychological rehabilitation. The Als et al. study provides a prototype of how this research could be conducted.

> Neuropsychologists need to conduct outcome studies to demonstrate that neuropsychological interventions with patients not only reduce disability and improve the quality of life of the patient, but also improve the quality of life of caregivers.

Prigatano et al. (1984) demonstrated that patients who received a holistic neuropsychological rehabilitation program were described as having significantly less frequent psychiatric symptoms than patients who did not receive such treatment. Moreover, these patients had an increased likelihood of returning to work. These findings were in part replicated by two other investigations (Klonoff, Lamb, & Henderson, 2001; Prigatano et al., 1994). Not captured in these studies was the fact that treated patients often were able to maintain gainful employment for longer periods of time and showed much less psychiatric morbidity. Helping these patients also resulted in substantially reducing the distress level of their family members. This was not systematically documented, but is frequently seen clinically and is an important area of investigation. Recently, Prigatano and Gray (2007) noted that a major source of distress of parents of children with traumatic brain injury is they do not know what the long-term outcome will be for their child. If neuropsychologists can refine their neuropsychological assessment skills, and predict a child's course of recovery and the needs they will have at different times of their development, this information will help parents and caregivers appropriately plan and manage the patient's problems over a lifetime. The economic and personal benefits (both objective and subjective markers of value) need to be documented.

Another area of work is providing services to patients with mild cognitive impairment (MCI) and early Alzheimer's disease. Presently, there is a dearth of services available between the time that individuals are diagnosed with early-stage Alzheimer's disease and when they require higher levels of care (Yale, 1999). The excess disability rate that occurs with cognitive impairment is high (one study cited 66% of patients), which includes treatable coexisting physical and psychiatric disturbances (Walstra, Teunisse, van Gool, & van Crevel, 1997).

Studies have begun to apply memory rehabilitation techniques to reduce disability in these patients. Belleville et al. (2006) taught episodic memory strategies to patients with mild dementia. The intervention effect (pre–post intervention difference) was significant on two primary outcome measures (delayed list recall and face–name association). They also demonstrated improved subjective memory and well-being, which was especially meaningful to the patients. This and other studies (Davis, Massman, & Doody, 2001; Loewenstein, Acevedo, Czaja, & Duara, 2004; Requena et al., 2004) suggest that such intervention programs may have substantial benefit for improving and extending the period of functional competence in patients with MCI and early dementia, as well as reducing the costs associated with inpatient care.

Complimentary studies, such as those presented by Suhr, Andderson, and Tranel (1999), have shown that patients with Alzheimer's disease who learn progressive muscle relaxation techniques show a decrease in psychiatric and behavioral disturbances. Collectively, these studies suggest that neuropsychologists have much to offer in reducing the costs associated with the care of patients who have dementia. The economic benefits of these types of interventions also need to be clearly documented. A key consideration is whether interventions generalize to improve quality of life.

> Neuropsychologists need to conduct outcome studies to demonstrate the economic impact of not receiving neuropsychological assessments and interventions in a timely fashion.

Recently, the American Cancer Society put out a Request for Applications (RFA) entitled: "The role of healthcare and insurance in improving outcomes." The purpose of this RFA was to "investigate the impact of healthcare costs, healthcare system and capacity, insurance status, social factors and delivery of health care services, on outcomes in cancer prevention, early detection, and treatment". The upshot of this RFA was to point out that limiting appropriate services for patients because of insurance issues might result in a larger economic burden for our entire healthcare system. Neuropsychology should take a lead from this RFA and recognize that similar studies should be conducted to demonstrate that when patients are denied neuropsychological services there is a greater cost to the healthcare system. This can readily be seen in the detection of patients with dementia, allowing patients with brain injury to go back to driving and work prematurely, and not providing services for children in a time-efficient way that ultimately results in greater morbidity for those children over the course of their lifetime.

Another area to consider is the impact of not providing neuropsychological services for inpatient neurorehabilitation units, since failure to do so can result in loss of CARF accreditation. This can have substantial economic consequences for a hospital. It is for this reason that hospitals will either employ neuropsychologists to provide these services, or hire them on a contractual basis.

DEVELOPING THE CLINICAL AND PROFESSIONAL SKILLS OF NEUROPSYCHOLOGISTS

Primary clinical skills

While our clinical neuropsychological training focuses on the scientific basis of what we do, our clinical work demands a broader understanding of the patient, his or her life circumstances, and how to adequately engage the patient in both the assessment and rehabilitation process (Prigatano, 1999). There are primary clinical skills that need to be identified and developed in all clinicians. We suggest these primary skills reflect evolving capacities of individual clinicians. Many of these skills take years to develop. There is not a simple way of measuring these skills, but as we develop greater methods of assessing qualifications for board certification, we should attempt to find further methods of measuring the skills listed in Table 1. By developing these clinical skills, we will clearly develop and establish our value to the healthcare system.

All forms of training programs should ask how they are developing these skills and what is the evidence of their success.

Table 1 Clinical skills that make a difference for the viability of the profession of neuropsychology in the healthcare marketplace

(1)	Capacity to review the medical and psychosocial history of a patient and identify key variables that bear on the neuropsychological interview and the examination procedures
(2)	Capacity to carefully interview the patient and family and briefly reveal the complexity of the problem
(3)	Capacity to establish a therapeutic alliance with the patient and family member
(4)	Capacity to examine (via various neuropsychological tests or procedures) a broad range of abilities that are necessary to refine the diagnosis, clarify the patient's strengths and weaknesses, and develop possible interventions
(5)	Capacity to give verbal feedback regarding the test findings to the patient and family that is understandable and acceptable. The patient and family should have a clear understanding of what was found and the rationale for the interpretations that were arrived at
(6)	Capacity to write reports that are concise (not necessarily short) and clear, which identify the next step in the patient's care and provide practical suggestions
(7)	Capacity to perform cognitive rehabilitation as a method of either compensation or restoration of function
(8)	Capacity to conduct psychotherapeutic interventions to help the patient struggle with his or her personal losses
(9)	Capacity to educate the patient, family, and physician regarding how the underlying brain disorder impacts neuropsychological functioning
(10)	Capacity to elucidate the next step in the patient's care

Table 2 Professional skills that make a difference for the viability of the profession of neuropsychology with other professions and the public at large

- Demonstrated acknowledgement of the limits of our knowledge with the capacity to advocate for the patient given the knowledge that is available
- Demonstrated capacity to negotiate conflicts within and between professions
- Demonstrated steadfastness in learning one's profession over several years
- Seeking out fair reimbursement for our services, but never putting economic gain over patient needs
- Self-monitoring of our personal and professional behavior (including our appearance, our office space, and how we talk to and relate to other healthcare providers)
- Demonstrated capacity to conduct ongoing clinical research to check on the validity of our clinical assumptions, even though the time needed to do this may not be financially reimbursed by an employer or a granting agency

PROFESSIONAL SKILLS

In addition to developing our clinical skills that are applied to patient care, neuropsychologists need to develop professional skills that describe how they relate to other professions and how we relate to one another. Table 2 lists professional skills that are important for the practice of clinical neuropsychology. While many of these skills may appear "obvious," we would encourage post-doctoral residency programs to specifically focus on fostering these skills. Identifying them and discussing them during seminar time may be especially useful. They are learned, however, mainly by observing experienced clinical neuropsychologists.

FINAL POINTS

For our profession to grow and for individual neuropsychologists to develop, many forms of outcome research need to be conducted. We conclude our paper with some final points that we feel should be kept in mind. These simple admonishments provide a summary of what we consider to be important for our field.

(1) *Find your professional niche.* A major goal for clinical neuropsychologists when it comes to being successful is to find their appropriate professional niche. This means doing something that meets your professional needs while meeting the needs of others. This often can result in challenging ideas that can cause some distress (see Prigatano, 2003). Nevertheless, this is important in your professional development and ability to survive in the face of adversity.
(2) *Recognize that neuropsychologists are not "mini" neurologists, psychiatrists, or radiologists.* Keep your identity as a psychologist interested in brain–behavior relationships, which includes the problem of human consciousness. To be a good clinical neuropsychologist, you need to be both a "good" clinical psychologist and a "good" neuropsychologist.
(3) *Evaluate the concept of value in healthcare economics.* A major point of this paper has been to emphasize the need to assess both objective and subjective markers of value. Value is a term used to reflect the "worth" of some service or commodity. When economists and stockbrokers, for example, refer to a stock as

being "a good value," what they mean is the amount of money paid for that stock is less than the actual or potential worth of that stock. The same is true when applied to services that neuropsychologists provide. You should always strive to provide "good value" for your services. Psychologists who charge huge and unrealistic amounts of money for a neuropsychological examination may line their pockets early, but ultimately are dismissed by many as simply having interest in business rather than an interest in patients. Having people come to you because they get good value for their dollar is exactly the business of healthcare economics, in which neuropsychologists are embedded.

REFERENCES

Als, H., Duffy, F. H., McAnulty, G. B., Rivkin, M. J., Vajapeyam, S., Mulkern, R. V., et al. (2004). Early experience alters brain function and structure. *Pediatrics*, *113*, 846–857.

Anonymous. (1983). Intermittent positive pressure breathing therapy of chronic obstructive pulmonary disease. A clinical trial. *Annals of Internal Medicine*, *99*(5), 612–620.

Attix, D. K., & Welsh-Bohmer, K. A. (2006). *Geriatric neuropsychology: Assessment and intervention*. New York: Guilford Press.

Belleville, S., Gilbert, B., Fonatine, F., Gagnon, L., Menard, E., & Gautheir, S. (2006). Improvement of episodic memory in persons with mild cognitive impairment and healthy older adults: Evidence from a cognitive intervention program. *Dementia and Geriatric Cognitive Disorders*, *22*, 486–499.

Bookheimer, S. (2007). Pre-surgical language mapping with functional magnetic resonance imaging. *Neuropsychological Review*, *17*, 145–155.

Davis, R. N., Massman, P. J., & Doody, R. S. (2001). Cognitive intervention in Alzheimer disease: A randomized placebo-controlled study. *Alzheimer Disease and Associated Disorders*, *15*, 1–9.

Dikmen, S. S., Machamer, J. E., Winn, H. R., & Temkin, N. R. (1995). Neuropsychological outcome at 1-year post head injury. *Neuropsychology*, *9*, 80–90.

Dodrill, C. B., & Ojemann, G. A. (2007). Do recent seizures and recent changes in antiepileptic drugs impact performances on neuropsychological tests in subtle ways that might be easily missed? *Epilepsia*, *48*, 1833–1841.

Drummond, M. F., O'Brien, B., Stoddart, G. L., & Torrance, G. W. (1998). *Methods for the economic evaluation of health care programmes* (2nd ed.). New York: Oxford University Press.

Fargo, J. D., Schefft, B. K., Szaflarski, J. P., Dulay, M. F., Testa, S. M., Privitera, M. D., et al. (2004). Accuracy of self-reported neuropsychological functioning in individuals with epileptic or psychogenic nonepileptic seizures. *Epilepsy & Behavior*, *5*, 143–150.

Goodglass, H. (1994). Diversity and unity in neuropsychology: A perspective on the discipline. *The Diplomate*, *13*, 5–7.

Håberg, A., Kvistad, K. A., Unsgård, G., & Haraldseth, O. (2004). Preoperative blood oxygen level-dependent functional magnetic resonance imaging in patients with primary brain tumors: Clinical application and outcome. *Neurosurgery*, *54*, 902–914; discussion 914–915.

Hamberger, M. J., McClelland, S., McKhann, G. M., Williams, A. C., & Goodman, R. R. (2007). Distribution of auditory and visual naming sites in nonlesional temporal lobe epilepsy patients and patients with space-occupying temporal lobe lesions. *Epilepsia*, *48*(3), 531–538.

Hamberger, M. L., Seidel, W. T., Goodman, R. R., Perrine, K., & McKhann, G. M. (2003). Temporal lobe stimulation reveals anatomic distinction between auditory naming processes. *Neurology*, *60*, 1478–1483.
Hamberger, M. J., Seidel, W. T., McKhann, G. M., Perrine, K., & Goodman, R. R. (2005). Brain stimulation reveals critical auditory naming cortex. *Brain*, *128*, 2742–2749.
Hargreaves, W. A., Shumway, M., Hu, T., & Cuffel, B. (1998). *Cost-outcome methods for mental health*. San Diego, CA: Academic Press.
Holtzer, R., Friedman, R., Lipton, R. B., Katz, M., Xue, X., & Verghese, J. (2007). The relationship between specific cognitive functions and falls in aging. *Neuropsychology*, *21*, 540–548.
Howe, L. L. S., Sweet, J. J., & Bauer, R. M. (2010). Advocacy 101: A step beyond just complaining: How the individual practitioner can become involved and make a difference. *The Clinical Neuropsychologist*, *24*, 373–390.
Johnson, S. C., Bigler, E. D., Burr, R. B., & Blatter, D.D. (1994). White matter atrophy, ventricular dilation, and intellectual functioning following traumatic brain injury. *Neuropsychology*, *8*, 307–315.
Klonoff, P. S., Lamb, D. G., & Henderson, S. W. (2001). Outcomes from milieu-based neurorehabilitation at up to 11 years post-discharge. *Brain Injury*, *15*, 413–428.
Levin, H. S., Gary, H. E., Eisenberg, H. M., Ruff, R. M., Barth, J. T., Kreutzer, J., et al. (1990). Neurobehavioral outcome 1 year after severe head injury: Experience of the Traumatic Coma Data Bank. *Journal of Neurosurgery*, *73*, 699–709.
Lezak, M. D., Howieson, D. B., & Loring, D. W. (2003). *Neuropsychological assessment* (4th ed.). New York: Oxford University Press.
Loewenstein, D. A., Acevedo, A., Czaja, S. J., & Duara, R. (2004). Cognitive rehabilitation of mildly impaired Alzheimer disease patients on cholinesterase inhibitors. *American Journal of Geriatric Psychiatry*, *12*, 395–402.
Martin, R., Bell, B., Hermann, B., & Mennemeyer, S. (2003). Nonepileptic seizures and their costs: The role of neuropsychology. In G. P. Prigatano & N. H. Pliskin (Eds.), *Clinical neuropsychology and cost outcome research: A beginning* (pp. 15–33). New York: Psychology Press.
Morgan, J. & Ricker, J. (Eds.). (2008). *Textbook of clinical neuropsychology*. New York: Taylor & Francis.
Pillon, B. (2002). Neuropsychological assessment for management of patients with deep brain stimulation. *Movement Disorders*, *17*(Suppl. 3), S116–S122.
Prigatano, G. P. (1999). *Principles of neuropsychological rehabilitation*. New York: Oxford University Press.
Prigatano, G. P. (2000). Neuropsychology, the patient's experience and the political forces in our field: Presidential address for National Academy of Neuropsychology. *Archives of Clinical Neuropsychology*, *15*, 71–82.
Prigatano, G. P. (2003). Challenging dogma in neuropsychology and related disciplines. *Archives of Clinical Neuropsychology*, *18*, 811–825.
Prigatano, G. P. (2008). Neuropsychological rehabilitation and psychodynamic psychotherapy. In J. Morgan & J. Ricker (Eds.), *Textbook of clinical neuropsychology* (pp. 985–995). New York: Taylor & Francis.
Prigatano, G. P., & Caples, H. (2003). Memory complaints and depression in a young adult: Case report. *Barrow Quarterly*, *19*, 28–31.
Prigatano, G. P., Fordyce, D. M., Zeiner, H. K., Roeuche, J. R., Pepping, M., & Wood, B. C. (1984). Neuropsychological rehabilitation after closed head injury in young adults. *Journal of Neurology Neurosurgery and Psychiatry*, *47*, 505–513.
Prigatano, G. P., & Gagliardi, C. (2005). Memory and anxiety: Neuropsychological test findings and subjective complaints in a 51-year-old woman. *Barrow Quarterly*, *21*, 9–12.

Prigatano, G. P., & Gray, J. A. (2007). Parental concerns and distress after pediatric traumatic brain injury: A qualitative study. *Brain Injury*, *21*, 721–729.

Prigatano, G. P., Klonoff, P. S., O'Brien, K. P., Altman, I., Amin, K., Chiapello, D. A., et al. (1994). Productivity after neuropsychologically oriented, milieu rehabilitation. *Journal of Head Trauma Rehabilitation*, *9*, 91–102.

Prigatano, G. P., & Pliskin, N. H. (Eds.) (2003). *Clinical neuropsychology and cost outcome research: A beginning*. New York: Psychology Press.

Prigatano, G. P., & Wong, J. L. (1997). Speed of finger tapping and goal attainment following unilateral CVA. *Archives of Physical Medicine and Rehabilitation*, *78*, 847–852.

Prigatano, G. P., & Wong, J. L. (1999). Cognitive and affective improvement in brain dysfunctional patients who achieve inpatient rehabilitation goals. *Archives of Physical Medicine and Rehabilitation*, *80*, 77–84.

Prigatano, G. P., Zigler, L. Y., & Rosenstein, L. D. (2003). The clinical neuropsychological examination: Scope, cost, and health-care value. In G. P. Prigatano & N. H. Pliskin (Eds.), *Clinical neuropsychology and cost outcome research: A beginning* (pp. 15–33). New York: Psychology Press.

Requena, C., Lopez Ibor, M. I., Maestu, F., Campo, P., Lopez Ibor, J. J., & Ortiz, T. (2004). Effects of cholinergic drugs and cognitive training on dementia. *Dementia and Geriatric Cognitive Disorders*, *18*, 50–54.

Rizzo, J. A., Friedkin, R., Williams, C. S., Nabors, J., Acampora, D., & Tinetti, M. E. (1998). Health care utilization and costs in a Medicare population by fall status. *Medical Care*, *36*, 1174–1188.

Stuss, D. T., Winocur, G., & Robertson, I. H. (1999). *Cognitive rehabilitation*. New York: Cambridge University Press.

Suhr, J., Anderson, S., & Tranel, D. (1999). Progressive muscle relaxation in the management of behavioural disturbance in Alzheimer's disease. *Neuropsychological Rehabilitation*, *9*, 31–44.

Sweet, J. J., Nelson, N. W., & Moberg, P. J. (2006). The TCN/AACN 2005 "Salary survey:" Professional practices, beliefs, and incomes of U.S. neuropsychologists. *The Clinical Neuropsychologist*, *20*, 325–364.

Walstra, G. J. M., Teunisse, S., van Gool., W. A., & van Crevel, H. (1997). Symptomatic treatment of elderly patients with early Alzheimer's disease at a memory clinic. *Journal of Geriatric Psychiatry and Neurology*, *10*, 33–38.

Westervelt, H. J., Brown, L. B., Tremont, G., Javorsky, D. J., & Stern, R. A. (2007). Patient and family perceptions of the neuropsychological evaluation: How are we doing? *The Clinical Neuropsychologist*, *21*, 263–273.

Yale, R. (1999). Support groups and other services for individuals with early-stage Alzheimer's disease. *Generations*, *23*, 57–61.

The Clinical Neuropsychologist, 24: 481–492, 2010
http://www.psypress.com/tcn
ISSN: 1385-4046 print/1744-4144 online
DOI: 10.1080/13854040802360566

Psychology Press
Taylor & Francis Group

WOMEN AND ADVANCEMENT IN NEUROPSYCHOLOGY: REAL-LIFE LESSONS LEARNED

Robin C. Hilsabeck[1] and Eileen M. Martin[2]
[1]*South Texas Veterans Health Care System, University of Texas Health Science Center at San Antonio, TX and* [2]*University of Illinois at Chicago, IL, USA*

The number of women in neuropsychology has been increasing over the past 20 years while the number of women in senior and leadership positions within neuropsychology has not. The field of neuropsychology has much to gain by facilitating the advancement of women into leadership roles, including access to some of the brightest and creative minds in the field. The purpose of this article is to offer practical advice about how to overcome barriers and advance within neuropsychology. Suggestions for professional organizations, women, and mentors of women are provided that will likely benefit trainees and junior colleagues regardless of their gender.

Keywords: Leadership; Advancement; Advocacy; Women; Neuropsychology.

INTRODUCTION AND BACKGROUND

The number of women in the neurosciences in general and neuropsychology in particular has skyrocketed over the past two decades. According to available APA membership statistics for Division 40 (Clinical Neuropsychology), women's membership increased 7.0%, from 34.7% (1361/3918) in 1997 to 46% (2012/4378) in 2007. A similar trend was noted in its junior membership, with the percentage of women rising 7.5%, from 41.9% in 1997 to 49.4% in 2006 (M. Rivera-Mindt, Division 40 Membership Committee Chair, personal communication, January 10, 2008; 2007 data for junior membership were not available). Despite this shifting demography, there has been a lag in the number of women in senior or leadership positions in the field. For example, only three women have been elected President of Division 40 since its inception in 1980, and the percentage of women Fellows has held relatively steady since 1997, increasing only slightly from 22.1% (46/208) to 24.4% (66/270) in 2006. Similar trends are seen within the National Academy of Neuropsychology (NAN). Although 46% of its general membership in 2007 was comprised of women, only 14% (44/239) of Fellows were women. Since 1975, only two women have been elected President of NAN, and only 15 positions on the Board of Directors have been held by women, some of which were held by the same women (P. Zeifert, Member-At-Large and task force chair of Women in NAN,

Address correspondence to: Dr Robin C. Hilsabeck, Ph.D., ABPP-CN, South Texas Veterans Health Care System, Psychology Service (116B), 7400 Merton Winter Blvd., San Antonio, TX 78229, USA. E-mail: Hilsabeck@uthscsa.edu
Accepted for publication: July 22, 2008. First published online: September 1, 2008.

personal communication, November 16, 2007). An informal survey of the editorial boards of five of the major journals in neuropsychology (i.e., *Archives of Clinical Neuropsychology*, *Journal of Clinical and Experimental Neuropsychology*, *Journal of the International Neuropsychological Society*, *Neuropsychology*, and *The Clinical Neuropsychologist*) revealed only one woman editor-in-chief and three women associate editors. Percentages of women on the editorial boards of these journals ranged from 20% to 50%.

Additionally, not only are women under-represented in senior and leadership positions, they are often paid less than men at the same level. The 2007 salary figures for psychologists show the median salary for women with 0–1 years of experience is $4500 less than the median salary for men with the same level of experience (http://research.apa.org/t15asalaries07.pdf). This salary gap holds relatively steady through 4 years of experience but then widens significantly over time so that after 30 years of experience the median salary of women psychologists averages $15,000 less per year than men with 30+ years of experience. Although 2007 salary data specific to neuropsychology were not available, data from a joint survey conducted by Division 40 and the NAN in 2000 documented a gender gap in pay with women neuropsychologists earning a median income $25,000 less than men (Sweet, Peck, Abramowitz, & Etzweiler, 2003). However, this discrepancy in income is most likely multiply determined: women neuropsychologists were significantly younger with fewer years of experience than men completing this survey and more likely to be working part-time and in non-private practice settings, both of which are variables associated with lower income levels (Sweet, Peck, Abramowitz, & Etzweiler, 2002).

Neuropsychology is not alone in this regard, however. Academic medical centers recruit comparable percentages of men and women to junior faculty positions but fewer women advance to the associate or full professor levels (Ash, Carr, Goldstein, & Friedman, 2004; Bickel et al., 2002). Women who do achieve associate or full professorship often take longer to attain promotion and then are not compensated equally (Ash et al., 2004; Bickel et al., 2002). The proportion of women decreases further at the level of department chair and dean (Andrews, 2007; Cheng, Promes, Clem, Shah, & Pietrobon, 2006). This pattern persists even when considering influencing factors such as attrition rates and productivity (Ash et al., 2004; Cheng et al., 2006).

The paucity of women in senior positions has been attributed to a number of personal, environmental, and social constraints sometimes referred to as the "glass ceiling." The U.S. Department of Labor (1991, p. 1) defines the glass ceiling as "those [collective] artificial barriers based on attitudinal or organizational bias that prevent qualified individuals from advancing upward in their organization into management level positions." Some barriers may be more blatant and obvious, such as sexual harassment and gender discrimination, while others are more subtle and unintentional, such as gender stereotyping, lack of effective mentorship, and a natural resistance to power sharing (Bickel et al., 2002; Pololi & Knight, 2005).

Disparities are not attributed to external forces in the workplace alone but may often be influenced by factors associated with female gender roles or characteristics, which Bickel (2004, p. 289; 2007a, p. 684) has referred to as the "personal glass ceiling." These factors include increased family responsibilities, lack of assertiveness, tendencies to personalize and internalize difficulties and underestimate abilities, and failure to negotiate (or negotiate well), all of which contribute to the slower advancement of women (Ash et al., 2004; Bickel, 2004, 2007a). Differences in career aspirations are another potential explanation, but this topic has not been well studied (Bickel, 2007a). Finally, women more often than men place their career aspirations on hold in order to raise their children, although this pattern is increasingly changing (Wright et al., 2003).

Regardless of the reasons, the field of neuropsychology suffers when women fail to advance into senior and leadership positions since some of its brightest and most creative minds are not utilized fully. On a more pragmatic note, since a growing percentage of neuropsychologists are women it is only wise to invest in the advancement of the field's up-and-coming constituents and to promote women's abilities to reach their career potential. In other words, the development of women leaders in neuropsychology is central to its longevity and financial success. Women leaders are essential for effective marketing to women looking for women neuropsychologists and to trainees seeking female role models (Bickel et al., 2002). Although at present women do not reach leadership positions as readily as men, the good news is that medical specialties with higher proportions of women have more women in leadership positions (Cheng et al., 2006; Kværner, Aasland, & Botten, 1999). In fact, organizations have increased their emphasis on preparing women as leaders and developed intensive training programs (e.g., Executive Leadership in Academic Medicine; ELAM). In 2008, APA's Committee for Women in Psychology (CWP) hosted the inaugural meeting of the Institute on Leadership for Women in Psychology. Given the large percentage of women neuropsychologists, neuropsychology is a specialty field where women are well positioned to advance into leadership roles. The purpose of this article is to offer guidance about how to overcome barriers and advance within the field of neuropsychology.

FOCUSED GOALS

Since none of the research investigating barriers to advancement among women is specific to neuropsychology, the focus of this article will not be an in-depth review of available literature. Rather, combining lessons learned from pioneering women in our field, peers, and personal experience, along with relevant literature across multiple professions, the focused goal of this article is to facilitate the advancement of women into leadership positions by:

(1) calling attention to existing efforts of professional organizations;
(2) reiterating and suggesting ideas for future efforts of professional organizations;
(3) offering guidance to individuals about how to reach their career potential; and
(4) highlighting the significance of mentoring and assisting earlier career level women to move up the ranks.

We emphasize that the primary focus of this article is facilitating the advancement of women; however, many of the suggestions in this article should prove helpful to advancing the careers of our male colleagues and trainees as well. This article is intended for both those seeking to advance or to assist others in advancement.

PREVIOUS AND CONTINUING EFFORTS

Within neuropsychology, Division 40 of the APA has made some important inroads in increasing the representation of women in leadership positions. For example, the gender composition of their board of directors has been approximately 50/50 for the past several years. In addition, they were the first to organize a concerted effort to address the unique needs in facilitating the advancement of women. Women in Neuropsychology (WIN) was established as a standing subcommittee of Division 40 in 2000 to a large degree by the work of Dr. Paula Shear. WIN sponsors workshops at the annual conferences of APA and the International Neuropsychological Society (INS) to support early and mid-career level members (Shear & Marcotte, 2002). Topics addressed by WIN include "The do's and don'ts of career development: What I wish someone had told me," "Women pioneers in neuropsychology: A perspective from the beginning," "Tips for Successful Job Negotiating," and "How to become a journal reviewer." WIN also hosts a list serve open to women and men, pairs mentors and mentees with similar career goals, and surveys the needs of its membership. In 2006 NAN appointed a task force to explore how the organization can better meet the needs of its women members. This task force became an advisory committee to the NAN Board of Directors in 2008 and sponsors an event at the NAN annual conference. Many of the suggestions below resulted from discussions at WIN and NAN events.

FUTURE EFFORTS

Advice for professional organizations in neuropsychology

The initial efforts of APA's Division 40 and NAN are encouraging and highlight the pivotal role professional organizations can play in advancing women leaders. Neuropsychological organizations can further promote women's advancement by clearly defining leadership competencies and then providing workshops or seminars that promote such competencies through hands on training and role modeling. In addition, because women often have less exposure to the hierarchical systems of leadership that currently characterize many academic departments (e.g., following the chain of command), they must develop a clear understanding and a pragmatic approach to working within these types of systems in order to follow a successful career trajectory. Thus, women's opportunities to advance will be enhanced when they are better educated about leadership competencies and how to navigate hierarchical systems successfully, both of which can be addressed through broad educational efforts.

Another suggestion for professional organizations is to continue to focus efforts on facilitating connections between current and future women leaders. Because there are few women in leadership positions, a potential avenue toward achieving this goal could be sponsorship of ongoing peer mentoring groups at annual meetings. Peer mentoring groups work by compensating for the limited number of women leaders, developing self awareness, facilitating spontaneous mentoring relationships, and providing training in the process of mentoring (Pololi & Knight, 2005). Participants benefit from the diverse wisdom of their peers in a safe, collaborative environment.

Suggestions for women in neuropsychology

Because changing the culture of organizations and modifying one's behavior take time and considerable effort and insight, below are suggestions for individuals who want to play an active role in facilitating this change for the better of neuropsychology as a whole.

Find mentors. The value of mentoring cannot be over-emphasized. Identify early a group of mentors (of both genders) with which you can develop a lasting professional relationship. At the bare minimum, find a mentor within neuropsychology who has the accomplishments or the background you are seeking to develop. It is entirely appropriate to ask this person to mentor you. These types of spontaneous mentoring relationships almost always work because they are characterized by respect, support, and compatibility that lead to long-term, mutually satisfying relationships that are not initiated or structured by an institution. It is also helpful to find a mentor within your institution who can advise you on specific rules or criteria for advancement such as the promotion process. If you cannot identify a clear candidate, ask a trusted colleague for suggestions.

Network. Networking is a key activity for finding mentors, and you should network with a goal in mind. For example, identify women whom you would like to emulate based on their having a successful clinical practice or a tenured faculty appointment and find out how they accomplished their goals. Make alliances with forward-thinking male colleagues and ask them to introduce you to others, suggest your name as a reviewer for grants or articles, or invite you to speak at their institutions. In addition to attendance at conferences and membership in professional organizations that promote women, such as WIN, NAN, and Women in Neuroscience, seek out more specific meetings and resources (e.g., HIV research; addiction research and treatment) that will facilitate your ability to navigate through a variety of networking situations within your areas of specialty interest.

Set goals. With the help of your mentors, set career-specific short-term (3–5 years) and long-term (5–10 years) goals. For example, if your career goal is to have a successful private practice, some possible short-term goals may be to develop marketing materials, build a strong referral base, and secure your own office space or join a group practice. Long-term goals may include achieving and maintaining a specific salary range, recruiting additional staff, and opening a second office. For individuals interested in research careers, short-term goals may include identifying supportive collaborators, submitting a pilot grant, and writing an average of three manuscripts per year. Long-term goals may be to obtain release time from clinical and teaching activities, obtain research funding, and mentor other clinician-scientists. Regardless of your goals, it will be important to monitor your progress regularly and to adjust your goals or strategies for achieving them when needed.

Keep your eyes on the prize. Once you have set your goals, stay focused on them and base choices about use of time and resources on whether or not they will get you closer to your goals. For example, if you are working toward a research career in Alzheimer's disease, attending an all-day workshop on traumatic brain injury may not be the best use of your time. In your day-to-day work setting, identify those tasks that you absolutely must do yourself and delegate out those that can be done by others (for example, your presence is not critical for successful literature searches). Remain cognizant of the current literature and do not spend precious time reinventing the wheel. Protect your time and limit your distractions! Turn off your phone, close your door, and limit time spent reading email to a specified time each day. Be mindful of how much time you are spending assisting others and the risk of neglecting your own work.

Identify (and conquer!) barriers. As indicated above, barriers to advancement come both from within and without. With regard to barriers without, be cognizant of possible gender discrimination within your particular work setting and work toward neutralizing it. If you are searching for a new job, look for settings that have women in leadership positions, programs for developing junior faculty, including guidance for men in mentoring women, and a women's professional group supported by the institution. Look for clues suggesting that unrestricted accessibility at work (i.e., neglect of personal life) is rewarded, flexible work hours are discouraged, and preconceived notions about what women are willing to do to advance are present.

One of the first steps toward identifying barriers involves soul-searching. What are your personal strengths and weaknesses? Do you tend to get overly emotional or personalize professional matters? Do you have trouble separating from your identity as a junior colleague or trainee rather than embracing new horizons afforded by leadership opportunities? How do you feel about managing family versus professional commitments? The point is not to dwell on your weaknesses but to know yourself and draw on your strengths to counter them. For example, if you are a busy mother of two in a dual career household, draw on your experiences as the household leader with multiple roles and use those well-honed skills of time management, planning, and prioritizing to identify and achieve career goals.

Another important topic to soul-search is what you want out of life. What are your personal and professional aspirations? Decide what is negotiable and what is non-negotiable and use this information to guide your decisions. For example, it may not be wise to take a job that will not allow you flexibility in your schedule when you have children and one of your priorities is to be available when they have school events. Putting yourself in a position that causes emotional angst could interfere with your work productivity, as well as your personal goals and overall well-being.

Know the "rules" of your work setting (Do your homework!). Because each work setting has its own system or set of rules for doing business, make sure you understand how the system works and what is needed and expected to advance. This includes knowing both the explicit rules, such as requirements for tenure and promotion, and the implicit rules, such as departmental politics and alliances. If you are in a medical school department, for example, understand the hierarchy of the system (e.g., whether or not you agree with your boss, you must respect the position if not the person you report to) and learn to work within it, even if you do not agree with it. Next, be prepared to ask and negotiate for the resources that you need to succeed. The worst that will happen is that you will not get them. However, to increase the likelihood of getting what you need, be sure to ask the right person. You will know who the "right" person is once you learn the hierarchy of your setting. Learn also how, when, and with whom to pick your battles. This, again, is an essential part of doing your homework, i.e., knowing what is worth standing up for and what is better left alone.

Do not personalize. In order to advance within any field, you must be prepared to face resistance and criticism. Do not take this personally! Accept constructive criticism in the spirit in which it is meant—that is, to provide you with feedback that may be useful for improving a particular area or skill set—do not respond with apologies or defensiveness. Information about what to improve is crucial for advancing, and learning how to respond appropriately to this type of feedback will enhance personal and professional characteristics necessary for competent leadership. Additionally, your goal is not to have everyone like you; in fact, if you are attaining success, some individuals will definitely not like you. They dislike that you have attained a position they themselves may have desired. Many times it may have nothing to do with you as an individual. You have to learn to let things roll off your back and move forward.

Show initiative and persistence. Verbalize your desire to advance and ask for what you need to do so. Offer to take the lead on activities that will get you closer to targeted career goals. For example, if you aspire toward a research career, send your CV to journal editors and offer to review articles in your areas of expertise. If education and training is your passion, volunteer to serve on the educational committee of your favorite professional organization. If you seek to be involved in broader service to neuropsychology, campaign for election to a desired position, and if you are not elected the first time, try again. Persistence is key. Odds are that in your efforts to win an election the first time around, you gained supporters and name recognition that will help you succeed on the next attempt. Not succeeding on your first attempt does not equal failure. Also, be willing to start small. Run for office or volunteer in regional or state organizations. Get your name out through well-articulated posts on neuropsychology listserves.

Be resourceful and practical. At the same time that you are seeking opportunities to advance, be selective and do not accept every opportunity that comes your way or you will quickly find yourself overextended and burned out. In determining whether an opportunity is right for you, ask questions about the time commitment involved and the perceived value to you and your organization. Stay away from committee work that does not further your career goals, entails a lot of time, and is not valued by your department. Accept also that perfection does not exist; painstaking attention to reference sections will only delay your publishing. Mistakes cannot be avoided but can take you down the path of experience to wisdom. Own up to your mistakes and view them as lessons learned. Never be afraid to ask questions, especially of your mentors. Just be sure to ask the "right" person. Your search for answers will minimize mistakes and precious time taken to meet your goals.

Advocate for yourself (Toot your own horn!). It is critical to be your own advocate. Assuming that your achievements will simply be "noticed" with no effort on your part is doomed to failure. No one knows your achievements better than you, so do not be afraid to take the credit you deserve. Notify supervisors and mentors about awards or recognition earned and take advantage of opportunities to highlight achievements when they present themselves. Because women are not socialized to highlight individual achievements, you may feel uncomfortable with this advice. However, you are the best person to inform others about your unique qualities and achievements. Advocate for yourself by applying for awards and/or seeking fellowship status in professional organizations. If you are not successful on your first attempt, then apply again. Remember, lack of success in these endeavors is not personal and does not equal failure. Persistence is key.

Support women colleagues. It is all too common, unfortunately, for women to discount the achievements of other women by neglecting to offer congratulations or by making disparaging remarks. Support your women colleagues by pointing out to others their successes, especially since you know first-hand how hard it is for women to toot their own horn, and by complimenting and encouraging their efforts to achieve and advance. Women will go farther faster when their "sisters" support them along the way.

Suggestions for mentors of women in neuropsychology

One of the most important methods for increasing the number of women in leadership positions is mentoring. Mentoring has been shown to contribute significantly to professional development in health care professionals, particularly in the areas of research, career satisfaction, and perceived support (Pololi & Knight, 2005). Mentoring women in neuropsychology can help them identify, set, and reach their career goals, as well as learn how to balance professional and personal commitments. Mentors, on the other hand, can benefit through personal enrichment, intellectual stimulation, and even rejuvenation for the profession. Mentoring also is a way to give back to neuropsychology, and by mentoring junior colleagues you will increase the likelihood that your mentees will mentor others, thus continuing the cycle (Pololi & Knight, 2005). This section highlights some of the activities of successful mentors and action items that trainees can ask their mentors to provide for them.

Identify strengths and foster them. Recognize strengths in protégés and find opportunities to showcase them. For example, if strong communication and organizational skills are displayed by a mentee whose career goal is to direct a residency program, encourage her to volunteer for education-related task forces or committee work where her skills will be recognized and utilized and her enthusiasm for education will be appreciated and rewarded. If strengths in manuscript writing are observed in a mentee who aspires toward a research career, ask her to take the lead on more manuscripts and provide her the time to follow through.

Give a gentle shove. Due to the way women are socialized and the low number of women in leadership positions, women are unlikely to pursue leadership positions or to make waves when they are not considered for leadership positions for which they are qualified. What is needed from you is encouragement and sometimes even a gentle shove in the right direction.

Nominate deserving women. Although women are just as interested in attaining leadership positions, they are less likely to be asked to serve in leadership positions (Wright et al., 2003). Thus, ask capable women to serve as leaders and suggest the same to your colleagues. Use your status to legitimatize that of women deserving of recognition. Research shows that an individual's status as a leader can be increased if endorsed by someone perceived as having higher status (Hogue, Yoder, & Ludwig, 2002). To help women overcome their status disadvantage and be perceived as competent and deserving, it also is important to highlight the specific achievements or qualifications that warrant consideration.

Introduce women to colleagues. Because there are fewer women in leadership positions and both men and women tend to seek out and maintain relationships with similar others, women may be left out of informal social gatherings of the male-dominated leadership where important information is exchanged. Mentors can help combat this disconnect by supporting socialization activities that appeal to both men and women, such as leadership retreats and quarterly dinners. Introduce women colleagues to those in leadership positions and foster these relationships by organizing cross-gender social activities. These interactions will facilitate communication and increase familiarity with those in leadership, opening doors to future interactions and opportunities. These efforts will promote an inclusive atmosphere and reduce turnover of women who may otherwise feel disenfranchised or marginalized.

Promote an unbiased, collaborative environment. Raise awareness of department chairs or other organization leaders to the necessity of mentoring and career development. Advocate for parental leave policies and temporary stops on the tenure track, which will enable women to navigate family and work roles more easily. Suggest rewarding outcomes that include behaviors often displayed by women, such as promoting teamwork, advising others, providing information, and mentoring that leads to grant or manuscript submissions (Morahan & Bickel, 2002).

Seek training in supervision and mentoring. Begin by recognizing that much of the advice that worked for you may not work for your mentee due to gender and generational differences. If you are a man, realize also that gender inequities exist and often go unrecognized (Bickel, 2004). There is a growing recognition that mentoring is not always intuitive, and this is particularly true when mentoring nontraditional professionals, such as women. Seek opportunities to gain expertise in mentoring by attending training and mentoring workshops at annual conferences or by conferring with experts within the area.

Suggestions to all who are invested in advancing neuropsychology as a field

In closing, women are a growing source of intellectual capital within neuropsychology as well as other health care specialties (Bickel, 2007b). The responsibility to help women achieve their leadership potential is a shared one, as the entire field of neuropsychology stands to benefit. Future generations will be provided an equitable professional environment where differences in women's and men's leadership styles are embraced and groomed and where options for balancing work and family responsibilities are many. A variety of resources that may be helpful in facilitating the advancement of women in neuropsychology are available in the Resource section.

RESOURCES

Books

Babcock, L., & Laschever, S. (2007). *Women don't ask: The high cost of avoiding negotiation–and positive strategies for change*. Princeton, NJ: Princeton University Press.

Chin, J. L., Lott, B., Rice, J. K., & Sanchez-Hucles, J. (Eds.). (2007). *Women and leadership: Transforming visions and diverse voices*. New York: Wiley.

Donaldson, M. C., & Frohnmayer, D. (2007). *Negotiating for dummies* (2nd ed.). Hoboken, NJ: Wiley Publishing, Inc.

Evans, G. (2001). *Play like a man, win like a woman: What men know about success that women need to learn*. New York: Random House.

Fisher, R., Patton, B. M., & Ury, W. R. (1992). *Getting to yes: Negotiating agreement without giving in*. New York: Houghton Mifflin Company.

Frankel, L. P. (2005). *Nice girls don't get the corner office: 101 Unconscious mistakes women make that sabotage their careers*. New York: Warner Books.

Heim, P., & Golant, S. K. (2005). *Hardball for women*. New York: Penguin Books.

Heim, P., Murphy, S., & Golant, S.K. (2001). *In the company of women: Indirect aggression among women: Why we hurt each other and how to stop*. New York: Penguin Books.

Miller, L. E., & Miller, J. (2002). *A woman's guide to successful negotiating: How to convince, collaborate, & create your way to agreement*. New York: McGraw-Hill.

Websites

2007 psychology salary tables
http://research.apa.org/07salariestables.html

Glass Ceiling Final Report:
http://www.dol.gov/oasam/programs/history/reich/reports/ceiling2.pdf

Society for Neuroscience – Women in Neuroscience:
http://www.sfn.org/index.cfm?pagename=WomeninNeuroscience

Association for Women in Science:
http://www.awis.org/

Association of American Medical Colleges – Women in Medicine:
http://www.aamc.org/members/wim/start.htm

American Psychological Association–Division 40 Women in Neuropsychology:
http://www.div40.org/Committee_Activities_Pages/Advisory_Committee/win.htm

ACKNOWLEDGEMENTS

We acknowledge that many of the ideas reflected in this article have been discussed both semi-formally in various workshops, particularly those of Division 40's WIN, and informally around tables of peers, in offices of mentors, and on the WIN listserve. We gratefully acknowledge the continuing financial support and commitment shown by APA's Division 40/INS and NAN, which provides a forum for these important exchanges.

Our thanks and deepest admiration go out to all the women "pioneers" in neuropsychology who have advocated for the advancement of women by taking leadership positions themselves and by initiating concerted efforts within professional organizations to address the unique needs of women. Special recognition in this regard must go to the following women for their substantial efforts as either current or past chair of the WIN Steering Committee or NAN Advisory Committee on Women or past president of Division 40, NAN, and/or INS (in alphabetical order): Ida Sue Baron, Martha Denckla, Eileen Fennell, Leslie Gonzalez-Rothi, Kathleen Haaland, H. Julia Hannay, Edith Kaplan, Sandra Koffler, Cynthia Kubu, Muriel Lezak, Cheryl Luis, Ann Marcotte, Freda Newcombe, Paula Shear, Barbara Uzzell, Elizabeth Warrington, Barbara Wilson, and Penelope Ziefert. The authors would also like to thank Kira Armstrong, Cheryl Luis, and two anonymous reviewers for their very helpful comments.

This work was supported by grants from the National Institutes of Health (K23 NS051244 to RCH and R01 DA12828 to EMM).

REFERENCES

Andrews, N. C. (2007). Climbing through medicine's glass ceiling. *New England Journal of Medicine*, *357*, 1887–1889.

Ash, A. S., Carr, P. L., Goldstein, R., & Friedman, R. H. (2004). Compensation and advancement of women in academic medicine: Is there equity? *Annals of Internal Medicine*, *141*, 205–212.

Bickel, J. (2004). Women in academic psychiatry. *Academic Psychiatry*, *28*, 285–291.

Bickel, J. (2007a). The work that remains at the intersection of gender and career development. *Archives of Physical Medicine and Rehabilitation*, *88*, 683–686.

Bickel, J. (2007b). Turning intellectual capital into leadership capital: Why and how psychiatrists can take the lead. *Academic Psychiatry*, *31*, 1–4.

Bickel, J., Wara, D., Atkinson, B. F., Cohen, L. S., Dunn, M., Hostler, S., et al. (2002). Increasing women's leadership in academic medicine: Report of the AAMC Project Implementation Committee. *Academic Medicine*, *77*, 1043–1061.

Cheng, D., Promes, S., Clem, K., Shah, A., & Pietrobon, R. (2006). Chairperson and faculty gender in academic emergency medicine departments. *Academic Emergency Medicine*, *13*, 904–906.

Hogue, M. B., Yoder, J. D., & Ludwig, J. (2002). Increasing initial leadership effectiveness: Assisting both women and men. *Sex Roles*, *46*, 377–384.

Kværner, K. J., Aasland, O. G., & Botten, G. S. (1999). Female medical leadership: Cross sectional study. *British Medical Journal*, *318*, 91–94.

Morahan, P., & Bickel, J. (2002). Capitalizing on women's intellectual capital in the professions. *Academic Medicine*, *77*, 110–112.

Pololi, L., & Knight, S. (2005). Mentoring faculty in academic medicine. A new paradigm? *Journal of General Internal Medicine*, *20*, 866–870.

Shear, P. K., & Marcotte, A. C. (2002). The evolution of the APA Division 40 Women in Neuropsychology (WIN) Interest Group. *Svensk Neuropsykologi*, *3*, 26–27.

Sweet, J. J., Peck III, E. A., Abramowitz, C., & Etzweiler, S. (2002). National Academy of Neuropsychology/Division 40 of the American Psychological Association practice survey of clinical neuropsychology in the United States, Part I: Practitioner and practice characteristics, professional activities, and time requirements. *The Clinical Neuropsychologist*, *16*, 109–127.

Sweet, J. J., Peck III, E. A., Abramowitz, C., & Etzweiler, S. (2003). National Academy of Neuropsychology/Division 40 of the American Psychological Association Practice Survey of Clinical Neuropsychology in the United States Part II: Reimbursement experiences, practice economics, billing practices, and incomes. *Archives of Clinical Neuropsychology*, *18*, 557–582.

United States Department of Labor (1991). *A report on the Glass Ceiling Initiative*. Washington, DC: United States Department of Labor.

Wright, A. L., Schwindt, L. A., Bassford, T. L., Reyna, V. F., Shisslak, C. M., St. Germain, P. A., et al. (2003). Gender differences in academic advancement: Patterns, causes, and potential solutions in one US College of Medicine. *Academic Medicine*, *78*, 500–508.

The Clinical Neuropsychologist, 24: 493–505, 2010
http://www.psypress.com/tcn
ISSN: 1385-4046 print/1744-4144 online
DOI: 10.1080/13854040902802947

Psychology Press
Taylor & Francis Group

BOARD CERTIFICATION IN PROFESSIONAL PSYCHOLOGY: PROMOTING COMPETENCY AND CONSUMER PROTECTION

David R. Cox
American Board of Professional Psychology, Chapel Hill, NC, USA

Board certification in psychology provides an opportunity for increased assessment of and demonstration of competence in the profession. In addition to serving as a means of consumer protection, it can serve the professional psychologist by providing the opportunity for increased income, professional satisfaction, facilitated mobility, and professional development. Jurisdictional and organizational recognition of the importance of board certification is increasing. This article uses the model and experience of the American Board of Professional Psychology, with particular attention to the American Board of Clinical Neuropsychology and the American Academy of Clinical Neuropsychology, to illustrate these benefits. Recent developments regarding board certification are described, as well as how to become involved in the process.

Keywords: Board certification; Specialization; Neuropsychology.

INTRODUCTION

Competency, and the assessment thereof, has been the focus of several psychological organizations as well as national and international conferences in recent years. Board certification through ABPP has historically been one method of measuring competency in professional psychology. As the field continues to mature, the conceptualization and measurement of competency is an ongoing and evolving process. The ABPP specialty board in neuropsychology is the American Board of Clinical Neuropsychology (ABCN). This article is intended—by way of using the ABPP and ABCN boards as illustrative—to present board certification as a natural stage of professional development for the individual psychologist and the profession as a whole. Psychology is becoming more specialized. Board certification is a mechanism for defining and measuring competency. Board certification is beneficial for the profession, individual psychologists, and the consumers of psychological services.

The American Board of Professional Psychology (ABPP), established in 1947 through sponsorship of the American Psychological Association (APA), provides board certification through credentials review and competency-based examination

Address correspondence to: David R. Cox, PhD, ABPP, Executive Officer American Board of Professional Psychology, 600 Market Street, Suite 300, Chapel Hill, North Carolina 27516, USA. E-mail: drcox@abpp.org

Accepted for publication: February 5, 2009. First published online: August 12, 2009.

processes for psychologists in multiple specialty areas within psychology, including clinical neuropsychology. The purpose and process of board certification through ABPP is reviewed here, as well as recent developments in the area of credentialing and board certification of psychologists and the benefits thereof.

As psychology has grown, efforts to regulate the profession and provide for consumer protection have led to the establishment of licensure, which in most jurisdictions is generic in nature. In most of the jurisdictions within North America licensure is based on assessment of *knowledge* (as opposed to competency) through the Examination for Professional Practice in Psychology (EPPP), is *generic*, and does not identify a *specialty* area of practice, much less provide for assessment of *competence* within that area.

As areas of specialty have emerged, professionals and consumers have sought to be better able to identify competent psychologists within specialty areas. Rodolfa et al. (2005) identify public accountability and a public demand for identification of specialty competence as fundamental reasons for the need to define competency and specialty. Psychological *specialty* practice has been defined by the APA (1995), the Council of Specialties in Professional Psychology (CoS), and ABPP, yet only ABPP (as the only credentialing body among them) uses the term *competency* in its definition (Rodolfa et al.).

Competence is often a core expectation within a profession. Many professions (among them medicine, law, psychology) have established methods to recognize competence. The APA *Ethical Principles of Psychologists and Code of Conduct* (2002) addresses consumer protection and states one should practice within one's area of *competence*.

Board certification is an outgrowth of this attention to competency and consumer protection. It serves as one method for addressing competency to provide services in a specialty area. As a way of serving the public and the profession, one of ABPP's primary purposes is certifying specialists through competency-based examinations.

Recent developments related to board certification

Board certification developments are ongoing that affect individual psychologists, the profession of psychology, and the general consumer public. Recent developments include implicit encouragement to become board certified (e.g., salary increases for ABPP board certified psychologists), limitations on who can describe themselves as board certified, and consideration of the issues around licensure and board certification (e.g., ASPPB).

Department of Veteran's Affairs recognition. The Department of Veteran's Affairs has recently enacted policy that provides for potential salary increases based on a psychologist becoming board certified through ABPP. The Special Advancement for Achievement criteria of the Hybrid Title 38 within the DVA allows for a one step increase within GS level for becoming ABPP (it also permits that increase for existing ABPP specialists as the program initiates).

US Department of Defense recognition. On October 14, 2008, President Bush signed into law Senate Bill 3001, the "Duncan Hunter National Defense

Authorization Act for Fiscal Year 2009". This legislation, recognizing a need for competent and qualified psychologists within the US Armed Forces, approved a significant accession bonus (up to $400,000 payable in increments of up to $100,000 per year over 4 years) for psychologists targeting for employment those who are board certified through the American Board of Professional Psychology.

Florida Legislation and Board of Psychology rules/regulations. The State of Florida recently enacted limitations on when a psychologist can identify themselves as board certified. The *legislative language* of F.S. 490.0149 is provided in Table 1; the Board of Psychology *rule language* is in Table 2. The legislative language has direct impact on individual psychologists, whereas the board rule has direct impact on credentialing organizations.

In January 2008 the Florida Board of Psychology reviewed the petitions submitted for recognition as a board-certifying organization. The American Board of Professional Psychology was among those approved. The ABPP was recognized in its entirety as an organization with several psychology specialty boards under its governance, thereby granting recognition to all psychology specialties within the ABPP.

Council of Specialties in Professional Psychology (CoS). Recognizing that the public may become confused by the variety of labels that different groups use, concerns about the use of the label "board certified" and activities of non-psychologists has led the Council of Specialties (CoS) to address the issue of board certification within psychology. Among the concerns expressed by CoS was the proliferation of individuals, many of whom are reportedly non-doctoral-level and non-licensed individuals, engaging in behavior analysis and indicating some sort of

Table 1 Florida legislative language about psychology board certification 490.0149 specialties

(1) As used in this section, the term "certified psychology specialist," "board-certified psychology specialist," or "psychology diplomate" means a psychologist with recognized special competency acquired through an organized sequence of formal education, training, experience, and professional standing that is recognized by a certifying body approved by the board pursuant to criteria adopted under subsection (3).

(2) A person licensed as a psychologist may not hold himself or herself out as a certified psychology specialist, board-certified psychology specialist, or psychology diplomate unless the person has received formal recognition from an approved certifying body.

(3) The board shall adopt rules to establish criteria for approval of certifying bodies that provide certification for specialties in psychology as provided in subsection (1). The criteria shall include that a certifying body:
   (a) Be national in scope, incorporate standards of the profession, and collaborate closely with organizations related to specialization in psychology.
   (b) Have clearly described purposes, bylaws, policies, and procedures.
   (c) Have established standards for specialized practice of psychology.
   (d) Provide assessments that include the development and implementation of an examination designed to measure the competencies required to provide services that are characteristic of the specialty area.

(4) A person licensed as a psychologist under this chapter may indicate the services he or she offers and may indicate that his or her practice is limited to one or more types of services when this accurately reflects his or her scope of practice.

Table 2 Florida Board of Psychology Rule

64B19-18.008 Board Approval of Specialty Certifying Bodies.

To obtain Board approval as a certifying body, eligible to grant formal recognition declaring a licensed psychologist to be a "certified psychology specialist," board-certified psychology specialist," or a "psychology diplomate," pursuant to Section 490.0149, F.S., an applicant shall file a petition demonstrating that it:

(1) Is an independent body, national in scope, that incorporates standards of the profession, collaborates closely with organizations related to specialization in psychology, and only certifies doctoral-level, licensed psychologists as having advanced qualifications in a particular psychological specialty through demonstrations of competence in the specialty being recognized;
(2) Has clearly described purposes, bylaws, policies, and procedures, that include an internal review and budgetary practices, to ensure effective utilization of resources with an administrative staff, housed in dedicated office space that is appropriate for the certifying body's program and sufficient for responding to consumer or regulatory inquiries;
(3) Has established standards for specialized practice of psychology and adopts the American Psychological Association (APA) "Ethical Principles of Psychologists and Code of Conduct," effective June 1, 2003, to guide the practice of its members. The code is incorporated by reference and available for inspection at the Board office as well as at: www.apa.org/ethics/code2002.html; and
(4) Has implemented and documented a comprehensive assessment procedure, designed to measure the competencies required to provide services characteristic of the specialty area, that describes security and grading standards, and consists of an oral examination and peer-review of practice samples and may include a written examination.

Specific Authority 490.0149, 490.004(4) FS. Law Implemented 490.0149 FS. History–New 11-1-07.

board certification. CoS has indicated that it recognizes the American Board of Professional Psychology (ABPP) as the only national organization of specialty boards to certify specialists in professional psychology, and believes that licensed psychologists who wish to identify themselves as board certified should be board certified by the American Board of Professional Psychology (CoS, 2006, 2007).

ABPP Early Entry Program: Encouraging certification and diversity. ABPP has recognized that students, interns, and residents are increasingly interested in the board certification process. In an effort to assist in increasing awareness of the process of board certification, and the competency models in education, training, and experience that lead to possible board certification, and in an effort to facilitate a cultural change within psychology toward board certification as the *expected* rather than the *exception*, ABPP initiated the ABPP Early Entry Program. This program also has a goal of increasing diversity with the ranks of board certified specialists. The program has been met with widespread enthusiasm, and many training institutions are sponsoring students in the process. Essentially, the program permits students, interns, and post-doctoral residents to initiate filing credentials with ABPP earlier in their professional training. This program does not grant any exception to the credentials review or examination process, and all requirements for successful attainment of ABPP board certification remain the same.

The opportunity to establish board certification as one of the goals of professional training, and incorporate identified areas of competency throughout the education and training experience fits well with the models and suggestions of the Competencies Conference (Kaslow et al., 2004) and the Assessment of Competency Benchmarks Work Group (American Psychological Association, 2007). Identification of competencies, with benchmarks for attainment of them within professional development is one of the aims of those working in this area.

Benefits related to board certification

Potential for higher income. As reviewed above, the Department of Veteran's Affairs has recently enacted policy that provides for potential salary increases, and the Department of Defense offers an accession bonus, targeting for employment those psychologists that are board certified through ABPP. As a specialty board within ABPP, ABCN is the neuropsychology board certifying entity recognized by a variety of organizations including the Department of Veterans Affairs, Department of Defense, Public Health Service, and others for potential salary increases and promotions. Similarly, some academic settings offer incentives to become board certified. Sweet, Nelson, and Moberg (2006) found that neuropsychologists board certified through ABCN reported greater psychology income (likely due to a variety of factors such as seniority and more forensic consultation, for example) than did neuropsychologists not board certified through ABCN.

Decreased malpractice liability costs. Some malpractice insurance carriers offer a discount to psychologists who are board certified through ABPP. For example, the American Professional Agency provides a 20% discount to such individuals.

Streamlined licensing. Over 35 states recognize ABPP in some fashion with respect to licensing of individual psychologists. Often the usual paperwork and forms necessary for licensure are reduced for a psychologist already board certified by ABPP. Many states continue to require a jurisprudence examination covering that jurisdiction's laws, rules, and regulations. Some states recognize ABPP explicitly in law (i.e., the licensing act for psychology), while others may recognize ABPP in rule. For example, Florida law (State of Florida, 2007) indicates that the Board of Psychology shall license an individual who demonstrates to the board that s/he is "...a diplomate in good standing with the American Board of Professional Psychology, Inc." (F.S. 490.006 (1)(b)).

Increased practice mobility. The ASPPB, a membership organization comprised of state, provincial, and territorial psychology licensing boards, accepts ABPP board certification as evidence that the essential criteria for education, training, and experience have been met. The ASPPB Certificate of Professional Qualification in Psychology (CPQ) process, used as a means of inter-jurisdictional mobility, is simplified for psychologists credentialed by ABPP.

A way for programs to demonstrate credibility. The Association of Psychology Postdoctoral and Internship Centers (APPIC) indicates that one necessary criterion for member programs is that the program director "...has expertise in an area of postdoctoral training offered and has credentials of excellence such as the American Board of Professional Psychology diploma..." (Association of Psychology Postdoctoral and Internship Centers, 2006, p. 1).

Increased job satisfaction and marketability. As indicated in part above, and likely due to a number of factors in addition to board certification, a survey of neuropsychologists found that respondents who are board certified through ABCN reported having greater psychology income, greater job satisfaction, and greater income satisfaction than did those not certified through ABCN (Sweet et al., 2006). In addition, many institutions hiring neuropsychologists are requesting that the psychologist be board certified, or attain board certification through ABPP as of a certain date. A recent review of employment opportunity ads for clinical neuropsychology positions revealed that 31% specified that ABPP-ABCN board certification was expected or desired (Lee, personal communication, December 6, 2007).

Helping to reduce public confusion. As more and more practitioners become board certified, the public can look to board certified practitioners as a way of determining that psychologists have obtained the required training and undergone evaluation by peers.

Consolidation of skills learned throughout the career. Studying for the ABPP-CN provides a good opportunity for the practitioner to consolidate and refresh information learned throughout their career. It encourages a breadth of knowledge in multiple areas.

Focused goal of this article

The focused goal of this article is to present board certification as a natural stage in the professional development of the individual psychologist and the field as a whole. The benefits of board certification to the individual psychologist, the field, and the consumer will be reviewed.

PREVIOUS AND CONTINUING EFFORTS

Establishment of the American Board of Professional Psychology

The American Board of Professional Psychology (ABPP) was established in 1947, originally as the American Board of Professional Examiners in Psychology (ABEPP) following recognition of such a need by the American Psychological Association (APA) (Bent, Packard, & Goldberg, 1999). As continues to be true, membership in a division of the APA is identified as an expression of *interest* in the subject area, as opposed to a measure of *competency* in that subject area (APA, 1946). Funding for the establishment of ABPP was provided through a loan from APA and early expenses (in the 1950s) were met through APA's continued financial support. Bent et al. (1999) provide a history of the development and growth of ABPP up through the late 1990s, covering the first 50 years of the organization's existence. That article documents the organizational evolution of ABPP, characterizing and describing several developmental phases through which the organization has grown.

Table 3 Specialty boards of the American Board of Professional Psychology

American Board of Clinical Child and Adolescent Psychology
American Board of Clinical Health Psychology
American Board of Clinical Neuropsychology
American Board of Clinical Psychology
American Board of Cognitive and Behavioral Psychology
American Board of Counseling Psychology
American Board of Couple and Family Psychology
American Board of Forensic Psychology
American Board of Group Psychology
American Board of Organizational and Business Consulting Psychology
American Board of Psychoanalysis in Psychology
American Board of Rehabilitation Psychology
American Board of School Psychology

Current structure and function of ABPP

Having grown from an initial field of two specialty areas (Clinical Psychology and Counseling Psychology), ABPP presently recognizes 13 specialty boards (listed alphabetically in Table 3). Each specialty board has its own governance and operates as a member board of the ABPP. The specialty boards are charged with defining the specialty, determining its competencies, reviewing applicants, and examining candidates. Many of the ABPP specialty boards have developed an affiliated academy, an independent organizational entity that may engage in activities such as providing continuing education, information about its specialty board certification process, and other such specialty-specific activities. The specialty academies have established the Council of Presidents of Psychology Specialty Academies (CPPSA) to facilitate inter-academy communication and activities.

The ABPP Board of Trustees (BOT) is responsible for the activity of the overarching activities of ABPP. The ABPP BOT is comprised of the ABPP Executive Committee (comprised of elected officials: President, Past-President, President-elect, Secretary, and Treasurer; and the non-voting Executive Officer), a representative from each specialty board, the president of the CPPSA, and a public member (non-psychologist). The BOT operates as do most corporate boards, overseeing operations, budgets, and the like. The BOT has established a number of committees that oversee issues including standards, affiliation, ethics, and other areas. Ultimately it is the Executive Committee and BOT that are the structures through which organizational change proposals pass; for example, including review of liaison relationships and consideration of applications for affiliation. If a new specialty area is proposed, for example, it is the BOT that considers the proposals (following review by the Affiliation Committee) and takes action.

Participation with other organizations in professional psychology

Recognition of a board-certifying organization by other entities and organizations involved in professional psychology is an important aspect of establishing and maintaining credibility. Ongoing inter-organizational activities help maintain relative consistency in expectations and standards, and facilitate advancement of the profession as well as protection of the public. Such inter-organizational interaction can be used to improve an organization's own processes and ongoing quality improvement efforts.

ABPP participates as a formal liaison and/or observer in many activities within APA and other organizations. Examples of committees with which ABPP interacts within APA are the Committee for the Advancement of Professional Psychology (CAPP), Board of Professional Affairs (BPA), Board of Educational Affairs (BEA), and the Taxonomy Work Group. ABPP has a liaison position with the ASPPB, and serves as a member organization of the Council of Credentialing Organizations in Professional Psychology (CCOPP). In addition, ABPP is actively involved with the Trilateral Psychology Executive Roundtable (TPER), comprised of executives from psychological organizations in the Canada, Mexico, and the United States.

This interaction with other professional psychology organizations works to increase ABPP's ability to incorporate current thinking and policies developing throughout professional psychology into its own activities and structure, facilitating its internal quality improvement efforts. ABPP's multiple boards are each individually subject to comparison with other ABPP and non-ABPP boards that may exist. Quality and standards are reviewed within and across the ABPP boards on a regular basis through a process called Periodic Comprehensive Review (PCR). The ABCN has recently (ABCN, 2007b) undergone such review. This process ensures an ongoing intra- and inter-board review of processes, materials, and performance of each of the boards. That ABPP has multiple boards, is national in scope, maintains active relationships with other professional psychology organizations, and is widely recognized within the profession of psychology has been a factor in recognition of ABPP by other various entities leading to some of the benefits of obtaining board certification.

Engaging in these types of ongoing inter-organizational professional activities is considered a vital part of ABPP's commitment to improving professional psychology and consumer protection. Over the years, much of the inter-organizational focus has had to do with the issues of *competency* and *competency assessment*.

Competency and assessment of competency

The APA Task Force on Competency Assessment in Professional Psychology (American Psychological Association, 2006) identified organizations involved in addressing the issues of competency and specialty within psychology. It identified a historical backdrop within society indicating a desire for review of provision of healthcare services in general, as well as the providers of those services. Historically, organizations such as the Association of State and Provincial Psychology Boards (ASPPB), the National Register of Health Service Providers in Psychology (NRHSPP), the Council of Credentialing Organizations in Professional Psychology (CCOPP), Committee for the Recognition of Specialties and Proficiencies in Professional Psychology (CRSPPP), National Council for Schools and Programs of Professional Psychology (NCSPP), Council of Specialties (CoS),

APA, ABPP, and others have cooperatively and collaboratively worked on issues that affect professional psychologists and consumers with regard to licensure, recognition as a health service provider, specialty definition, and board certification.

Competency is not a static state; it is developed over the course of a professional's education, training, and experience. The Competencies Conference, 2002: Future Directions in Education and Credentialing in Professional Psychology was convened with sponsorship, support and participation of the APA, the Association of Psychology Postdoctoral and Internship Centers (APPIC), and roughly 30 other groups. It provided a forum for inter-organizational discussion of the needs of the profession with respect to competencies (Kaslow et al., 2004).

That conference led to a model of understanding the developmental nature of competency across the professional life-span: a cube model of *foundational* (knowledge, skills, and attitudes foundational to competence) and *functional* (what competent psychologists are expected to do) domains of competency (Rodolfa et al., 2005). One axis of the cube includes foundational competency domains: reflective practices/self-assessment, scientific knowledge and methods, relationships, ethical and legal standards/policy issues, individual and cultural diversity, interdisciplinary systems. Another axis includes the functional competency domains: assessment/diagnosis/conceptualization, intervention, consultation, research/evaluation, supervision/teaching, management/administration. The final axis is comprised of stages of professional development: doctoral education, internship/residency, postdoctoral residency, and continuing competency.

The APA Task Force on Assessment of Competency in Professional Psychology (American Psychological Association, 2006) report provides a significant contribution to current thinking about competency in psychology. Models within other healthcare professions were reviewed, citing strengths and weaknesses. It is reported that healthcare professions have largely set in place four systems in an attempt to produce competent providers: (1) entry-level education and training, (2) licensure and practice regulation; (3) continuing professional education; and (4) specialty certification. The latter are programs recognizing competencies in specialty areas that reach beyond those basic standards required for licensure. Four models of assessment were described: (1) measures of knowledge, (2) measures of professional decision making, (3) measures of practice performance including professional attributes, and (4) integrated assessments of practice-based skills and tasks.

Within psychology, all four methods of assessment are used at one or more points during professional development. Measures of practice performance and practice-based skills and tasks are integrated into professional development through education, training, and supervision. The EPPP may be considered as fitting into the "measures of knowledge" category. ABPP has long used case examples that fit into the "measures of professional decision making" model. The APA Task Force (American Psychological Association, 2006, p. 46) wrote: "The practice sample and oral examination used by the ABPP specialty boards to assess competence in a given specialty area may reflect higher fidelity approaches than those used elsewhere in the profession. In other words, these assessment strategies may tap competence in a manner that reflects actual practice."

Overview of board certification through ABPP

The ABPP board certification process includes several phases: credentials review, submission of practice samples, and oral examination. These aspects of the process are similar for each ABPP specialty board. At the discretion of the specialty board, a written examination (e.g., multiple choice) may also be included in the process. Presently, Forensic Psychology and Clinical Neuropsychology include such exams.

All specialty boards of the ABPP have *generic* requirements, yet different specialty-specific requirements. Criteria for the boards can be reviewed at www.abpp.org. Applicants who meet the generic criteria are advanced to specialty board review. Specialty boards define the education and training required of candidates as well as the areas of competence that are expected. The ABCN has adopted The Houston Conference Guidelines (Hannay et al., 1998) for graduates of programs as of 2005, for example (see www.theabcn.org).

Upon approval of applicant's credentials, a practice sample is requested. The nature of the practice sample most often requires two case presentations or a similar sample of professional work. Particulars of the practice samples required are beyond the scope of this article and the reader is referred to the specialty board materials for details (e.g., www.theabcn.org for ABCN, or www.abpp.org).

The clinical neuropsychology example

ABCN formally affiliated with ABPP in 1983. ABCN (www.theabcn.org) has board certified 680 neuropsychologists. Relative to the number of potential candidates for board certification, this is quite likely the largest percentage of any specialty board. This number continues to grow and the specialty of neuropsychology has clearly led the way in promoting a "culture change" toward board certification as an expectation, largely through the efforts of ABCN and AACN.

Affiliation with ABPP as of 1983, following its initial incorporation in 1981, has been mutually valuable. ABCN became formally associated with the larger "umbrella organization" of ABPP and thereby benefited from the recognition already provided to ABPP. ABPP has benefited from the association through the increased interest in ABPP, in part due the growing interest in the field of neuropsychology and the relative success of ABCN as a specialty board. ABCN established the American Academy of Clinical Neuropsychology (AACN; www.theaacn.org) in 1996. The AACN has served to provide educational opportunities within the profession and provide guidance regarding consumer protection/education and contributes input into public policy through various publications. Basic standards and aspirational guidelines for providing quality neuropsychological services to the public may be found in *Practice guidelines for neuropsychological assessment and consultation* (AACN, 2007a). AACN joined with APA Divisions 22 and 40 and the National Academy of Neuropsychology (NAN) to develop the *Official position of the Military TBI Task Force on the role of neuropsychology and rehabilitation psychology in the evaluation, management and research of military veterans with traumatic brain injury* (McCrea et al., 2008).

The AACN has arguably been the most active of any ABPP affiliated academies and has instituted numerous professional benefits available to its members and others. A group has formed to help educate psychologists about how to become ABCN board certified (BRAIN: Be Ready for ABPP in Clinical Neuropsychology) and out of those and AACN efforts there is a book on board certification in clinical neuropsychology (Armstrong, Beebe, Hilsabeck, & Kirkwood, 2008). The academy has an excellent website with useful resources including practice guidelines and position statements, and has adopted *The Clinical Neuropsychologist* as the official journal of AACN. The AACN has been an incredibly strong advocate of the board certification process, and has helped ABCN become the fastest-growing ABPP specialty board. Sweet (2008) reports that 97% of ABCN board certified psychologists are also members of AACN. An annual conference established by the AACN has continuously grown in size and been given high marks for quality from attendees. The recently formed ABPP Board–Academy Relations Committee specifically sought to have a representative from clinical neuropsychology due to the significant achievements arising out of the ABCN/ AACN relationship. Combined, the AACN and ABCN set forth an exemplary relationship of academy and board from which other ABPP boards and academies can learn much.

FUTURE EFFORTS

Psychology continues to define itself and its practitioners as it grows. As with other fields, continued growth is likely to lead to continued distinctions between practices and practitioners within the field. The emergence of subspecialties is an anticipated result of these growing areas. Indeed, ABCN has been actively reviewing this in conjunction with ABPP, examining whether separate subspecialty designations might be appropriate and if so, how they might be adopted. This is an issue that all specialty boards are likely to face, as other areas of possible subspecialty designation are likely to arise in the future.

As part of those efforts, the ABPP Board of Trustees recently agreed in concept on a mechanism for possible implementation of a subspecialty. In short, individuals already board certified through ABPP would be able to propose to a specialty board that subspecialty designation was warranted. An ABPP specialty board could choose to "sponsor" an application for recognition of a subspecialty, and all ABPP specialty boards would have the opportunity to be involved in the review of such an application. The application, which would have to arise from within ABPP, would be procedurally reviewed in a process akin to an application for affiliation of a new specialty board—requiring vetting by a variety of ABPP committees and all specialty boards within ABPP.

Another area in which psychologists will likely encounter issues related to board certification is that of hospital bylaws. Some hospitals already require that psychologists on staff be board certified just as are physicians on staff. The culture of some institutions are built on expectation of high standards; for the past 10 to 15 years, the Department of Psychiatry and Psychology of the Mayo Clinic has informally made the expectation clear that any psychologist hired is expected to obtain an ABPP in their chosen field of expertise (Rohe, personal communication, January 10, 2008).

The issue of maintenance of certification is one that is beginning to gain attention. Other than an annual attestation that the board certified psychologist is licensed and free of disciplinary action and ethical violations, ABPP has not yet established criteria for demonstrating continuing competence.

Florida has set an example of the type of legislation and rule that may well exist in many states in years to come. Specialization within psychology can be expected to be subject to similar rule and regulation as other jurisdictions review the effects of the Florida action on the profession as well as the consumers of psychological services.

HOW TO BECOME INVOLVED

Being an interested and informed educator, training director, or supervisor can provide valuable growth experiences to the students, interns, and supervisees with whom we interact. Defining board certification as a natural step in professional development and setting in place a culture of competency as a developmental process within professional growth can be instrumental for young psychologists. In these roles we serve as mentors, teaching important lessons in professional psychology in a way that sets the tone for the future of the profession of psychology. Certainly, becoming board certified oneself serves to convey a message of interest in competency within the profession and to those with whom we interact.

Participation by psychologists in their professional groups, board certification organizations, and related academies, as well as in consumer groups, is essential. Local, state, and national organizations interested in the profession of psychology are often much more active in legislative activities than many psychologists are aware. Although most involvement in these organizations comes at the cost of volunteering time and effort, over the long haul the cost of not being involved may well exceed that of volunteering.

Although many psychologists seem reluctant to engage in issues related to politics, public policy, health insurance issues, and such, these are areas that inevitably impact the practice of psychology. As public policy forms and reforms, involved psychologists will be the ones who set the stage for the direction of the profession within such policy.

RESOURCES

Information regarding neuropsychology board certification and related issues may be found through:

- The American Board of Professional Psychology www.abpp.org
- The American Board of Clinical Neuropsychology www.theabcn.org
- The American Academy of Clinical Neuropsychology www.theaacn.org
- BRAIN (Be Ready for ABPP in Clinical Neuropsychology) http://www.cincinnatichildrens.org/svc/alpha/n/neurobehavioral/brain/

REFERENCES

American Academy of Clinical Neuropsychology (2007a). Practice guidelines for neuropsychological assessment and consultation. *The Clinical Neuropsychologist*, *21*, 209–231.

American Board of Clinical Neuropsychology (2007b). *ABCN periodic comprehensive review*. Savannah, GA: American Board of Clinical Neuropsychology.

American Psychological Association (1946). *Report of the Policy and Planning Board on Certification of Professional Psychologists*. Washington, DC: American Psychological Association.

American Psychological Association (1995). *Principles for the recognition of specialties in professional psychology*. Washington, DC: American Psychological Association.

American Psychological Association (2002). Ethical principles of psychologists and code of conduct. *American Psychologist*, *57*, 1060–1073.

American Psychological Association (2006). *American Psychological Association Task Force on the Assessment of Competence in Professional Psychology: Final report*. Washington, DC: American Psychological Association.

Armstrong, K., Beebe, D. W., Hilsabeck, R. C., & Kirkwood, M. W. (2008). *Board certification in clinical neuropsychology. A guide to becoming ABPP/ABCN certified without sacrificing your sanity*. New York: Oxford University Press.

Association of Psychology Postdoctoral and Internship Centers (2006). *APPIC membership criteria: Postdoctoral training programs*. Retrieved December 4, 2007 from the Association of Psychology Postdoctoral and Internship Centers website: (http://www.appic.org/about/2_3_2_about_policies_and_procedures_postdoc.html).

Bent, R. J., Packard, R. E., & Goldberg, R. W. (1999). The American Board of Professional Psychology, 1947 to 1997: A historical perspective. *Professional Psychology: Research and Practice*, *30*(1), 65–73.

Council of Specialties in Professional Psychology (2007b). *CoS Policy on Specialty Synarchies*. Retrieved December 3, 2007 from http://www.cospp.org/

Hannay, H. J., Bieliauskas, L. A., Crosson, B. A., Hammake, T. A., des Hamsher, K., & Koffler, S. P. (1998). Proceedings: The Houston Conference on Specialty Education and Training in Clinical Neuropsychology. *Archives of Clinical Neuropsychology*, *13*, 160–166.

Kaslow, N. J., Borden, K. A., Collins, F. L., Forrest, L., Illfelder-Kaye, J., Nelson, P. D., et al. (2004). Competencies conference: Future directions in education and credentialing in professional psychology. *Journal of Clinical Psychology*, *60*, 699–712.

McCrea, M., Pliskin, N., Barth, J., Cox, D., Fink, J., French, L., et al. (2008). Official position of the Military TBI Task Force on the role of neuropsychology and rehabilitation psychology in the evaluation, management and research of military veterans with traumatic brain injury. *The Clinical Neuropsychologist*, *22*, 10–26.

Rodolfa, E., Bent, R. J., Eisman, E., Nelson, P. D., Rehm, L., & Ritchie, P. (2005). A cube model for competency development: Implications for psychology educators and regulators. *Professional Psychology: Research and Practice*, *36*(4), 347–354.

State of Florida (2007). *The 2007 Florida Statutes, Chapter 490, Psychological Services. F.S. 490.006 (1)(b)*. Tallahassee: State of Florida.

Sweet, J. J. (2008). President's annual state of the Academy report. *The Clinical Neuropsychologist*, *22*, 1–9.

Sweet, J. J., Nelson, N. W., & Moberg, P. J. (2006). The TCN/AACN 2005 "Salary Survey": Professional practices, beliefs, and incomes of U.S. neuropsychologists. *The Clinical Neuropsychologist*, *20*, 325–364.

United States Congress (110th) (2008). *Duncan Hunter National Defense Authorization Act for Fiscal Year 2009*. Retrieved December 27, 2008 from: http://frwebgate.access.gpo.gov/cgi-bin/getdoc.cgi?dbname=110_cong_bills&docid=f:s3001enr.txt.pdf

The Clinical Neuropsychologist, 24: 506–517, 2010
http://www.psypress.com/tcn
ISSN: 1385-4046 print/1744-4144 online
DOI: 10.1080/13854040802531463

Psychology Press
Taylor & Francis Group

THE POLITICS OF TECHNICIANS

Joanne R. Festa[1], William B. Barr[2], and Neil Pliskin[3]
[1]*Department of Neurology, Columbia University Medical Center, New York,* [2]*Departments of Neurology and Psychiatry, New York University Medical Center, New York, and* [3]*Departments of Psychiatry and Neurology, University of Illinois Medical Center, Chicago, IL, USA*

An unintended consequence of the New York psychology Scope of Practice legislation led to a restriction in the use of testing technicians that has yet to be reversed after 4 years. The misperception of neuropsychology by state legislators and psychology colleagues was a key obstacle to achieving a timely solution. We discuss how the political agenda and practice philosophies of New York neuropsychologists were at odds with those of our psychology colleagues, and how that brought about a protracted struggle affecting both patient care and the practice of clinical neuropsychology. Neuropsychologists must maintain an active role in professional and political organizations with equal attention at the local, state, and national levels to avoid similar restrictions to their clinical practice.

Keywords: Technicians; Advocacy; Professional Organizations; Practice Regulations; Politics.

INTRODUCTION AND BACKGROUND

The decade of the brain further enhanced neuropsychology's prominence, attracting psychologists to the discipline and increasing practitioners' involvement with the national organizations. However, neuropsychologists must also establish and retain a strong voice in their state's political process or they may be restricted in professional practice and activities that are in accordance with empirically derived, national standards.

The battle waged by neuropsychologists in New York to re-establish the use of neuropsychology technicians in clinical practice demonstrates that, while neuropsychology may have gained prestige on a national level, our political influence at the state level may be much less than we realize. This article will highlight a case in which neuropsychologists' political agenda and practice philosophy were at odds with those of our psychology colleagues, creating a situation in which the practice of neuropsychology within the entire State of New York was faced with specific and unprecedented restrictions.

Each state addresses professional practice issues in the context of its own political zeitgeist. New York neuropsychologists' fight to reinstate the use of testing technicians is a story of the perfect political storm: A long struggle to gain a Scope

Address correspondence to: Joanne R. Festa, Department of Neurology, Columbia University Medical Center, 710 West 168th Street, New York, NY 10032, USA. E-mail: jf2128@columbia.edu
Accepted for publication: July 31, 2008 First published online: January 28, 2009

of Practice law, the impending licensing of Masters-level therapists, and continued cutbacks from insurers threatening the livelihood of psychotherapists created a fearful, uncertain atmosphere among licensed psychologists. A convergence of many factors caused New York psychologists to ignore the concerns of their neuropsychology colleagues when a strict interpretation of the new Scope of Practice law in 2003 effectively outlawed the use of neuropsychology technicians in the state. The result has been 4 years of continued struggle among psychologists within the New York State Psychological Association (NYSPA) and the creation of a new state organization for neuropsychology that operates outside the confines of NYSPA. In the end, however, after much effort New York neuropsychologists were successful in working with other members of NYSPA to draft legislation that, if passed by the state legislature, will once again allow neuropsychologists to exercise the option of utilizing technicians as part of their clinical practice.

TECHNICIAN USE IN THE UNITED STATES

Psychologists' utilization of testing technicians (also known as psychometrists, test extenders, or psychological assistants) in performing assessment services has been an established standard of practice in the field of clinical neuropsychology for more than three decades. In fact, other doctoral-level health-care practitioners also routinely employ trained non-doctoral technical personnel (e.g., medical laboratory personnel, radiology and EEG technicians). Practice surveys indicate that approximately 50% of neuropsychologists utilize technicians in their work settings, and that paid nondoctoral-level technicians are the most commonly used testing assistant (Sweet, Peck, Abramowitz, & Etzweiler, 2002). Psychologists utilize technicians in a manner analogous to "physician-extenders" in the medical field, enabling psychologists to extend professional services to a wider range and larger number of patients, particularly those who otherwise might not have been likely to receive such services due to the abnormally low reimbursement rate for testing.

In the late 1980s, the Division 40 Executive Board commissioned a Task Force on Education, Accreditation, and Credentialing to evaluate and develop standards for technician use in neuropsychological assessments. The work of the task force is reflected in two publications:

- Division 40 Task Force on Education Accreditation, and Credentialing. (1989). Guidelines regarding the use of nondoctoral personnel in clinical neuropsychological assessment. *The Clinical Neuropsychologist*, *3*, 23–24.
- Division 40 Task Force on Education, Accreditation, and Credentialing (1991). Recommendations for education and training of nondoctoral personnel in clinical neuropsychology. *The Clinical Neuropsychologist*, *5*, 20–23.

These standards, in place for close to 20 years, affirm that the primary responsibility of the test technician is the acquisition of data upon which the licensed doctoral-level professional bases his/her evaluation and opinions. Technician training and supervision, test selection, data interpretation and analysis, report writing, and consultation are the sole responsibility of the licensed psychologist. At no time is the technician considered an independent provider of mental health services. Technicians working in a clinical setting must have at minimum, a Bachelor's degree in psychology and training in test administration and scoring. Moreover, technicians must obtain specialized training in confidentiality issues, HIPAA guidelines, the APA Ethics Code, and sensitivity to cultural and demographic differences.

The practice of using technicians in psychological and neuropsychological practice has been supported by the American Academy of Clinical Neuropsychology (Policy on the Use of Non-Doctoral Level Personnel in Conducting Clinical Neuropsychological Evaluations, 1999) and is also consistent with policies and procedures defined by the American Psychological Association (*General Guidelines for Providers of Psychological Services*, 1987; *Speciality Guidelines for the Delivery of Psychological Services by Clinical Psychologists*, 1981; *Ethical Principles of Psychologists and Code of Conduct*, 2003). The use of technicians as an established standard of practice was recently recognized by the federal government through the creation of CPT codes specifically designed for psychologists' use of technicians when assisting in the evaluation of their patients. Prior to the 2003 issue that arose in New York and is described below, technician use was allowed in all 50 states in the US.

NEW YORK'S HISTORICAL BACKGROUND

For more than a decade New York psychologists struggled to pass legislation that would safeguard a psychology scope of practice. The proposed Scope of Practice bill was introduced to the New York legislature with the stated intent of not changing the practice of psychology in New York. After protracted lobbying, NYSPA achieved their goal and the Mental Health Licensing Bill (Chapter 676 of the Laws of 2002) was ratified in the fall of 2003. The new law came into effect in January 2004. New York psychologists were pleased that consumers of mental health services had adequate protection by providing a clear definition of the profession's legal scope of practice.

However, this news was not necessarily good for New York state neuropsychologists. Up to and including 2003, psychologists in New York had used technicians in the supervised administration and scoring of psychological and neuropsychological tests. Not long after the passage of the Scope of Practice bill, questions arose from neuropsychologists, hospitals, and rehabilitation centers who had grave concerns that the new law might be interpreted in a manner that would prohibit the use of testing technicians. They sought clarification of the Scope of Practice bill from the New York State Education Department (NYSED), the state body that oversees and regulates the professions, to ensure the continued employment of technicians in clinical practice. Appeals to support the continued use of technicians were made by practitioners, institutions, and neuropsychology organizations. APA's Senior Director of Legal and Regulatory Affairs for the APA Practice Directorate, Billie Hinnefeld, J.D., Ph.D., wrote to the NYSED to urge extensive consultation on the topic. The letter described the "safety net" that ensures protection of the consumer is the ultimate responsibility of the licensed doctoral level provider. In support of neuropsychologists' concerns, Rudy Nydegger, Ph.D., president of NYSPA at that time, requested official clarification regarding the use of technicians from the NYSED. The Executive Secretary of the State Board of Psychology was assigned the task of developing an opinion response.

A common misperception among some influential individuals at the NYSED and within NYSPA itself was that New York suffered from a proliferation of insurance fraud mills where neuropsychological assessments of school-aged children were being conducted by testing technicians without psychologists on site. In fact, a review of the Summaries of Regents Actions on Professional Misconduct and Discipline for the 10-year period from 1997 to 2006 revealed NO disciplinary actions against neuropsychologists for improper use of technicians. Nevertheless, the Executive Secretary of the NYSED wrote an opinion that interpreted the new Scope law in a manner excluding the use of technicians, stating that testing by technicians constituted the independent practice of psychology. Specifically, the response letter to Dr. Nydegger dated October 31, 2003 quoted the NYSED website published interpretation that asserts:

> "*. . . the use of unlicensed persons . . . to perform any services or activities that fall within the statutory definition of psychology could result in professional misconduct charges or in the criminal charge of aiding and abetting illegal practice. The statutory scope of practice of psychology includes psychological (including neuropsychological) testing.*" The letter further stated that "*the administration and scoring of psychological tests would require a license in this state*" and that "*a change in statute would be necessary to permit unlicensed persons to perform the services and activities in the profession's scope of practice.*" An interpretation by this single representative of the NYSED in 2003 had significantly altered the practice of clinical neuropsychology by restricting the use of technicians. The effect on patients, facilities, and practitioners was profound and widespread.

Although some believed that a restriction on technicians in New York would force hospitals to hire more psychologists, increases in psychology staff did not occur. Large facilities could not bear the financial burden of hiring a psychologist to fill the gap of a technician. Rather, in the absence of technicians, services were cut to patients and there were longer wait times for medically necessary evaluation services. Neuropsychologists in institutional settings simply could not meet the demand for services without the aid of technicians. Waiting times for appointments became protracted; one upstate New York rehabilitation center indicated their wait time went from 2 months to 5 months overnight. Those who could least afford to pay were the most affected. Patients from ethnic minority groups were especially impacted by the technician ban in New York (Peery & Barr, 2007). Neuropsychologists who provided services to patients of diverse backgrounds with the aid of bilingual technicians were no longer able to fill the needs of non-English-speaking patients in New York, resulting in decreased access to neuropsychological services. Likewise, the restriction on technician use seriously impacted patients in rural areas, smaller cities, and remote locations within the state where fewer neuropsychologists practice.

Ironically, physicians in New York were not restricted from supervising technicians, and medical doctors in New York continue to use technicians to perform neuropsychological testing in their offices. The time for advocacy and intervention by neuropsychologists was at hand.

FOCUSED GOALS

Neuropsychologists need to maintain an active role in professional and political organizations with equal attention at the local, state, and national levels. Fundamental to the NY technician struggle was neuropsychology's relative obscurity: despite the growth of our field, information about the discipline of neuropsychology and its methods of practice is not widely known, and perhaps, somewhat misunderstood by our colleagues and by the public at large. In this special issue of *The Clinical Neuropsychologist*, Howe, Sweet, and Bauer describe the extent of neuropsychology's national public relations problem. The misperception of neuropsychology by state legislators and psychology colleagues was a key obstacle to achieving the support from our state psychological association necessary to reverse the interpretation that restricted neuropsychologists from employing technicians. This situation might have been avoided if more members of our profession had participated in activities at the state level. It is our hope that neuropsychologists across the country will learn from our experience in New York and become more active in both state and local affairs.

PREVIOUS AND CONTINUING EFFORTS

By the end of 2003 it was clear that the New York State Education Department's opinion on technicians would ban technician use in clinical neuropsychology practice. In January 2004, NYSPA leadership changed and with the new officers came a significant shift in support for neuropsychologists. Since that time, neuropsychologists in the state have continued to work toward reversing the NYSED's opinion through the Neuropsychology Division of NYSPA, despite the overt lack of support and the covert tactics on the part of some people within the state organization. National practice organizations, particularly APA's Division 40 and the National Academy of Neuropsychology (NAN), were abreast of the events and immediately offered support to state neuropsychologists. Although national neuropsychologists were unified in their support for affecting a reversal of the NYSED's opinion, it was evident that a small group of well-placed, highly involved, New York psychologists within NYSPA were against any attempts to resolve the technician ruling. Sadly, the agenda of neuropsychologists appeared at odds with that of the leadership of our state psychology association. Many individuals within NYSPA believed that the use of technicians would have a negative impact on the practice of psychology through the involvement of non-doctoral personnel in testing. Others in the school psychology community worried that if technicians were available in the state, school systems would hire these individuals to replace doctoral-level personnel.

Early in January 2004, as information about a ban on the use of technicians was slowly disseminating, NYSPA members and non-members, in-state and out-of-state practitioners, were reaching out to learn more about what actions were being undertaken. Although many complained, few offered assistance. A subcommittee of NYSPA's Neuropsychology Division (itself about 160 members) was immediately formed to address the use of technicians in clinical practice. A separate meeting of the committee convened and several action points were developed. The committee decided to poll the NYSPA Neuropsychology Division membership and assess their opinions about reversing the ruling on technicians. In reviewing the records at that time, we recognized that a large proportion of neuropsychologists in New York were not members of NYSPA. Further education of the membership was needed: it appeared that the new restriction was not widely known, even among practicing neuropsychologists. A paragraph summarizing the technician issue was developed to accompany a poll to the NYSPA Neuropsychology Division membership.

Early in the process, NYSPA's Neuropsychology Division had the opportunity to meet with neuropsychologists from around the country at the 2004 INS meeting to gain a historical perspective, gather information, and develop the necessary tools for meeting the challenges ahead. Representatives from national organizations, aware of the implications of the New York technician restriction, marshaled efforts to increase neuropsychologists' participation in the process, both locally and nationally. As a result, 39 new members were recruited to NYSPA and its Neuropsychology Division, giving neuropsychology a greater presence within NYSPA.

NYSPA's Neuropsychology Division set out to engage and educate its membership. The division reinstated a newsletter to maintain communication and improve the education of neuropsychology members while keeping them abreast of progress on the "technician issue." With a recent surge in membership, the poll was mailed to Neuropsychology Division members. The mailer included information about the role of a technician in clinical practice based on the Division 40 guidelines as well as links to the position paper on the NAN PAIO website. The poll asked: "Should the Neuropsychology Division (of NYSPA) pursue an amendment to Section 7601-A of the Education Law to support a neuropsychologist's right to appropriately use and supervise psychometricians in clinical practice?" The respondent simply answered "Yes I support" or "No, I do not support... the Neuropsychology Division's efforts to pursue and amend psychology's Scope of Practice Law allowing for the use of unlicensed technicians." The poll had a 51% response rate with 78% of responders in favor and 22% of responders not in favor.

With a mandate from its members, the division was empowered to request that NYSPA approach the State Education Department asking for a review of the technician opinion and a reversal of the ban on technicians. A letter to the Legislative Committee of NYSPA presented in person by the neuropsychology division president requested that, based on the evidence from the poll, the problem be addressed by seeking an amendment to the Scope of Practice bill. The request was made in May 2004, only 5 months after the restriction on technicians went into effect.

Later that year the first of two task forces was appointed by a president of NYSPA. The message that outlined the group's agenda included inflammatory wording and misinformation, setting the tone for future events. The same NYSPA president later addressed the NYSPA Legislative Committee stating that while she sympathized with neuropsychologists, the issue of technicians was "troublesome." The president warned of problems with the training and qualifications of technicians, noting that tests were sometimes administered by "high school drop-outs" and "office secretaries."

Frustrated neuropsychologists, with no immediate relief in sight, sought other solutions. An Article 78 proceeding was considered that would bring a law suit against the NYSED for their interpretation. Given that our state organization was still not behind a reversal of the opinion, it was assumed that NYSPA's Neuropsychology Division could not support such an action independent of the NYSPA council. State neuropsychologists considered initiating a lawsuit on the part of a patient who was denied or delayed services due to the circumstances created by the ruling. This approach was seriously and thoughtfully examined but it was deemed a back-up plan while other strategies were prioritized. A lawsuit was considered inordinately expensive and protracted: NY neuropsychologists sought to first pursue more immediate relief.

In Albany, New York's state capitol, psychologists had not always enjoyed a stellar professional reputation in the eyes of the legislature. Fifteen years of pursuing a Scope of Practice bill, a contentious merge of psychology with the teachers' union, and a last-minute repeal of a continuing education bill, cemented psychology's reputation as a fractious, if not eccentric group. Adding to the political landscape, in recent years NYSPA's management had come under scrutiny by its constituents: state psychologists voiced anger and resentment over being disenfranchised. Many psychologists believed that the merge with a teachers union and the proposed (but squelched) continuing education bill were implemented without proper input from state psychologists. With negative feedback on multiple fronts, NYSPA's leadership had become cautious about taking any legislative action that might endanger the hard-won Scope of Practice bill or incur further complaints and scrutiny from state psychologists.

Among NYSPA council members there was no clear consensus regarding a solution to the use of technicians. Several seasoned NYSPA council members suggested a legislative fix: NYSPA's lobbyists had indicated that a legislative change to the Scope of Practice law was achievable. Others argued that neuropsychologists should employ the newly-licensed Master's-level therapists to administer tests, while others warned that this could lead to unintended consequences: Master's-level providers taking over psychologist testing. Opposition to restoring the use of technicians continued from various NYSPA divisions. The APA's Practice Directorate as well as neuropsychologists from around the country and state came to offer information and assistance to NYSPA's council and to express concerns about the need for a solution.

For more than 2 years NYSPA's attempts to resolve the technician problem did not produce measurable success. The results of the first NYSPA task force were accepted by the NYSPA council "with thanks" in 2005: the recommendations were not acceptable to neuropsychologists or to the NYSPA council. The council instead asked the NYSPA Legislative Committee to make recommendations. In 2006, members of council and the Legislative Committee met with representatives from the NYSED seeking a 3-year moratorium while NYSPA determined how to best define and regulate technicians. The request was denied. Instead, the NYSED suggested that legislation be submitted to address the problem. Yet another task force was appointed in 2006 to develop this legislation.

Over the course of 3 years, the Neuropsychology Division of NYSPA worked diligently to address concerns raised by New York State psychologists and to provide them with information on how psychology technicians are utilized in other states across the country without creating an erosion in the quality of psychological assessment services. The opposition from other psychology divisions within NYSPA did not change in response to the Centers for Medicare and Medicaid Services (CMS) ruling in 2005 that enabled psychologists across the country to bill for technician services under Medicare and Medicaid. They were also not persuaded by the changes in the Current Procedural Terminology (CPT) codes that were developed specifically for psychological and neuropsychological assessment services provided by psychology technicians. New York remains the only state with a current Scope of Practice interpretation that prohibits its psychologists from using procedure codes used by psychologists in the rest of the country and from providing services consistent with federally mandated guidelines.

LESSONS LEARNED FROM THE NEW YORK TECHNICIAN EXPERIENCE

The natural first step in addressing practice issues is to enlist the help of one's state psychological association. New York neuropsychologists assumed that support for a reversal of the ban on technicians and actions to achieve relief would be forthcoming. Those assumptions proved inaccurate. The Neuropsychology Division is only one part of the larger NYSPA organization: the division did not have the clout to affect immediate support. Furthermore, neuropsychologists were not part of NYSPA's Executive Committee, thereby reducing the division's influence. Although the Neuropsychology Division was somewhat marginalized and regular attempts were made to derail its efforts, neuropsychologists persisted in addressing the issue with the state organization. By continually keeping the pressure on NYSPA's council, they recognized that neuropsychologists would persist until they achieved a tenable solution.

Although every state has its own unique set of circumstances, similar problems have likely occurred elsewhere in the United States. Advocacy for a local problem can often be assisted by representatives from other states who have had similar issues, and from national organizations who have assisted in brokering a solution. In the case of New York, the technician ban was a problem greater than local grassroots efforts could manage. Advocacy on behalf of New York from national organizations, including APA Practice Directorate, APA Division 40, and NAN, lent credence to the arguments in support of technicians and underscored the message that technician use is an important national issue in psychology. Political pressure, particularly on the part of APA Practice, conveyed the message to key council members that sabotaging the process would not be tolerated and support for neuropsychologists was expected.

In this special issue of *The Clinical Neuropsychologist*, Howe, Sweet, and Bauer emphasize the importance of educating others in the process of advocacy. New York neuropsychologists learned that sometimes the education required is very fundamental. Most psychologists have very limited knowledge about clinical neuropsychology, neurocognitive testing, and the role of technicians. When other efforts to inform council members failed, the Neuropsychology Division made a presentation to the NYSPA council, educating them on the very basics of our discipline. However, the educational process remained a moving target: every year new council members are elected and the collective knowledge of the council decreases.

There are times when even the most persistent efforts in advocacy cannot trump the political zeitgeist of a state organization and alternative solutions must be sought. Frustrated by the lack of progress achieved through NYSPA, neuropsychologists developed a new practice organization: the New York State Association of Neuropsychology (NYSAN). The new organization was intended as a necessary complement to NYSPA's Neuropsychology Division: NYSAN could more freely and forcefully address the advocacy needs of New York neuropsychologists. NYSAN was formed by neuropsychologists to retain a lobbying firm that would address the NYSED on behalf of clinical neuropsychology practice. Charter members contributed start-up funds to maintain a viable organization from which to effectively address the technician issue as well as other future practice-related matters. Knowing that lobbying efforts are costly, NYSAN immediately sought support from national organizations. Applications were made to APA's Psychology Defense Fund, the National Academy of Neuropsychology, the American Academy of Clinical Neuropsychology (AACN), American Board of Professional Neuropsychology (ABPN), and APA's Division 40. All applications were generously funded. A lobbying firm was retained and NYSAN immediately developed a course of action. In part, what a lobbyist offers is a network of existing relationships with well-placed officials. Selection of an appropriate lobbyist with established connections was therefore critical.

NYSAN's primary goal is to arrive at a solution that will enable state psychologists to return to practice as it was prior to the 2003 Scope of Practice Law. After initial consultation with its lobbyist, NYSAN's strategy was to first educate the state policy makers. Yet again, education was a crucial component of these political advocacy activities. Educating the NYSAN lobbyist was the first step. NYSAN's lobbyist was essentially given a crash-course on both clinical neuropsychology and technicians. Position papers, communications, and historical data were made available during the initial phase of the process. An important aspect of the lobbyist's education was observing a mock examination where he could witness first-hand the mechanical aspects of testing administration. Having seen the actual activities of a technician, the lobbyist was convinced that officials from the NYSED required the same experience in order to grasp the true nature of a technician's activities. Having become an expert in the use of technicians, the lobbyist's work involved educating the policy makers.

DIRTY POLITICS

Be prepared for the unexpected. No battle is waged without scars and advocates in New York have suffered their share of battle wounds. For reasons ranging from perceived professional threats to personal proclivities, a group of psychologists continued to work against the interests of finding a solution using a variety of what neuropsychologists considered dirty political tactics. In the process of advocating for technicians there were personal attacks in which neuropsychologists with long histories of service to NYSPA had their characters maligned. There was also rumor-mongering, use of fear tactics, stonewalling, and back-room dealing. Some psychologists even pledged their support for a solution in public forums while explicitly stating their desire to short-circuit the process in more confined settings.

WORKING TOWARD A SOLUTION

For over 2 years a group of New York neuropsychologists have been working on multiple fronts, through NYSAN and NYSPA, to achieve a solution to the technician restriction. NYSAN has been instrumental in gaining access to state policy makers, educating them on the problems imposed by the restriction on technicians and proposing the potential solution. NYSAN has kept technicians on NYSED's agenda and engendered the goodwill and support from key executives to assist with implementing a resolution.

Simultaneously, state neuropsychologists have worked within NYSPA to hammer out draft legislation that would enable the use of technicians in the state. Through the negotiations involved in drafting the bill it became apparent that every state's psychology legislation is critical to the process: Although state and national neuropsychologists suggested that legislation from Arkansas served as a good model for drafting a New York bill, psychologists in New York continually reverted to New Jersey's legislation that restricts technicians from administering IQ tests, the only state to do so. Four years of persistent advocacy and several task forces finally yielded draft legislation from NYSPA that was adopted by the NYSPA Council in 2007. It is currently being discussed with state legislators. The draft adopts the educational and training requirements of the national guidelines, but additionally restricts technicians from administering intelligence tests. Although long debated and not the preferred solution, the restriction on IQ testing became a necessary concession to advance a resolution.

FUTURE EFFORTS

There are still several steps to reaching the final goal of reinstating the use of technicians in New York. Through the course of the legislative process, the draft bill will inevitably be rewritten. NYSPA council has threatened to remove their support should any substantive changes to the bill result from the re-drafting. NYSAN has laid the necessary groundwork to expedite a bill: meetings with the NYSED have educated the key officials about the importance of this issue.

To date, the NYSED's opinion has effectively banned the use of psychology technicians in New York State with few exceptions. Qualified individuals who were employed as psychology technicians have lost their jobs. The ban on technicians has not resulted in new jobs for psychologists; rather, it has resulted in lack of services. It has been particularly difficult for patients in remote areas, for underinsured patients, and for patients who do not speak English.

Several problems arose in advocating for technicians that have spurred new considerations for protecting the practice of neuropsychology. These are some things to consider: Should neuropsychologists have separate licensure or a separate designation (as is the case in the State of Louisiana)? If so, the age-old issue of defining a neuropsychologist must be resolved in order to advance separate licensing forward. Should the title "Neuropsychologist" be protected and should it be under the "psychologist" umbrella? Should certification or licensure for Bachelor's-level technicians be considered? Time and again, technicians were an easy target for derogatory comments, such as describing them as "high-school drop outs." There is a legitimate concern over the rigor and standardization of training for technicians. To make neuropsychologist/technician analogous to physician/nurse, radiologist/technician, dentist/dental assistant, our technicians may need to be licensed or certified.

HOW TO BECOME INVOLVED

Woefully few neuropsychologists are active in their state psychology association. Less than one-third of all psychologists in New York State belong to NYSPA. In 2005 there were just over 450 psychologists in the state identifying themselves as having a professional interest in neuropsychology, through membership in one of several neuropsychology organizations. Less than half of these individuals (44%) were members of the NYSPA Neuropsychology Division. Join your state organization and participate in its activities. Vote for officers who will support clinical neuropsychology. Get neuropsychologists elected to the state association's Executive Committee and to the state's psychology board. Newsletters will help you stay abreast of legislative activities that may be relevant to your practice. Know your state licensing laws and be aware of pending legislative changes. Even if you do not use technicians in your clinical practice, protect the neuropsychologists' right to choose how they meet the demands of their practice.

ACKNOWLEDGMENTS

We have borrowed liberally from documents prepared over the years by New York psychologists involved in this fight. We acknowledge the work of Shane Bush, Charles Zaroff, and Shelley Peery. Several New York neuropsychologists have worked tirelessly on this process, whether in writing, in meetings, or in spirit. Special recognition must go to these professionals for their advocacy efforts: Larry Thomas, Steve Honor, Stan Singer, Maria Lifrak, Tony Puente, Michael Santa Maria, Dominic Carrone, Tony Wong, June Feder, and Gayle Berg. We also acknowledge the valued expertise of our lobbyist, Richard Leckerling.

REFERENCES

American Academy of Clinical Neuropsychology. (1999). Policy on the use of non-doctoral-level personnel in conducting clinical neuropsychological evaluations. *The Clinical Neuropsychologist*, *13*(4), 385.

American Psychological Association. (1981). Speciality guidelines for the delivery of services clinical psychologists. *American Psychologist*, *36*, 640–651.

American Psychological Association. (2003). Ethical principles of psychologists and code of conduct. *American Psychologist*, *57*, 12–28.

American Psychological Association Board of Professional Affairs, Committee on Professional Standards. (1987). General guidelines for providers of psychological services. *American Psychologist*, *42*, 712–723.

Division 40 Task Force on Education, Accreditation, and Credentialing. (1989). Guidelines regarding the use of non-doctoral personnel in clinical neuropsychological assessment. *The Clinical Neuropsychologist*, *3*(1), 23–24.

Division 40 Task Force on Education, Accreditation, and Credentialing. (1991). Recommendations for education and training of non-doctoral personnel in clinical neuropsychology. *The Clinical Neuropsychologist*, *5*(1), 20–23.

National Academy of Neuropsychology. (2000). The use of neuropsychology test technicians in clinical practice. *Archives Of Clinical Neuropsychology*, *15*(5), 381–382.

Peery, S., & Barr, W. B. (2007). On the absence of neuropsychology technicians in NY State: The differential impact on minorities. *NYSPA Notebook*, *12*(4), 16–17.

Sweet, J., Peck, E., Abramowitz, C., & Etzweiler, S. (2002). The NAN/Division 40 Practice Survey. *The Clinical Neuropsychologist*, *16*, 109–127.

The Clinical Neuropsychologist, 24: 518–537, 2010
http://www.psypress.com/tcn
ISSN: 1385-4046 print/1744-4144 online
DOI: 10.1080/13854041003775347

Psychology Press
Taylor & Francis Group

THIRD PARTY OBSERVATION DURING NEUROPSYCHOLOGICAL EVALUATION: AN UPDATE ON THE LITERATURE, PRACTICAL ADVICE FOR PRACTITIONERS, AND FUTURE DIRECTIONS

Laura L. S. Howe[1] and Robert J. McCaffrey[2,3]
[1]VA Palo Alto Health Care System, Palo Alto, CA, [2]University at Albany, State University of New York, and [3]Albany Neuropsychological Associates, NY, USA

A clash between neuropsychology and the law may exist when a demand is made for third party observation during forensic neuropsychological evaluation. Third party observation includes any person or observational process present during a neuropsychological evaluation aside from the psychologist and the examinee, including electronic devices (e.g., video and audio recordings). The goal of this paper includes succinctly providing to practitioners the scientific, ethical, and pragmatic (i.e., test security and coaching) reasons to not allow third party observation. Practitioners at the individual level need to be aware of the reasoning and be willing and able to advocate protecting the boundaries of neuropsychological practice and test security. We present practitioners with options when confronted with a request, provide a list of resources to educate the legal system and submit with motions, provide responses for some of the more common myths/reasoning used to support a request for a TPO, and encourage more global solutions such as state-by-state legislation.

Keywords: Neuropsychology; Advocacy; Third Party Observer.

INTRODUCTION

When two distinct professional systems meet, the possibility for misunderstandings and clashes exists. This dynamic is evident when a member of any profession enters the legal system as an expert. The law has many rules and a set structure and procedure with which many professionals are not familiar. It is important for the neuropsychologist who becomes involved in the legal system to understand the legal culture (Greiffenstein & Cohen, 2005). Greiffenstein and Cohen (2005) identified three basic conflicts between neuropsychological and legal methods, which include conflicting agendas, conflicting methods, and conflicting relationships. These conflicts are due to core ways in which each discipline is structured and cannot be changed in any significant manner, and thus must be

Address correspondence to: Laura L. S. Howe, VA Palo Alto Health Care System, Psychology Service (116B), 3801 Miranda Avenue, Palo Alto, CA 94304, USA. E-mail: lauralshowe@yahoo.com
Accepted for publication: March 12, 2010.

adjusted to (Greiffenstein & Cohen, 2005) as outlined in the APA Ethical Principles of Psychologists and Code of Conduct (Section 1.02 Conflicts Between Ethics and Law, Regulations, or Other Governing Legal Authority) (APA, 2002).

In contrast, however, there are other situations where neuropsychology and the law conflict but the individual clinical neuropsychological practitioner may have input into how he or she proceeds in a specific situation. Importantly, how the individual practitioner proceeds will impact the resolution of the initial conflict and the potential final outcome. For example, when requested to produce raw data practitioners may engage in several different behaviors, outlined in other papers and position statements (e.g., Barth et al., 2003; Kaufmann, 2009), which would lead to the data being turned over without any stipulations, or to the data being inspected "in camera", or the most extreme solution wherein the data are not released at all in some situations. In each scenario, how the individual clinical neuropsychological practitioner decides to proceed may significantly impact the specific outcome (e.g., what happens with the raw data), how the field of neuropsychology is impacted (e.g., legal precedence may be created), and perception of the field by the legal community (e.g., increased or decreased understanding of issues particular to neuropsychology). Familiarity with potential options and informed decisions on how to proceed is a form of advocacy for the field of neuropsychology as well as a professional responsibility if one chooses to enter into the forensic realm (APA Ethical Principles of Psychologists and Code of Conduct, 2002, 2.01 Boundaries of Competence).

A clash between neuropsychology and the law may exist when a demand is made for a third party observer (TPO) during a forensic neuropsychological evaluation. A TPO is any person or observational process that is present during a neuropsychological evaluation aside from the psychologist and the examinee, and includes electronic devices (e.g., video and audio recordings). Attorneys, most often plaintiff attorneys, sometimes demand to be present during a client's neuropsychological evaluation. These demands range from having another psychologist present (the ethical issues with this option will be described in detail later), or the attorney themselves (creating a situation in which counsel may be called as a witness at the time of trial), a paralegal, a court stenographer, or a videographer present to having the interaction monitored by extenders or any combination of the aforementioned.

While TPOs are excluded in federal courts from being present during psychiatric, psychological, and neuropsychological evaluations, there are some jurisdictions such as New York and Florida that have statutes and case law (cf. Broyles v. Reilly, 1997) permitting attorneys to attend independent medical evaluations (IMEs) or compulsory medical evaluations (CMEs), absent a good showing that they should be excluded from the evaluation. The research literature with regard to neuropsychological evaluations and TPOs has consistently demonstrated that third party observation adversely impacts the validity of the obtained neuropsychological data, which in turn impacts the usefulness and reliability of the evaluation. In addition, the presence of TPOs raises ethical considerations as well as pragmatic concerns regarding test security and coaching. TPOs is an area in which the individual practitioner has some control over the resolution of the dispute. How the practitioner responds to the request will impact the field and the legal system's understanding of neuropsychology.

Decreased Validity of Obtained Results Due to Social Facilitation and Inhibition

The fundamental reason TPOs should not be present during neuropsychological evaluations is the inherent impact on the validity of standardized psychological tests. The foundation of neuropsychological practice is extensive training to understand brain–behavior relationships, which results in an ability to understand brain–behavior relationships when viewing obtained data. When the data are obtained in non-standardized conditions it is sometimes not clear how much the data's reliability has been impacted. Most psychological/neuropsychological tests are developed under standardized conditions that include an assumption that only the examiner and the examinee are present during the evaluation, which is stated specifically in some manuals (e.g., *Wechsler Adult Intelligence Scale – Third edition manual*, Wechsler, 1997; *Wechsler Memory Scale – Third Edition manual*, Wechsler, 1997).

Every departure from standardized conditions has the potential to render the normative data no longer applicable and to decrease the validity of the test measures (cf. Lee, Reynolds, & Willson, 2003). Alterations that significantly impact the obtained data in unpredictable ways result in data from which clear and confident conclusions often cannot be made. The research literature has consistently demonstrated that the presence of TPOs results in changes to the obtained data. With regard to TPOs, the phenomenon of social facilitation is what impacts the data collected. More precisely, based on the effects shown, the term used to describe the dynamic should be social facilitation and inhibition. In general, social facilitation and inhibition causes individuals to perform better on tasks requiring over-learned or simple skills, while performing more poorly on novel or more difficult tasks (McCaffrey, Fisher, Gold, & Lynch, 1996). With regard to memory tasks, the average effect size has been shown to be approximately three-quarters of a standard deviation but can be as large as one and a half standard deviations (Gavett, Lynch, & McCaffrey, 2005). Therefore the social facilitation effect could diminish an average memory score of 90 ($M = 100, SD = 15$) to an impaired memory score of 75 or less.

Changes in performance due to factors not associated with brain dysfunction make the data difficult to interpret and conclusions have to be hedged with one or more caveats. One of the skills of a neuropsychologist is knowing what circumstances may impact neuropsychological test performance that are not directly related to the patient's brain functioning (e.g., effort, an open door, anxiety) and then trying to minimize those influences. The presence of TPOs is a factor that impacts the data, and can be controlled by not allowing a TPO.

One of the most important impacts when the reliability and validity of a neuropsychological evaluation is compromised due to a TPO is that the individual examinee was denied the opportunity for the best measurement of their cognitive functioning (Kaufmann, 2005) due to factors that could easily have been controlled by not allowing a TPO. The areas of cognitive performance most impacted by the presence of a TPO are attention, sustained concentration, verbal fluency, learning, and memory (Gavett et al., 2005). Studies have demonstrated that the mere presence of a TPO effects performance even if the TPO does not subjectively appear to be disruptive (e.g., observers sitting quietly in the room and out of sight). The effects of social facilitation and inhibition even exist when the TPO is an electronic device such as an audio recorder (Constantinou, Ashendorf, & McCaffrey, 2002) or a video recorder (Constantinou, Ashendorf, & McCaffrey, 2005). Social facilitation and inhibition effects extend to when the observer is a significant other (Kehrer, Sanchez, Habif, Rosenbaum, & Townes, 2000), or someone posing as the examiner's supervisor (Yantz & McCaffrey, 2005). A more in-depth review of the social facilitation literature can be found in other articles (e.g., McCaffrey et al., 1996; McCaffrey, Lynch, & Yantz, 2005). Appendix A lists relevant scientific studies regarding TPOs and neuropsychology, position and policy statements from organizations, and commentaries and other sources that discuss the TPO issue and would be helpful to submit with motions to quash a request for a TPO.

A second important impact is that the field of neuropsychology is placed in a position that compromises its ability to function as well as it can and contribute on a level it should be able to when aiding the court. In addition, it presents a situation where the field on a larger level can be negatively impacted through violations of test security that can result in coaching and a diminishment of the usefulness of assessment measures.

Test Security

TPOs result in a breach of test security that may lead to misuse of materials and increase the potential for public access to test items. Many neuropsychological tests depend on an examinee's unfamiliarity with the items, which necessitates protecting the test items from general circulation to preserve their uniqueness and usefulness (Axelrod et al., 2000b). Psychologists are bound by their ethics to protect psychological materials and they often have to sign purchasing agreements when obtaining materials, stating they will uphold test security. When non-psychologists have access to testing materials no similar restraints are placed on the individuals, which places the test materials in a vulnerable position. Test development and standardization is a lengthy and expensive process. For example, re-standardization of the WAIS-III and WMS-III took over 5 years and cost several million dollars (Axelrod et al., 2000b). Additionally, even though retesting was expected to cost the school system hundreds of thousands of dollars, Michigan's Department of Education in 2007 made thousands of fifth and sixth graders retake part of the state's standardized writing test due to a breach in test security—caused by a newspaper publishing a brief article about the test that revealed the topics for two of the questions and could have resulted in an unfair advantage for some students (Bunkley, 2007). Knowing questions contained on neuropsychological assessment measures ahead of time likewise creates an unfair advantage that can impact scores and interpretation.

Coaching

Breaches in test security may lead to the coaching of examinees, which describes when examinees are given information about psychological tests that could lead to their being able to alter their presentation to appear a certain way.

Wetter and Corrigan (1995) surveyed 70 practicing attorneys and 150 law students, and found that 22% of students and 42% of attorneys responded that an attorney should provide as much specific information as possible about psychological assessment. This is concerning, since coaching can impact assessment procedures. For example, providing detailed information on the validity scales was shown to enable a third of examinees to successfully elevate their responses on the MMPI-2 clinical scales but not the validity scales (Rogers, Bagby, & Chakraborty, 1993). In real life, coaching does occur. Youngjohn (1995) reported a case in which an attorney admitted that he deliberately coached his client before testing. For a recent review of the coaching literature, see Suhr and Gunstad (2007). Additional helpful references regarding coaching are listed in Appendix A (cf. Abeles, 2001; Victor & Abeles, 2004; Wydick, 1995).

Ethical Conflicts

Most psychologists in the United States are bound by the Ethical Principles of Psychologists and Code of Conduct (APA, 2002). Allowing TPOs during assessments may conflict with several psychological ethical code sections. Psychologists are encouraged to adhere to standardized procedures and utilize test materials in a manner appropriate based on the current research (APA at ES 9.02. Use of Assessments). As shown, the state of the current research shows that TPOs impact performance levels, in addition to some tests making explicit recommendations to not have TPOs during evaluations. The *Standards for Educational and Psychological Testing* [AERA] (1999) state "test users have the responsibility of protecting the security of test materials at all times" (AERA at St. 5.7) which includes making "reasonable efforts to maintain the integrity and security of test materials and other assessment techniques consistent with law and contractual obligations" (APA at ES 9.11 Maintaining Test Security). Additionally, "psychologists do not promote the use of psychological assessment techniques by unqualified persons" (APA at ES 9.07 Assessment by unqualified persons) and they must protect against misuse and misrepresentation of their work (APA at ES 1.01 Misuse of Psychologists' Work). Each of these may occur when unqualified individuals observe psychological examinations. Neuropsychologists obtain extensive training in brain–behavior relationships, which is necessary to understand, integrate, and correctly interpret behavior that occurs during an evaluation. Someone without such expertise may misinterpret the examinee's performance, not placing it in the context of clinical history, which may lead to incorrect attributions for test results. Finally, "psychologists take reasonable steps to avoid harming their clients/patients ... and others with whom they work, and to minimize harm where it is foreseeable and unavoidable" (APA at ES 3.04 Avoiding Harm).

Due to the importance of this issue within the field of neuropsychology and the potentially far-ranging negative impacts, the National Academy of Neuropsychology and the American Academy of Clinical Neuropsychology have each published official statements on the topic of TPOs (Axelrod et al., 2000a; Hamsher, Lee, & Baron, 2001).

FOCUSED GOALS

The goal of this paper includes succinctly providing to practitioners the scientific, ethical, and pragmatic (i.e., test security and coaching) reasons not to allow third party observation during forensic neuropsychological evaluation. Practitioners at the individual level need to be aware of the reasoning, and be willing and able to advocate protecting the boundaries of neuropsychological practice and test security. We present practitioners with options they can utilize when confronted with a request for a TPO and provide a list of resources that practitioners can use to educate the legal system and submit with motions. In addition we provide responses for some of the more common myths used to support a request for a TPO during a forensic neuropsychological evaluation. Lastly we encourage more global solutions to the TPO problem such as state-by-state legislation.

PREVIOUS AND CONTINUING EFFORTS

It is important to note that, regardless of ethical, scientific, and pragmatic concerns associated with TPOs, state and federal statutes and case law dictate how the legal system will resolve the dilemma when it arises. Jurisdictional law supercedes professional ethics. This is one reason why it is crucial to educate the legal system because, when gaps in information exist, laws may be created and perpetuated that contradict developing and established science. State statutes and case law regarding TPOs are variable between jurisdictions. The individual practitioner must be aware of the rules in the jurisdiction in which he/she practices. For example, Texas and the federal courts do not allow TPOs during neuropsychological evaluation (Bennett v. State, 1989; see also Lagrone v. State, 1997). In contrast, in Florida no distinction is currently made between psychological and medical evaluation. Florida courts apply a two-part test to determine if an involved TPO should be excluded during a medical legal evaluation. The party seeking to prevent the TPO's presence must demonstrate with case-specific facts why a TPO will be disruptive to the evaluation, AND that no other qualified provider in the area would be willing to conduct the evaluation with a TPO (Broyles v. Reilly, 1997).

In jurisdictions that do not prohibit TPOs, the previous and continuing efforts are for the most part engaged in on a case-by-case basis by the individual clinician. Some practitioners may allow a TPO because they are not familiar with the adverse effects, while others object and present the technical and ethical concerns, but then accept the judge's final ruling and either withdraw from the case or conduct the evaluation and add caveats to the report regarding the presence of a TPO. More globally, some state and national professional organizations have written policy and position statements regarding TPOs (Axelrod et al., 2000a; Colorado Neuropsychological Society, 2008; Hamsher et al., 2001). While these statements function to educate psychologists and the legal system and create professional standards, they do not create enforceable legal dictats. In 2007 some individuals in

Florida advocated having their state psychological association support legislation that would prohibit TPOs in civil forensic neuropsychological evaluations. However, this goal was not adopted by the Florida Psychological Association at that time.

FUTURE EFFORTS

Individual practitioners need to be aware of the scientific, ethical, and pragmatic reasons not to allow TPOs. We present steps practitioners can take when confronted with a request for a TPO, and also specific responses to counter reasons people sometimes use for why a TPO should be permitted during a forensic neuropsychological evaluation. We then present more global strategies that can be utilized in jurisdictions that permit TPOs. Practitioners should always check the applicable rules that govern in their specific jurisdiction, as some of the advice given may not be applicable.

Steps for the individual practitioner

Foremost, education of all parties is crucial. Individual practitioners must be aware of the problems inherent in allowing TPOs during forensic neuropsychological evaluations, and be able to present the arguments in an articulate way to other practitioners, the retaining attorney, the opposing attorney, and the court itself. When confronted with a request for a TPO, the practitioner should explain the reasons for opposition. If educative efforts are not sufficient, an affidavit explaining the negative effects of TPOs should be presented to the court along with the relevant articles and position statements. Affidavits from colleagues can bolster one's persuasive power. Since some states (e.g., Florida) may require case-specific reasons why a TPO should not be permitted, affidavits should also contain case-specific reasons why a TPO will negatively impact this particular examination. For example, if the examinee has complained of attention difficulties, neuropsychological literature stating that individuals with attention difficulties should be assessed in an area as free from distraction as possible should be included in the affidavit. Appendix A lists the relevant neuropsychological TPO articles. If the court orders that a TPO is permissible, the practitioner may choose to withdraw from the case, or continue and allow a TPO. If the practitioner determines to allow a court-ordered TPO after exhausting all potential appeals, then the practitioner should require a protective order. The report should indicate a TPO was present and indicate how this may have impacted the data.

Specific responses to counter assertions that TPOs should be permitted

Regardless of the particular state's specific legal stance on TPOs, practitioners have an obligation to be informed regarding the effects of TPOs and be familiar with the arguments for and against them. To help practitioners articulate clear responses to reasons often given for requesting them, below are some of the common arguments for TPOs and the corresponding response arguments.

Transparency. Transparency has been stated as a reason to permit TPOs during forensic evaluations (cf. Witt, 2003). Due to potentially life-changing and significant outcomes that can occur in the legal system, the idea exists that procedures should be open and accountable to full scrutiny to aid investigation and questioning. Additionally, some argue the field and individual practitioners should be held up for scrutiny. It has been suggested this keeps the process honest; however, interestingly this standard is only applied to the defense evaluation and not the plaintiff evaluation.

Response. The authors agree that important rights are at stake in the legal environment and professionals should be held to high standards. However, the route to ensuring high standards should not be at the expense of destroying or significantly diminishing the evidence. There comes a point where providing protections destroys the very evidence that is being sought. The film-developing analogy illustrates why transparency is not a good reason to allow TPOs. The presence of TPOs when collecting neuropsychological data is akin to having the lights on when developing film. Imagine that a roll of film exists which has crucial information that will help to resolve a legal issue. Since so much hinges on what is on the film, one lawyer wants to ensure it is developed properly with standardized procedures and nothing out of the ordinary occurs during development. The other lawyer asks to have the lights on when the film is developed so the process will be transparent. Against advice that the lights may negatively impact the quality of the film, the judge orders that the lights be kept on when the film is developed. All procedures are strictly followed with regard to the film developing and nothing unusual happened during the process, which pleases all sides to the controversy. When the final images are investigated, however, the film is ruined and there are no useful images. Allowing a TPO during a neuropsychological evaluation is akin to developing film with the lights on. All can see the procedure, but the cost is high.

Other procedures, such as having an expert review the obtained data, deposition, and cross-examination, are in place to allow review of the neuropsychologist's work product. Either side can also request a separate evaluation by an opposing expert. If there is a concern regarding a specific examiner, and that specific examiner is thought to be unethical or incompetent, that concern should be pursued via other routes, since TPOs decrease neuropsychology's ability to clearly articulate the examinee's true level of performance; which limits its usefulness in consultations.

The risk of "coaching" is balanced against the right of the attorney to have a reviewable record of the evaluation. It has been proposed that the risk of future coaching should be balanced against the right of the attorney to have a permanent record of the evaluation for cross-examination and review by an opposing expert (Witt, 2003).

Response. This reasoning posits two items that cannot be directly compared, and begins with the faulty premise that coaching is the only concern. This argument ignores the diminished validity of the obtained data, which is the crux of the matter for neuropsychology. Additionally, requiring a retrievable record of the neuropsychological evaluation implies that the retained experts who perform the evaluation may be untrustworthy. An opposing expert can review the obtained data and the conclusions of the expert in the report and deposition, which allows an ample foundation of data. When an examinee gets an x-ray or MRI, the opposing expert reviews the obtained films and reviews the report of the other expert. The opposing expert does not view a videotape of the person preparing for and then getting the MRI or x-rays.

No consensus exists on the topic and there is not that much evidence showing the detrimental impacts. Some sources have stated that no consensus exists on the topic of TPOs and that there is not that much evidence showing the detrimental impacts (Witt, 2003) or that additional evidence is needed to draw conclusions (Otto & Krause, 2009).

Response. Although there may not be a consensus in the overarching field of forensic psychology, there is a majority consensus within the field of forensic neuropsychology that TPOs should not be permitted during forensic neuropsychological evaluations, and that when they are the quality of the data obtained is diminished (cf. Axelrod et al., 2000a; Hamsher et al., 2001). Additionally, numerous studies specific to neuropsychology have been published within the last 10 years that amply demonstrate the negative impacts of TPOs on neuropsychological evaluation with healthy controls and also diagnostic populations (e.g., brain-injury survivors and a patient with seizures) in many different situations. The introduction describes the various research studies, and Appendix A lists the citations for research studies investigating the effects of TPO.

Since some policy statements allow some observers but disallow others, all should be allowed. Otto and Krause (2009) argued it was problematic that the NAN and AACN position statements appeared to allow some observers, such as trainees, and disallow other observers such as attorneys. Although the authors did not directly state that this meant all observers should be allowed, they infer this conclusion.

Response. The fact that the policy statements did not disallow all observers does not negate findings that TPOs negatively impact neuropsychological assessment.

Many factors can impact the psychological evaluation process, so TPOs should not be singled out and prohibited. Otto and Krause (2009) stated it was "odd to single out third party presence as a prohibitive threat to psychological assessment when more serious threats to the examinee's responses are tolerated" (p. 367). Initially they refer to items such as race, sex, and SES as also having an impact on the assessment process.

Response. This argument appears to be using the logic that if something is problematic with a situation then it is acceptable to add additional problematic elements. In contrast, it is a psychologist's duty to be attentive to elements that may negatively impact the interaction with and assessment of an individual. It is prudent psychological practice to minimize factors that negatively impact one's ability to fulfill one's professional responsibilities.

Neuropsychological and psychological instruments have not been normed with individuals involved in legal proceedings, so practitioners cannot say they are obtaining valid data anyway. Otto and Krause (2009) stated they believed psychological and neuropsychological measures not being normed on those involved in a legal proceeding was likely the most important factor that limited the applicability of norms to the obtained data, rather than TPOs. According to Otto and Krause (2009), due to the fact that individuals in legal proceedings are more likely to malinger, feign symptoms, or display an altered response style, and that the impact of TPOs is allegedly less documented and the effect size of TPOs may be less than the legal context itself, the arguments against TPOs are faulty.

Response. Neuropsychology readily accepts that malingering, altered response style, and feigning and embellishment of symptoms occurs in most populations and likely with a greater frequency in a forensic situation. Many papers have documented this finding (for overview see AACN consensus conference statement; Heilbronner et al., 2009). Otto and Krause's (2009) argument ignores the development and utilization of symptom validity measures in neuropsychology to assess response style and malingering. Practitioners have methods to aid the determination of when examinees are performing abnormally due to embellishment or decreased task engagement. Often, when examinees are determined to be malingering or embellishing symptoms, the obtained data are considered invalid and unrepresentative of the examinee's true cognitive abilities. Also, the impact of TPOs being less well documented than the impact of malingering is irrelevant to whether TPOs introduce a negative aspect into the assessment that can be controlled for to increase the validity of the evaluation. Additionally, as reviewed in a section below, the impact of a TPO cannot be systematically controlled for since the impact is variable. The two situations—a patient malingering for secondary gain (the patient purposely introducing error into the assessment) and a patient being assessed in the presence of a TPO (the examination situation introducing error into the assessment)—are not comparable.

The TPO is for the patient's benefit to protect them and to ensure a valid assessment. Some argue a TPO is needed to protect the patient and to ensure a valid assessment. This is similar to the transparency argument. However, this argument focuses on making sure proper assessment procedures are followed and that the examinee is not confronted with inappropriate procedures. Some have suggested the interfering impacts of a TPO can minimized by establishing ground rules prior to the examination, such as having the TPO sit outside of the examinee's line of vision (cf. Otto & Krause, 2009).

Response. First, the majority of lawyers are not trained in brain–behavior relationships and would not know if deviations from standard procedure are occurring. Additional queries and alternative phrasing of questions are sometimes part of a standard administration based on specific answers a patient gives, or patient factors. Information could be easily misperceived and not understood by an observer who is not familiar with the nuances of the assessment process. The observer may not understand why questions are rephrased, and interpret the situation as badgering the patient or asking the question multiple times and multiple ways in an effort to inflate a score. Attempting to protect the examinee may interfere with and ruin standard administration if the attorney interrupts the examination. An alternative means of protecting the examinee's civil rights is for the attorney to meet with the examinee before the examination and advise their client regarding the limits of what the psychologist may reasonably request during the evaluation. It is also acceptable to have the examinee's legal representative remain on site in the waiting room.

Additionally, it must be considered that TPOs intended to ensure standardized assessment procedures are followed are actually breaking with standardized administration. Reducing the validity of an examination negatively impacts all concerned, especially the examinee. Performances due to factors not associated with brain dysfunction render the test findings difficult if not impossible to interpret, and conclusions have to be hedged with one or more caveats. The presence of test scores outside of the normal range could be due to true brain pathology, or simply the effects of the TPO. Examinees are denied an assessment clearly showing their strengths and weaknesses by the individuals claiming to want to help and protect them. Forensic neuropsychological evaluation may involve individuals who are claiming some type of brain injury. Since a common symptom of brain injury is distractibility, it has been suggested that when testing individuals with potential brain injury the assessment should be conducted in an environment as free from distraction as possible, to maximize the individual's attention and therefore obtain data that are a better indicator of the brain–behavior relationship under examination (Lezak, Howieson, & Loring, 2004). Since attention is the foundation for learning, and is required for all other abilities such as learning and memory, the testing environment must minimize distractions as much as possible. Additionally, scientific studies have demonstrated that the mere presence of a TPO affects performance even if the TPO does not subjectively appear to impact the testing environment (supervisor in the room; significant other). For these reasons, having a TPO does not function to protect the examinee.

Trained TPOs eliminate the problematic nature of TPOs. Some argue the reasons for not allowing a TPO are eliminated when it is a trained TPO, such as another neuropsychologist or a trained technician, since they are familiar with standardized procedures and protocol (cf. Blase, 2008) and a trained TPO eliminates the concern regarding test security (Otto & Krause, 2009).

Response. This line of reasoning ignores the fact that mere presence of a third party in the room has been demonstrated in studies to impact the examinee's performance, even if the TPO is not engaged in any disruptive behavior(s) (significant other; supervisor). The standardization of the testing environment is important, and manuals of some of the more well-known test batteries (e.g., The WAIS-III, WMS-III administration manuals, 1997) specifically state TPOs should be excluded from the examination room to keep it free from distraction. Many sources review the importance of standardized administration (e.g., Anastasi & Urbina, 1997). Also eliminating or reducing concerns regarding test security will not eliminate the problematic psychometric aspects of TPOs.

Based on early social facilitation literature, the effect stems from the first additional person, so having two people shouldn't make a difference. Blase (2008) opined that, since the early social facilitation literature demonstrated that the effect stems from the first additional person (beyond the person being alone), having two people (the examiner and the TPO) in the room with the examinee should not make a difference.

Response. This viewpoint may be restated as: Why does a third party have an impact on neuropsychological testing, yet the examiner does not? Since neuropsychological tests are standardized with the examiner and examinee present, according to Howe, Rice, and Hoese (2008, p. 21):

> ...any impact caused by the examiner, if present, is accounted for during the standardization process. This process systematically accounts for and controls for the presence of the examiner. Conversely, the impact of a third party is not systematically accounted for during standardization procedures. Studies comparing situations that have the examiner and examinee present and then the examiner, examinee, and a TPO present have repeatedly shown that adding a TPO causes increased performance on some measures (over learned and easy) and decreased performance on others (novel and more difficult). This is the crux of the matter as it pertains to neuropsychology.

Psychologists can determine a way to systematically control for the impacts of a TPO and apply a formula. It has been proposed that psychologists can determine a way to systematically control for the impacts of a TPO and apply a formula after the fact which would eliminate the detrimental impacts of TPOs.

Response. Based on relevant studies, the extent to which a given test is impacted by a TPO and the direction of change (e.g., higher obtained score vs lower obtained score) are variable (Gavett et al., 2005). There is no way to control systematically for the impact of a TPO on the neuropsychological data (Howe et al., 2008). "TPOs will introduce an unknown and uncontrollable change into a system in which degree of change is crucial," (Howe et al., 2008, p. 21).

A solution is to norm some tests with TPOs present. Some have argued that a simple solution would be to norm tests with a TPO present, so the concerns on each side of the debate are satisfied.

Response. This would unduly restrain the trade of neuropsychology. It takes much time, expense, and resources to norm tests. Additionally, if some tests were normed with a TPO and some were not, the researchers who normed the tests would decide what assessment procedures were used in the forensic realm and not the neuropsychologist. Test selection would not be based on clinical judgment but solely on what tests happened to get normed with a TPO present.

Attorneys assert that psychological evaluation should be treated the same as a medical evaluation when the state statute does not specify psychological evaluation. If the state's legislation and/or case law permits TPOs but does not distinguish between psychological and medical evaluation, the attorney may advocate that psychological evaluation should be treated the same as a medical evaluation.

Response. When the statute allows TPOs at medical evaluation but does not specify psychological evaluation, the practitioner should provide arguments for why a psychological evaluation should not be considered under the same rule as a medical evaluation, as well as providing information regarding why the particular evaluation is an exception to the medical observer rule. Approaching the problem from both ways allows the court to rule on either issue (e.g., psychological evaluations should be considered differently from medical evaluations, or this particular evaluation should not fall under the rule for case-specific reasons). The court may not be comfortable creating case law that states a psychological evaluation is different from a medical evaluation, but the court may be willing to disallow a TPO in the particular case.

From a conceptual viewpoint, there are many reasons why medical and psychological evaluation should be treated differently based on reasons inherent to each situation. Foremost, the environment required to facilitate a meaningful psychological evaluation differs significantly from what is required to obtain a meaningful physical medical evaluation. Physicians conduct procedures and evaluate responses that for the most part are not influenced by surrounding circumstances. For example, the examinee's reflexes and how their bones will look on an x-ray are not contingent on how the examinee feels about the examining doctor or how many people are in the room. In contrast, environmental conditions directly impact data collection during neuropsychological evaluation. Neuropsychological evaluation are utilized to measure the examinee's cognitive, emotional, personality, and/or adaptive functioning, which rely on observing behavior and interpreting responses to estimate the examinee's thoughts, feelings, understandings, and cognitive processes.

The APA Statement on Third Party Observers in Psychological Testing and Assessment: A Framework for Decision Making may be used to suggest TPOs are not barred from neuropsychological evaluations. The APA released an informational statement regarding TPOs (APA, 2007). When requesting TPOs not be allowed, practitioners may be confronted with the *APA Statement on Third Party Observers in Psychological Testing and Assessment: A Framework for Decision Making*, and the assertion that the Statement as well as the 2002 Ethical Standards do not explicitly bar third parties from attending evaluation, nor explicitly bar recordings of evaluation. The Statement may be used incorrectly as an authoritative stance of the APA. Several arguments are presented below for when practitioners are confronted with this informational statement.

Response. First, the informational statement is not an official policy. The Statement begins (p. 2) with: "This Statement does not constitute an official policy of the American Psychological Association (APA), does not purport to dispense legal advice, and is not intended to establish standards or guidelines for conduct by practitioners. The statement may prove useful in analyzing and responding to situations in which third parties request to be present, either in person or by electronic proxy, at the time that psychological evaluations are conducted." The statement clearly states it is not an official policy of the American Psychological Association. Practitioners should correct any assertions by attorneys or other psychologists that infer the Statement is an official policy, since it explicitly states it is not. It also explicitly states it is not a guideline or standard. The document by its very nature (i.e., informational) would not be able to explicitly bar or allow TPOs or recordings. *Attorneys cannot argue that since it does not disallow them it allows them, since it is not a policy.* Second, an informational statement or policy cannot negate substantial research findings. As demonstrated above, the mere presence of a TPO impacts the validity (e.g., supervisor study).

Global Solutions

Presenting research articles and organizational position papers allows practitioners to act on an individual basis, but these actions are time consuming and costly (Howe, Rice, & Hoese, 2007). Each time the TPO issue is appealed to an appellate level, there is the risk that a ruling will have a negative impact on neuropsychology (Howe et al., 2007). Therefore actions that are more preventative and global versus reactive and case specific would be beneficial. First, preventative education is needed. By routinely including a statement in every report, both clinical and forensic, regarding TPOs, practitioners are raising awareness of TPOs and educating referral sources by bringing it to their attention (e.g., MDs, attorneys, and the general public). For example, consider the following statement: "There were no third party observers present during formal neuropsychological testing, and as such the results of the current evaluation do not need to be interpreted in light of this known confounding factor." Practitioners can also volunteer to give talks at legal venues and conferences. In addition, practitioners can proactively educate legal referral sources by giving them articles such as this one, in case the issue arises in their practice.

The most effective way to handle the issue, however, is to write, gain support for, and pass legislation at the individual state level (sample legislation is included in Appendix B). This legislation should exclude TPOs during civil neuropsychological evaluations, except in cases with extenuating circumstances that lead the neuropsychological expert to determine that a TPO should be present based on their clinical judgment and expertise. This legislation would shift the burden of proof to the party requesting a TPO to show good cause for why one should be present based on the particular circumstances.

REFERENCES

Abeles, N. (2001). Challenges of test coaching in assessment. *Testing International, 11*(2), 4–6.

Anastasi, A., & Urbina, S. (1997). *Psychological testing* (7th ed.). New York: Macmillan Publishing Company.

American Psychological Association (2002). Ethical principles of psychologists and code of conduct. *The American Psychologist*, *57*, 1060–1073.

Axelrod, B., Barth, J. G., Faust, D., Fisher, J., Heilbronner, R., Larrabee, G., et al. (2000a). Presence of third party observers during neuropsychological testing: Official position statement of the National Academy of Neuropsychology. *Archives of Clinical Neuropsychology*, *15*, 379–380.

Axelrod, B., Heilbronner, R., Barth, J., Larrabee, G., Faust, D., Pliskin, N., et al. (2000b). Test security: Official position statement of the National Academy of Neuropsychology. *Archives of Clinical Neuropsychology*, *15*, 383–386.

Barth, J., Pliskin, N., Arffa, S., Axelrod, B., Blackburn, L., & Faust, D. (2003). Test security: An update. Official statement of the National Academy of Neuropsychology, approved by the NAN Board of Directors 10/13/2003.

Bennett v. State. 766 S.W.2d 227 (Tex.Cr.App.1989).

Blase, J. (2008). Trained third party presence during forensic neuropsychological evaluations. *Florida Psychologist*, *59*(2), 16–19.

Broyles v. Reilly. 695 So. 2d 832 (Fla. 2d DCA 1997).

Bunkley, N. (2007, October 13). After news article on test, Michigan orders retesting. *The New York Times*.

Colorado Neuropsychological Society. (2008). *Official position statement of the Colorado Neuropsychological Society regarding third party observers and neuropsychological evaluations*.

Committee on Psychological Test and Assessment (2008). Statement on third party observers in psychological testing and assessment: A framework for decision making. *Psychological Science Agenda*, *22*(1), 2.

Constantinou, M., Ashendorf, L., & McCaffrey, R. J. (2002). When the third party observer in a neuropsychological evaluation is an audio-recorder. *The Clinical Neuropsychologist*, *16*, 407–412.

Constantinou, M., Ashendorf, L., & McCaffrey, R. J. (2005). Effects of a third party observer during neuropsychological assessment: When the observer is a video camera. *Journal of Forensic Neuropsychology*, *4*, 39–47.

Gavett, B., Lynch, J., & McCaffrey, R. J. (2005). Third party observers: The effect size is greater than you might think. *Journal of Forensic Neuropsychology*, *4*, 49–64.

Greiffenstein, M. F., & Cohen, L. (2005). Neuropsychology and the law: Principles of productive attorney-neuropsychologist relations. In G. J. Larrabee (Ed.), *Forensic neuropsychology: A scientific approach* (pp. 29–91). New York: Oxford University Press.

Hamsher, K., Lee, G. P., & Baron, I. S. (2001). Policy statement on the presence of third party observers in neuropsychological assessments, American Academy of Clinical Neuropsychology. *The Clinical Neuropsychologist*, *15*, 435–449.

Heilbronner, R. L., Sweet, J. J., Morgan, J. E., Larrabee, G. J., Millis, S. R., & Conference Participants (2009). American Academy of Clinical Neuropsychology consensus conference statement on the neuropsychological assessment of effort, response bias, and malingering. *The Clinical Neuropsychologist*, *23*, 1093–1129.

Howe, L., Rice, W. J., & Hoese, V. (2007). Psychological ethics and third party observers (TPO): We've observed their effect and now need to act. *Florida Psychologist, Summer*, *58*(2), 18–19, 35.

Howe, L. L. S., Rice, W. J., & Hoese, V. M. (2008). Why allowing trained third party observers during forensic neuropsychological examinations is a misguided and harmful position for which psychologists should not advocate: A response to Dr. John Blase. *Florida Psychologist, Spring*, *59*(1), 16–17, 2; *59*(2), 20–21, 38.

Kaufmann, P. M. (2005). Protecting the objectivity, fairness and integrity of neuropsychological evaluations in litigation. A privilege second to none? *The Journal of Legal Medicine*, *29*, 95–131.

Kaufmann, P. M. (2008). Admissibility of neuropsychological evidence in criminal cases. In R. L. Denney & J. P. Sullivan (Eds.), *Clinical neuropsychology in the criminal forensic setting* (pp. 55–90). New York: Guilford Press.

Kaufmann, P. M. (2009). Protecting raw data and psychological tests from wrongful disclosure: A primer on the law and other persuasive strategies. *The Clinical Neuropsychologist*, *23*(7), 1130–1159.

Kehrer, C., Sanchez, P., Habif, U., Rosenbaum, J., & Townes, B. (2000). Effects of a significant-other observer on neuropsychological test performance. *The Clinical Neuropsychologist*, *14*, 67–71.

McCaffrey, R. J., Fisher, J. M., Gold, B. A., & Lynch, J. K. (1996). The ethical neuropsychologist. Presence of third parties during neuropsychological evaluations: Who is evaluating whom? *The Clinical Neuropsychologist*, *10*, 435–449.

McCaffrey, R. J., Lynch, J. K., & Yantz, C. L. (2005). Third party observers: Why all the fuss? *Journal of Forensic Neuropsychology*, *4*, 1–16.

Lagrone v. State. 942 S.W.2d 602 (Tex.Cr.App.1997).

Lee, D., Reynolds, C. R., & Willson, V. L. (2003). Standardized test administration: Why bother? *Journal of Forensic Neuropsychology*, *3*, 55–81.

Lezak, M. D., Howieson, D. B., & Loring, D. W. (2004). *Neuropsychological assessment*. Oxford, UK: Oxford University Press.

Lynch, J. K. (2005). Effect of a third party observer on neuropsychological test performance following closed head injury. *Journal of Forensic Neuropsychology*, *4*, 17–25.

Otto, R. K., & Krause, D. A. (2009). Contemplating the presence of third party observers and facilitators in psychological evaluations. *Assessment*, *16*(4), 362–372.

Rogers, R., Bagby, R., & Chakraborty, D. (1993). Feigning schizophrenic disorders on the MMPI-2: Detection of coached simulators. *Journal of Personality Assessment*, *60*, 215–226.

Standards for educational and psychological testing (1999). [American Educational Research Association, American Psychological Association, National Council on Measurement in Education.]. Washington, DC: AERA Publication Sales.

Suhr, J. A., & Gunstand, J. (2007). Coaching and malingering. In G. J. Larrabee (Ed.), *Assessment of malingered neuropsychological deficits* (pp. 287–311). Oxford, UK: Oxford University Press.

Victor, T., & Abeles, N. (2004). Coaching clients to take psychological and neuropsychological tests: A clash of ethical obligations. *Professional Psychology: Research and Practice*, *35*, 373–379.

Wechsler, D. (1997a). *Wechsler Adult Intelligence Scale – Third edition manual*. San Antonio, TX: The Psychological Corporation.

Wechsler, D. (1997b). *Wechsler Memory Scale – Third edition manual*. San Antonio, TX: The Psychological Corporation.

Wetter, M., & Corrigan, S. K. (1995). Providing information to clients about psychological tests: A survey of attorneys' and law students' attitudes. *Professional Psychology: Research and Practice*, *26*, 474–477.

Witt, P. H. (2003). Expert opinion: Some observations on observers of psychological testing. *American Psychology Law Society News*, *23*(3), 18–19.

Wydick, R. C. (1995). The ethics of witness coaching. *Cardozo Law Review*, *17*, 1–52.

Yantz, C., & McCaffrey, R. (2005). Effects of a supervisor's observation on memory test performance of the examinee: Third party observer effect confirmed. *Journal of Forensic Neuropsychology*, *4*, 27–38.

Youngjohn, J. (1995). Confirmed attorney coaching prior to neuropsychological examination. *Assessment*, *2*, 279–283.

APPENDIX A: TPO RELATED RESOURCES

Abeles, N. (2001). Challenges of test coaching in assessment. *Testing International*, *11*(2), 4–6.

American Academy of Clinical Neuropsychology (2001). Policy statement on the presence of third party observers in neuropsychological assessments. *The Clinical Neuropsychologist*, *15*, 433–439.

Binder, L., & Johnson-Greene, D. (1995). Observer effects on neuropsychological performance: A case report. *The Clinical Neuropsychologist*, *9*, 74–78.

Butler, J., & Baumeister, R. F. (1998). The trouble with friendly faces: Skilled performance with a supportive audience. *Journal of Personality and Social Psychology*, *75*, 1213–1230.

Colorado Neuropsychological Society (2008). *Official position statement of the Colorado Neuropsychological Society regarding third party observers and neuropsychological evaluations.*

Constantinou, M., Ashendorf, L., & McCaffrey, R. J. (2002). When the third party observer of a neuropsychological evaluation is an audio-recorder. *The Clinical Neuropsychologist*, *16*, 407–412.

Constantinou, M., Ashendorf, L., & McCaffrey, R. J. (2005). Effects of a third party observer during neuropsychological assessment: When the observer is a video camera. *Journal of Forensic Neuropsychology*, *4*, 39–47.

Constantinou, M., & McCaffrey, R. J. (2003). Using the TOMM for evaluating children's effort to perform optimally on neuropsychological measures. *Child Neuropsychology*, *9*, 81–90.

Duff, K., & Fisher, J. M. (2005). Ethical dilemmas with third party observers. *Journal of Forensic Neuropsychology*, *4*, 65–82.

Gavett, B. E., Lynch, J. K., & McCaffrey, R. J. (2005). Third party observers: The effect size is greater than you might think. *Journal of Forensic Neuropsychology*, *4*, 49–64.

Gavett, B. E., & McCaffrey, R. J. (2007). The influence of an adaptation period in reducing the third party observer effect during a neuropsychological evaluation. *Archives of Clinical Neuropsychology*, *22*, 699–710.

Hamsher, K., Lee, G. P., & Baron, I. S. (2001). Policy statement on the presence of third party observers in neuropsychological assessments. *The Clinical Neuropsychologist*, *15*, 433–439.

Harcourt Assessment Inc (2004). HIPAA position statement. *National Academy of Neuropsychology Bulletin*, *19*(1), 1–2, 7–8. [available at: www.nanonline.org].

Horwitz, J. E., & McCaffrey, R. J. (2008). Effects of a third party observer and anxiety on tests of executive function. *Archives of Clinical Neuropsychology*, *23*, 409–417.

Howe, L. L. S. (2006). *Amicus brief filed in the Fifth District Court of Appeal, Florida 5D06-2053, by the Group Protecting the Integrity of Psychological Examinations.*

Howe, L., Rice, W. J., & Hoese, V. (2007). Psychological ethics and third party observers (TPO): We've observed their effect and now need to act. *Florida Psychologist, Summer*, *58*(2), 18–19, 35.

Howe, L. L. S., Rice, W. J., & Hoese, V. M. (2008). Why allowing trained third party observers during forensic neuropsychological examinations is a misguided and harmful position for which psychologists should not advocate: A response to Dr. John Blase. *Florida Psychologist, Spring*, *59*(1), 16–17, 2; *59*(2), 20–21, 38.

Kehrer, C. A., Sanchez, P. N., Habif, U., Rosenbaum, J. G., & Townes, B. D. (2000). Effects of a significant-other observer on neuropsychological test performance. *The Clinical Neuropsychologist*, *14*, 67–71.

Lynch, J. K. (2005). Effect of a third party observer on neuropsychological test performance following closed head injury. *Journal of Forensic Neuropsychology*, *4*, 17–25.

Lynch, J. K., & McCaffrey, R. J. (2004). Neuropsychological assessments in the presence of third parties: Ethical issues and literature review. *NYS Psychologist*, *May–June*, 25–29.

McCaffrey, R. J. (2005). Some final thoughts and comments regarding the issues of third party observers. *Journal of Forensic Neuropsychology*, *4*, 83–91.

McCaffrey, R. J., Fisher, J. M., Gold, B., & Lynch, J. K. (1996). Presence of third parties during neuropsychological evaluations: Who is evaluating whom? *The Clinical Neuropsychologist*, *10*, 435–449.

McCaffrey, R. J., Lynch, J. K., & Yantz, C. L. (2005). Third party observers: Why all the fuss? *Journal of Forensic Neuropsychology*, *4*, 1–16.

McSweeney, A. J., Becker, B. C., Naugle, R. I., Snow, W. G., Binder, L. M., & Thompson, L. L. (1998). Ethical issues related to third party observers in clinical neuropsychological evaluations. *The Clinical Neuropsychologist*, *12*, 552–559.

Morel, K. M. (2009). Test security in medicolegal cases: Proposed guidelines for attorneys utilizing neuropsychology practice. *Archives of Clinical Neuropsychology*, *24*(7), 635–646.

National Academy of Neuropsychology Policy and Planning Committee (2000). Presence of third party observers during neuropsychological testing: Official statement of the National Academy of Neuropsychology. *Archives of Clinical Neuropsychology*, *15*, 379–380.

Suhr, J. A., & Gunstand, J. (2007). Coaching and malingering. In G. J. Larrabee (Ed.), *Assessment of malingered neuropsychological deficits* (pp. 287–311). Oxford, UK: Oxford.

Victor, T., & Abeles, N. (2004). Coaching clients to take psychological and neuropsychological tests: A clash of ethical obligations. *Professional Psychology: Research and Practice*, *35*, 373–379.

Wetter, M., & Corrigan, S. K. (1995). Providing Information to clients about psychological tests: A survey of attorneys' and law students' attitudes. *Professional Psychology: Research and Practice*, *26*, 474–477.

Wydick, R. C. (1995). The ethics of witness coaching. *Cardozo Law Review*, *17*, 1–52.

Yantz, C. L., & McCaffrey, R. J. (2005). Effects of a supervisor's observation on memory test performance of the examinee: Third party observer effect confirmed. *Journal of Forensic Neuropsychology*, *4*, 27–38.

Yantz, C. L., & McCaffrey, R. J. (2007). Social facilitation effect of examiner attention or inattention to computer administered neuropsychological test: First sign the examiner may affect results. *The Clinical Neuropsychologist*, *21*, 663–671.

Yantz, C. L., & McCaffrey, R. J. (2009). Effects of parental presence and child characteristics on children's neuropsychological test performance: Third party observer effect confirmed. *The Clinical Neuropsychologist*, *21*, 663–671.

Youngjohn, J. (1995). Confirmed attorney coaching prior to neuropsychological examination. *Assessment*, *2*, 279–283.

APPENDIX B: SAMPLE LEGISLATION

Third Party Observation Bill

A bill to be entitled

An act related to the presence of involved third party observers; creating hb/sb. governing the presence of involved third party observers in psychological evaluations; providing a definition; specifying the circumstances under which involved third party observers may be present in psychological evaluations; requiring the Board of Psychology to adopt rules and establish specific criteria for psychologists to admit third party observers into psychological evaluations and to provide an effective date.

Be It Enacted by the Legislature of the State of X

Section 1. Section X.XXXX State Statutes is created to read:
X.XXXX Presence of Involved Third Party Observers

(1) Definitions:

A. As used in this section, involved third party observers are defined as those who in the context of civil litigation, directly or indirectly, have an interest in the specific outcome of a particular plaintiff's evaluation. This interest may arise from any relationship or benefit including yet not limited to the legal, financial, family, and social domain and is irrespective of the level and/or absence of familiarity that the observer has with the party being examined. An employee or agent of the participating attorney is considered an involved third party observer under this condition.

B. As used in this section, uninvolved third party observers have no direct or indirect interest in the specific outcome of the particular plaintiff's examination and instead are concerned with one of more of the following; the behavior of the examiner, the examination process, or the behavior of the examinee as a teaching illustration. For all intents and purposes it is irrelevant to the uninvolved third party who the particular individual is that serves as an exemplar. An example of an uninvolved third party observer is a student or assistant, in training, to a licensed psychologist.

(2) The board shall adopt rules relating to the presence of third party observers and the exceptions by which each is permitted.

(3) Scope

A. The scope of this law applies to psychologists who conduct psychological examinations in a medico-legal context.

B. This law pertains to psychological examinations conducted for the purpose of civil litigation including but not limited to tort litigation and associated insurance matters related to third parties.

C. This law does not include criminal forensic consultations.
D. The scope of this law does not include clinical/medical consultations that are not currently within the civil litigation domain.

(4) This law accepts the presence of involved third party observers only under the following circumstances:

A. In the case of children or adults when physical and/or emotional separation from a caretaker results in dysfunctional behavior that may invalidate assessment results, it is permissible to allow a parent or other caretaker to be present until rapport is established and behavior stabilized so the evaluation may be undertaken.
B. Other extenuating circumstances are to be judged on a case-by-case basis where the psychologist involved makes a clinical decision based on their training and expertise that the harm involved in allowing the presence of the third party observer is outweighed in this particular situation by the need for the involved third parties presence to conduct the examination. The presence of the third party observer in these situations must be limited to the shortest time clinically indicated.

(5) Involved third party observers may not be present in the room physically or by extenders. Extenders include, yet are not limited to, items such as electronic or recording devices, agents, and observation through one-way mirrors.
(6) When involved third party observers are present during a psychological examination, the psychologist must note such presence in their evaluation report and that the attendance of third party observers may have impacted the validity of the test results.

Section 2. This act shall take effect on Date.

The Clinical Neuropsychologist, 24: 538–542, 2010
http://www.psypress.com/tcn
ISSN: 1385-4046 print/1744-4144 online
DOI: 10.1080/13854041003722307

Psychology Press
Taylor & Francis Group

ADVOCACY SPECIAL ISSUE: CONCLUSION

Laura L. S. Howe[1] and Neil Pliskin[2]
[1]*Palo Alto VA Health Care System, Palo Alto, CA and* [2]*University of Illinois School of Medicine, Chicago, IL, USA*

In this special issue of *The Clinical Neuropsychologist* we have attempted to: "(1) convey the importance of advocacy, (2) address and dispel unfounded mental obstacles that inhibit involvement in advocating for the specialty, and (3) aid neuropsychologists in preparing to join the advocacy process" (Howe, Sweet, & Bauer, 2010 this issue, p. 374). The 12 manuscripts in this special issue provide examples of broad areas and specific topics that require advocacy efforts. This special issue is organized into three main section headings that represent broad domain areas in which additional advocacy efforts would help advance the field of neuropsychology. Within these broad domain areas there are several articles that go into depth regarding a specific topic. The specific main section headings and the illustrative articles within them do not delineate finite areas of need—they are meant as exemplars to demonstrate areas that would benefit from individual efforts.

The first section heading is "Advocacy to Increase the Awareness of Neuropsychology." The opening article by Howe et al. (2010 this issue), stressed the importance of advocacy by demonstrating with concrete examples how lack of advocacy can negatively impact the field, individual practitioners, patients, and society. Howe et al. stressed that we are the stewards of our profession and "that *most critical decisions that affect neuropsychological practice are made by non-neuropsychologists*" (2010 this issue, p. 375, original italics). They deconstructed some of the common mental obstacles that prohibit individuals from becoming involved in advocacy, and put out a call to action for all individuals to self-assess their own strengths and determine how they could become involved in a way that is manageable for them.

Next, Attix and Potter (2010 this issue) reviewed ways to increase the awareness of neuropsychology in the general public, stressing that due to the current healthcare and funding climates increased awareness is crucial for the continued viability of our field. They identified three factors among the many reasons for inadequate information regarding neuropsychology in the public domain that could be modified: "(1) our own motivation and sense of responsibility to engage in public awareness education, (2) our knowledge of methods that can be utilized to this end,

Address correspondence to: Laura L. S. Howe, Palo Alto VA Health Care System, Psychology Service (116B), 3801 Miranda Avenue, Palo Alto, CA 94304, USA. E-mail: lauralshowe@yahoo.com
Accepted for publication: February 22, 2010.

and (3) our own limited awareness of tools that exist for such awareness efforts" (Attix & Potter, 2010 this issue, p. 392). They identified numerous methods of participation, from development of printed materials to public-speaking engagements to volunteering with associations that support psychology and neuropsychology. They also reviewed the process by which effective materials can be created since public awareness efforts are aided by communication tools. It is important to note that increasing the awareness of neuropsychology extends in many directions including educating politicians and government officials, general psychology colleagues, and medical and other health professionals. It also extends to fellow neuropsychologists who specialize in areas other than the area in which you specialize. It would be helpful for other neuropsychologists to understand and know additional various unique ways neuropsychology can contribute to the public.

Next, Goldstein (2010 this issue) used the Veterans Health Administration to exemplify how advocacy needs, goals, and acceptable routes to attainment differ within government agencies as compared to private practice and academic settings. Goldstein provided examples of initiatives at the local and the national level. Goldstein underscored the importance of educated advocacy. "Becoming involved in advocacy should obligate the advocate to understand what is legal and appropriate, have knowledge of the degree of support for the views taken, and have pertinent information about the characteristics of the target audience" (Goldstein, 2010 this issue, p. 413). It is important for individuals to assess if his/her stance is aligned with the field's broader goals. Also, even if the goals are aligned, it is helpful to determine if advocacy efforts are already under way for this specific topic. That would help avoid counterproductive efforts.

Next, Loring, Hermann, and Cohen (2010 this issue) delineated the means by which practitioners can utilize their specialized knowledge of the behavioral and cognitive effects associated with epilepsy to advocate for and improve the quality of life for individuals who have epilepsy. Loring et al. accentuated that communication is key since "epilepsy continues to be poorly understood, is often associated with varying degrees of stigma, and because even though there are a diversity of resources available that can minimize some of the negative consequences of epilepsy and its treatment, these resources are often underutilized" (2010 this issue, pp. 417–418). The authors expressed the viewpoint that it is incumbent upon the neuropsychologist to be knowledgeable and able to communicate pertinent information to patients, families, hospital staff, school staff, and the general public. Almost all other patient populations would also benefit from advocacy efforts to increase awareness of cognitive and behavioral profiles, reduce stigma, and encourage the assignment of societal resources needed to craft and implement interventions. Knowledge is incredibly powerful. In particular, increasing the general public's awareness and understanding of particular diagnoses can significantly reduce stigmatization of the individuals with those diagnoses. Some of the specific strategies and the general principles presented for epilepsy can be used with other patient diagnostic populations as well.

While Loring et al. discussed avenues to become involved in advocacy for patients belonging to a particular diagnostic group, Mindt, Byrd, Saez, and Manly (2010 this issue) provided advice for individuals to become involved and advocate for increasing the relevance, appropriateness, and applicability of neuropsychological services for ethnic minority populations in general, regardless of a specific diagnosis. Mindt et al. explicated practical ways to increase culturally competent neuropsychological services by increasing multicultural awareness and knowledge, education and training, and research.

In addition to increasing awareness of neuropsychology, the field needs to demonstrate its scientific value and improve and advance the product being delivered. For example, although a campaign may be able to increase the awareness of phrenology (study of bumps on the head), it is likely that most individuals would opt for more current and scientifically based forms of treatment. Clearly, advancing the science and practice of the field and being able to distil advances into practical patient outcomes is crucial. The second section heading of this special issue contains articles regarding "Advocacy to Advance the Science and Practice of Neuropsychology." Chelune (2010 this issue, p. 466) demonstrated how to "advance evidence-based approaches in both research and practice." Chelune provided ways in which researchers can present their data so clinicians can use the information for case-by-case clinical decisions. Suggestions for practitioners to move toward evidence-based practice and the manner in which research findings can be incorporated into report writing were also provided.

Prigatano and Morrone-Strupinsky (2010 this issue) described how neuropsychologists can demonstrate to stakeholders the value of neuropsychological services, which is crucial in today's healthcare climate. Similar to Chelune's paper, Prigatano and Morrone-Strupinsky advocated for and demonstrated ways to integrate clinical practice with research in ways that will advance the relevance and applicability of the field of neuropsychology, which is essential for the field to remain viable as a profession. Prigatano and Morrone-Strupinsky discussed some areas that are in need of additional outcomes studies and then provided specific examples of cost-outcomes research that could be conducted within each area.

Next, Hilsabeck and Martin (2010 this issue) delineated methods of advocacy that can be used to advance leadership positions for women within the field. They provided concrete advice for women practitioners to reach their goals, and how others can help to mentor women in the field and assist them in achieving their goals.

Another way to advocate for and advance the field of neuropsychology is to continue to define scope of practice and demonstrate unique skills and competences. Other papers in this special issue have described some of the core abilities neuropsychologists should possess for the discipline to flourish (see Prigatano & Morrone-Strupinsky, 2010 this issue). Cox (2010 this issue) discussed board certification by the American Board of Professional Psychology (ABPP) within professional psychology as a means of defining, assessing, and demonstrating competency in psychology. Having a means of assuring levels of basic competency in neuropsychology provides a level of consumer protection. Conceptualizing board certification as a natural stage in the professional development of psychology's specialists, as exemplified within neuropsychology by ABPP's American Board of

Clinical Neuropsychology, has benefits for the profession, the individual psychologist, and consumers of psychological services (Cox, 2010 this issue).

The final section heading in this special issue is "Advocacy at the Intersection of Neuropsychology and the Law." There are many opportunities for neuropsychologists to become involved at the interface of neuropsychology and the law. The two articles within this section provided discrete examples of two issues that are salient today for neuropsychology. Festa, Barr, and Pliskin (2010 this issue) provided a real-life example of the disastrous impact that can occur when state legislatures and psychological colleagues misunderstand neuropsychology practice. Festa et al. noted a chronology of events that led to the restriction of psychological testing technicians in New York State due to an interpretation of the New York Scope of Practice legislation. They discussed how this odd and seemingly capricious interpretation has had a lasting and negative impact, and described efforts to correct this wrong. This article underscores the need for neuropsychologists to be active in local, state, and national organizations to advocate for neuropsychology to avoid similar situations. The lessons learned from the New York testing-technician situation have important implications for the rest of the country.

Howe and McCaffrey (2010 this issue) updated practitioners on the current arguments regarding third party observation. Similar to Chelune's (2010 this issue) description that by integrating evidence-based practices all clinicians can become advocates for the field, Howe and McCaffrey demonstrated that practitioners at the individual level need to advocate protecting the boundaries of neuropsychological practice and testing security. Howe and McCaffrey also provided more global solutions to the issue at the state and legislative levels. The introduction article by Howe et al. (2010 this issue) suggested additional ways that neuropsychologists can become involved in this broad domain area.

Throughout this special issue of *The Clinical Neuropsychologist* we have presented the reader with concrete and practical ways to immediately get involved with advocacy for the field. As the articles in this special issue demonstrate, advocacy can take many different forms. The time commitment varies vastly depending on how one chooses to become involved. Many activities can be woven into one's everyday practice by making minor changes. The most important message is that we all need to be involved on some level and contribute in some manner. We have reviewed how the efforts of individuals can aid the field at large. Advocacy can also have a positive impact on the individual, even if the impact does not increase referrals or direct monetary gain. Advocacy for the field can result in the individual feeling more connected to the larger goals of the field, increase a sense of professional identify and pride, increase one's ability to be assertive, create a sense of empowerment and accomplishment, and increase self-awareness and self-efficacy.

Advocacy, no matter how zealous or well intentioned, will not always result in the goal being attained. However, without an attempt the probability increases that the goal will not be reached and necessary change will not be implemented (Howe & Pliskin, 2009). Instead of complaining and wondering if professional circumstances can be different, individuals should take action(s) toward making a difference. It is time to take control, mobilize, and work toward that in which you believe.

REFERENCES

Attix, D. K., & Potter, G. G. (2010). Increasing awareness of clinical neuropsychology in the general public. *The Clinical Neuropsychologist*, *24*, 391–400.

Chelune, G. J. (2010). Evidence-based research and practice in clinical neuropsychology. *The Clinical Neuropsychologist*, *24*, 466–479.

Cox, D. R. (2010). Board certification in professional psychology: Promoting competency and consumer protection. *The Clinical Neuropsychologist*, *24*, 505–517.

Festa, J., Barr, W., & Pliskin, N. (2010). The politics of technicians. *The Clinical Neuropsychologist*, *24*, 493–504.

Goldstein, G. (2010). Advocacy for neuropsychology in the public sector: The VA experience. *The Clinical Neuropsychologist*, *24*, 401–406.

Hilsabeck, R. C., & Martin, E. M. (2010). Women and advancement in neuropsychology: Real-life lessons learned. *The Clinical Neuropsychologist*, *24*, 454–465.

Howe, L. L. S., & McCaffrey, R. J. (2010). Third party observation during neuropsychological evaluation: An update on the literature, practical advice for practitioners, and future directions. *The Clinical Neuropsychologist*, *24*, 518–537.

Howe, L. L. S., & Pliskin, N. (2009). Advocacy for neuropsychology. *NAN Bulletin*, *24*(2), 7–9.

Howe, L. L. S., Sweet, J. J., & Bauer, R. M. (2010). Advocacy 101: A step beyond complaining: How the individual practitioner can become involved and make a difference. *The Clinical Neuropsychologist*, *24*, 373–390.

Loring, D. W., Hermann, B. P., & Cohen, M. J. (2010). Neuropsychological advocacy and epilepsy. *The Clinical Neuropsychologist*, *24*, 417–428.

Mindt, M. R., Byrd, D., Saez, P., & Manly, J. (2010). Increasing culturally competent neuropsychological services for ethnic minority populations: A call to action. *The Clinical Neuropsychologist*, *24*, 429–453.

Prigatano, G. P., & Morrone-Strupinsky, J. (2010). Advancing the profession of clinical neuropsychology with appropriate outcome studies and demonstrated clinical skills. *The Clinical Neuropsychologist*, *24*, 480–492.

The Clinical Neuropsychologist

The Official Journal of the American Academy of Clinical Neuropsychology

The Clinical Neuropsychologist is included in the following abstracting, citation, and information retrieval systems: Child Development Abstracts and Bibliography (CDAB). Current Contents/Social & Behavioral Sciences, EMBASE/Excerpta Medica, European Reference Index for the Humanities (ERIH), Exceptional Child Educational Resources (ECER), Linguistics and Language Behavior Abstracts (LLBA), MEDLINE, Neurosciences Citation Index, Psychological Abstracts, PsycINFO, PsycLIT, Research Alert, SciSearch, SCOPUS, Social Sciences Citation Index, Social SciSearch, VINITI.

The Clinical Neuropsychologist (USPS permit number pending) is published eight times per annum (in January, February, April, May, July, August, October, and November) by Psychology Press, 27 Church Road, Hove, East Sussex, BN3 2FA, UK. Periodicals Postage pending at Philadelphia, PA and additional mailing offices. **US Postmaster**: Please send address changes to *The Clinical Neuropsychologist*, T&F Customer Services, Informa UK Ltd., Sheepen Place, Colchester, Essex, CO3 3LP, UK.

Subscription rates to volume 24, 2010 (8 issues) are as follows (price inclusive of postage and packing):
Print ISSN 1385-4046

To Institutions (full subscription):	£826.00 (UK);	€1,089.00 (Europe);	$1,361.00 (Rest of the World).
To Institutions (online only):	£785.00 (UK);	€1,034.00 (Europe);	$1,293.00 (Rest of the World).
To Individuals:	£332.00 (UK);	€438.00 (Europe);	$548.00 (Rest of the World).

Dollar rates apply to all subscribers outside Europe. Euro rates apply to all subscribers in Europe, except the UK and the Republic of Ireland where the pound sterling price applies. If you are unsure which rate applies to you please contact Customer Services in the UK. Journals are sent by air to the USA, Canada, Mexico, India, Japan and Australasia. Subscriptions are entered on an annual basis, i.e. January to December. Payment may be made by sterling cheque, dollar cheque, euro cheque, international money order, National Giro or credit cards (Amex, Visa and Mastercard).

An institutional subscription to the print edition includes free access to the online edition for any number of concurrent users across a local area network.

Subscriptions purchased at the personal (print only) rate are strictly for personal, non-commercial use only. The reselling of personal subscriptions is strictly prohibited. Personal subscriptions must be purchased with a personal cheque or credit card. Proof of personal status may be requested. For full information please visit the Journal's homepage.

(Continued from the back cover)

II. Advocacy to Advance the Science and Practice of Neuropsychology

III. Advocacy at the Intersection of Neuropsychology and the Law

The Clinical Neuropsychologist now offers an iOpenAccess option for authors. For more information, see: www.tandf.co.uk/journals/iopenaccess.asp

For information about manuscript submission and layout, please visit the "Instructions for Authors" page of the Journal's website: **www.psypress.com/tcn**

For Product Safety Concerns and Information please contact our EU representative GPSR@taylorandfrancis.com Taylor & Francis Verlag GmbH, Kaufingerstraße 24, 80331 München, Germany

Batch number: 10748884

Printed by Printforce, the Netherlands